How to Be a Muslim

How to Be a Muslim

An American Story

HAROON MOGHUL

BEACON PRESS
BOSTON

BEACON PRESS
Boston, Massachusetts
www.beacon.org

Beacon Press books
are published under the auspices of
the Unitarian Universalist Association of Congregations.

20 19 18 17   8 7 6 5 4 3 2 1

This book is printed on acid-free paper that meets the uncoated paper
ANSI/NISO specifications for permanence as revised in 1992.

Text design and composition by Kim Arney

Conversations are recollected to the best of my ability. To protect people's
privacy, I've modified some names, circumstances, geographies, and
chronologies. Small sacrifices have been made for narrative coherence.
These were not fundamental to my journey.

All translations of the Qur'an, and the poetry of Rumi and Iqbal,
are my own.

Library of Congress Cataloging-in-Publication Data

Names: Moghul, Haroon, author.
Title: How to be a Muslim : an American story / Haroon Moghul.
Description: Boston : Beacon Press, 2017.
Identifiers: LCCN 2016041078 (print) | LCCN 2017006950 (ebook) |
    ISBN 9780807020746 (pbk. : alk. paper) | ISBN 9780807020753 (e-book)
Subjects: LCSH: Moghul, Haroon. | Muslims—United States—Biography. |
    Islam—Essence, genius, nature.
Classification: LCC BP80.M6155 A3 2017 (print) | LCC BP80.M6155
    (ebook) | DDC 297.092 [B] —dc23
LC record available at https://lccn.loc.gov/2016041078

CONTENTS

1 You Go To Sleep, and You Wake Up Dead ▪ 1

2 How the Hell the Apple Fell ▪ 7

3 Linda Was a Cheerleader ▪ 17

4 Judge None Choose One ▪ 25

5 Catholic Girls ▪ 33

6 Hi, I Am Not a Christian ▪ 43

7 Which of These Two Land Cruisers Will You Deny? ▪ 49

8 And Shams Is the Sun ▪ 59

9 "Are You There, Muhammad? It's Me, God." ▪ 63

10 A Planet Called Medina ▪ 71

11 The Falafel Philosophy ▪ 81

12 You Think You Need to Get Married ▪ 97

13 Between the Dome of the Rock and a Hard Place ▪ 105

14 Wake Me Up When September Ends ▪ 119

15 Make It Look Like You're Working ▪ 127

16 The Gravedigger Said ▪ 137

17 The Late, Great Mosque of Córdoba ▪ 147

18 How to Be an Idiot ▪ 157

19 The Bigamist ▪ 165

20 Emirate State of Mind ▪ 177

21 Jet Engine Oven ▪ 183

22 Matthew and Son ▪ 191

23 Who Shot the Shatri ▪ 201

24 Gazi Husrev Begging the Question ▪ 207

25 Muslim Prefers Virgin ▪ 217

Acknowledgments ▪ 229

· 1 ·

YOU GO TO SLEEP,
AND YOU WAKE UP DEAD

IN JUST OVER A DECADE, I'd gone from an inelegant twenty-one-year-old, compelled by an act of terror to enter a public spotlight he was terrified by, to a man sure-footedly navigating a privileged world of pundits, politicos, policymakers. That some of my new colleagues went in and out of the White House from time to time was considered unremarkable. I was thirty-one, and I had my dream job.

Hafsa and I chose a tidy one-bedroom in a vibrant neighborhood of Arlington. We had add-ons most New Yorkers could only dream of: a dishwasher, a washer and dryer, wall-to-wall carpeting, central air-conditioning, a balcony overlooking an interior courtyard. Our building had swimming pools, a garage, a doorman. Even a deli you could enter without having to step outdoors. Not much by my father's standards, but I felt I'd made it.

I'd knocked out my master's thesis (at an Ivy League); passed my oral examinations by unanimous consensus, scoring an MPhil; and successfully defended my prospectus. Through the philosopher Muhammad Iqbal, I'd seek to better understand non-Western modernity; framed by thinkers like Koselleck, Foucault, and Chakrabarty, I'd explore how spatiality and temporality functioned in an Indo-Islamic contemporaneity.

It felt fair to ask: Where would I be in ten years?
I can tell you where I was just six months later.

Just a few months after moving to Virginia, I was seeing a therapist twice or thrice a week, walking from work whenever the weather was nice enough—it was a pleasant hike from the New America Foundation's office to hers. Right before her block, I'd cross a very long, very exposed bridge. The asphalt had long since been bleached by the Southern sun. The guardrails, made of sooty stucco, failed to rise much higher than my waist. Below was a forest, and in the middle of that, a pathetic rivulet, which never shimmered no matter how bright the day. It was there I decided, one autumn afternoon, that I'd take my life back into my hands. By concluding it with the power of my own legs.

Because, as Sir Edmund Hillary might put it, it was there. A voice in my head, at least one of them, told me I should tell my therapist. I was paying her a lot of money, and I'd gone out of my way to find her. Tired of explaining the pressures of a Muslim life to the uninitiated, I went and found myself not just a Muslim therapist but a Punjabi like me. Here I was confessing to a woman I'd rather have been dating that I was a total fraud. I'd made my name talking about Islam; I would've told you in any public venue that suicide was indubitably a sin, and now I was considering it? When I'd first started researching suicide just weeks before, I told myself it was better to look it up than act it out. Theoretical exercises. Passive ideation. Until I found carbon monoxide. "You go to sleep," some kind anonymous soul wrote on a crowded message board, "and you wake up dead."

There was a painless way to go. Which meant there was a way to go. Which meant I could go. But it's not just that a mechanism presented itself and the conceptual became the potential. It's that I began to perceive my decision as Islamic. Darkly and cruelly so, the last revenge of a religious logic that had bedeviled me my entire life. By cutting short a reprobate existence, which if continued would only see me accumulate *more* misdeeds, I'd be more, not less, likely to go to heaven. After all, one big sin—suicide—is better than a lot of big sins. Although I was well into seeing my therapist when this train of thought left the station, I didn't tell her right away. I waited until that day, on that bridge, and then I decided I should tell someone. An old friend, Ali; I caught him outside the bookstore near where his train from Philadelphia had just come in—he was impossible to miss.

He was wide, stocky in the manner of a shorter man, but tall too. The kind of person you wouldn't want to come across in a dark alley—unless he was on your side. When we finally sat down to dinner, he asked me why I'd needed to meet this very night.

"Because I'm planning to kill myself," I announced.

Ali was quieter than I expected. He kept his distance, like the slightest move toward me might set me off. "Well." There went dessert. "Can you promise me you'll wait until tomorrow before making any irreversible decisions?"

If he'd told me suicide was *haram*, I might well have stabbed myself to death with my cutlery. I never wanted to hear of Islam again. So this approach was novel, and therefore appreciated. But: "How do you know I'll keep my word?"

"If you kill yourself tonight," Ali responded, "I'll be the last person you ever saw. Can you imagine how guilty I'd feel if I couldn't stop you from killing yourself?"

Since Ali had a wife, two adorable daughters, two very kind-hearted parents, and was himself a model human being, these words had their intended impact—he was an inestimable bastard for thinking of them on the fly. Dinner wasn't done until I promised not to make any immediate, irrevocable decisions—and then, just like that, I was home. Though we were technically still married, Hafsa was in New York and I was alone in Arlington. I usually spent my evenings by myself, in the dark, watching television, or leaving it on in the background so at least it sounded like there was someone in my life.

But I'd lied. Not intentionally, but I'd fibbed all the same. Ali knew enough about the problems that had piled up on me, but he wasn't there when they broke me. So just a few nights after swearing to Ali I would not, I sat at my desk, writing. I wrote for hours, inspired by the thought that I did not have to leave a suicide note, but could explain my decision through a suicide short story, a genre I hoped I had just invented. I wanted to leave something as heartrendingly unforgettable as the last paragraph of Tony Judt's *The Memory Chalet*. At least one thing I wrote would last longer than me. Then I slept well, for the first time in months: there was nothing to stay up and worry over. And I was awake by 7 a.m., starting the day like every Muslim does, by checking his phone and firing off an e-mail: I wasn't coming into work today. Breakfast passed uneventfully. A bagel, toasted and margarined.

Then it was down to the business center.

The downstairs decor of my apartment building was belied by the quality of its downstairs decoration—shocking-pink walls that belonged in a bed and breakfast somewhere several hundred miles south and west, and framed prints straight from a TJ Maxx remainders aisle. I printed out two copies of my story and went back up to my apartment, its eggshell-white walls and noncommittal gray carpets a jarring contrast to the exuberant lobby. I showered and shaved—remarkably motivated, all things considered—placed one copy of my story on my bedside table, put on a light jacket, and headed out the door.

From Starbucks, I ordered Awake tea and a coffee cake, warmed up and served in a crinkly pastry bag. I took my last ride on the Metro, but got off at the penultimate stop, deciding to walk the remainder of the way. Once I passed the Hilton, it was only a short distance to the bridge, a miracle of midcentury American engineering, suspending me in the air between this life and the next. Halfway across, I stopped, turned my back to traffic, sucked in a deep breath, and stared down below. Way down. Would it hurt? In theory, it'd be painless. Would it hurt anyone else? The only people who might care would be my father and my brother. But I hurt too much to stay for them. Would it offend Him?

But my whole life was offensive to Him.

Though you're reading this, not some suicide short story. Standing there, considering the height from which I'd have to fall, I took a few seconds to realize that my left leg was shaking not with nervousness but because the phone in my pocket was vibrating. A minute later, I was leaning against the concrete barrier, staring in disbelief at the texts I'd just received. Zhaleh was the last person in the world I expected to hear from, and the last one I wanted to hear from. But every beginning has an end. Every end has a beginning. Sometimes the one becomes the other and turns out to be neither. It depends on how far back you go, or how far ahead you try to look. In the sentence of my life, Zhaleh was the semicolon.

· 2 ·

HOW THE HELL
THE APPLE FELL

THERE ARE ALMOST NO BABY PICTURES. "Remembering you," my father once admitted, "would've been too painful." I don't begrudge him the feeling. When I was forty-eight hours old, I had my first surgery. The operation left a gnarled scar branded onto me, the only upside being the various fictions behind it—the shark I bit first, a gunfight in some foreign land, an otherworldly battle in Nargothrond.

The next medically necessary intervention? When I was ten months old. Mostly that gastrointestinal intervention reversed the first gastrointestinal intervention, which was itself a stopgap measure—no permanent cure existed, then or now.

At twelve weeks new, I was prescribed eyeglasses that unintentionally overcorrected my vision, leaving me at the intersection of cross-eyed (congenital) and near-sighted (statute of limitations rules out the lawsuit). When I was a toddler, doctors removed my tertiary thumb, thus severing any chance of a life like Hrithik Roshan's. When I was in kindergarten, my hips hurt so badly I was unable to walk. After a week the god-awful pain disappeared and nobody knew why. Come my third decade, I was jackknifed and hospitalized. Three months later I left a different hospital, minus half of two spinal disks.

On the very day in 2003 we went to war with Iraq for the ump-
teenth time, I was admitted to the emergency room.

Most people I knew enjoyed their youth. Or at least had one. I
was born dying. All I understood was deterioration. When I was in
middle school, I remember our imam told our congregation, "When
we feel sorry for ourselves, we should remember people worse off than
us." God made me, I remember concluding in that Massachusetts
mosque, so others could be grateful for what they had. "At least you're
not Haroon," some parent might remind his child. "That's so true," a
chastened young man would concede. His perspective restored, he'd
thank God and conquer the world. While I sat in my room.

In illness, some turn to God. Considering who I was, and where
I came from, you'd think I would've turned to God, too. But just as
there was only one God, so far as I knew there was only one way to
God, which was my parents': (Sunni) Islam. But that didn't work,
though apparently only for me. Just as my chronic infirmities contrasted to general good health all around, my personal impiety would
have stood out against the uniform righteousness I presumed to exist
everywhere around me. Had I not been so expert at concealing it.

Imagine a product everyone else seems to have successfully put to
good use. Day and night you rack your brain—it helps that you're
often too sick to do anything but, because the only thing you have
that works, or at least works well, is your mind. Why is it Islam comes
together for them, you ask? Is there something wrong with me? It
couldn't be Islam, which came from a perfect God. Then it was me,
and Who made me? He didn't want it to work out for me, then, because something in me was unworthy. Why would I have been born
so broken, except that I was disliked? Obviously I preferred other
existences. The future (*Star Trek*) or the past (*The Silmarillion*), but
always anywhere but here and anyone but me.

Worse, the present was merely prologue.

In Islam, death is not the end. Our expiration is our transition
from this circumscribed world to a far more elaborate and enduring

plane, grander or graver than the life we know now. Whoever thinks the afterlife is a fantasy made up to make us feel better has never contemplated ending up on the wrong side of God.

In middle school, because I never got picked for either team in gym, I'd be sidelined with the other marginals. Like Dave. One afternoon this left Dave and me talking all period. Dave was a big kid who'd been held back a grade, which in overripe public school lore had been exaggerated into several years. On the few occasions when Dave was picked to, say, bunt, his jog to first base would be accompanied by cries that his car was being towed. I laughed. (Sorry, Dave.)

But that day a benched Dave and Haroon got around to the subject of my religion, which also distinguished me from my classmates, inspiring endless fascination, the kind reserved for an exotic zoo animal.

"Are you Protestant or Catholic?" Dave asked.

"Umm, it's a separate religion."

Blank stare.

Hmm. I went on. "You know how Jews aren't Catholic or Protestant, because they're not Christian?"

Dave did not know any Jews. So he took a different tack. "What do you like most about Islam?"

Like many Americans, he took the s for an undercover z, believing it was his patriotic duty to call out the deceitful consonant. (Incidentally, Dave often seemed deeply concerned with the answer to any number of absurd conundrums—once he asked me whether I should prefer to die in a plane crash or of snakebite, with a seriousness that suggested this was a choice he would one day have to make.)

"The afterlife," I said, meaning heaven.

Then he asked what I most hated about Islam. In so many words.

"The afterlife," I offered.

After Raphael blows the trumpet and the world ends, humanity will be resurrected for judgment. All the billions who ever lived will be measured and found wanted (Elysium) or wanting (the fire). The garden, to be clear, isn't an abstract state of immortal contentment. We don't believe we'll sit on clouds with wings attached to our upper backs, unless I suppose someone really wanted to, in which case she could. The garden is a physical *and* spiritual space, where, as per the above, you need not ask to receive but merely conceive, and voilà. Those so fortunate will enjoy God's presence, but also the company of those they loved in their time on Earth and many other good things besides. Including copious sex—the attraction of which, to a pimply, perennially horny juvenile, cannot be underestimated. The corollary is that hell is not a nonconcrete state of psychic or spiritual separation from the Divine, but an actual and ongoing immolation— as well as the former. Most Muslims believe that most sinners who go to hell will not stay there forever. Still, they will be on fire until then.

I believed that while my life could continue in one of these two places, it was almost surely going to end in the latter. The circumstances of my birth, for one. My birth into which family, for two. Hell may be other people, but it's not for other people. Once someone has been instructed in Muhammad's message, she has to live up to it. Or face the flames. Good thing for me my parents had made sure I received a thorough indoctrination in the Islamic sciences. All of which came attached to outrageous penalties. The Qur'an opens with a vociferous condemnation of those who claim to follow Islam in public while deriding it in private. External adherence without internal conviction is the deepest deceit. But, that said, belief means nothing if it doesn't come joined to material action. In order to even be considered for heaven, you have to complete all the *salat*, the ritual prayers performed five times a day.

It's not a get-out-of-jail-free card, of course—the prayer has to be genuine, and your sins still count against you. *Salat* is necessary, in other words, but not sufficient, to get to heaven, or to avoid hell. Therein the problem.

Q: Did I pray five times a day? Even once a day? Even once a week? A: Only when my parents took me to the mosque or forced me to pray.

Like many of my Semitic cousins, I'd been taught that righteousness is embodied. You may not wear your faith on your sleeve, but the length of your sleeve may be part of your faith. I didn't quite fit the Qur'an's description of the casuist, of course. I didn't mock Islam in private. I merely despaired in private.

But I did pronounce Islam in public.

Outside Haroon could say all the right things, especially at the Islamic Center of Western Massachusetts. He always won Sunday-school quiz competitions even though, objectively speaking, the prizes were crap. He was a little clone of the obedient Muslim boy. I'd internalized all the arguments Islamic orthodoxy had going for it. I could increasingly quote source text, from the letter of the law to the spirit of the argument, in the manner of a parrot.

Inside Haroon just wondered how the hell the apple fell so far from the tree.

The older I got, the more aware I became of the contrast between what I told people I was, or what they assumed I was, and what I actually was (not). Nothing, I became increasingly aware, made me Muslim except my insistence that I was, the repeated performance of Islam for the consumption of others. It did not help that our social circle was so limited. I did not go out often. Very shy and awkward, making friends was a nightmare. I had one sibling, but he was many years older. When I turned eight, he left for boarding school, over an hour's drive north from us.

That left me mostly by myself, or circulating in small communities of mostly Indian or Pakistani Muslim families that lived across Pioneer Valley. Most of the aunties and uncles—which is what South Asians invariably call an elder who is *not* related to them— were also doctors or the spouses of same, and so could afford to live in widely spaced, magnificent homes. We were sprinkled like salt from another sea on someone else's land. To even admit to not praying would be sacrilege, and to ask any other kind of question would be wrong, too. About sex, for example. I thought about sex more than anyone my age.

To clarify, I knew approximately no one in my age group.

I can't tell you how many times I sat at a dinner party, in the men's section, of course, bored and eager to return home where I could at least be bored in private, while someone casually dismissed the *kuffar*, which meant non-Muslims, the people, but also the values of the people, right outside our doors. We were better because we believed in God and Muhammad. And not only were we better because we believed but because we *acted* on those beliefs, worshipping only in the way Muhammad did—a euphemistic condemnation of talismanic Islam, the closest you could get to saying Sufi, or Shi'a, or any other Islam, all of which were wrong, and most of which were irrational, effete, and inferior. Absorbing these self-congratulatory outbursts only increased my ire at my own insufficiency. I was the only person I could imagine was to blame for my faithlessness. And the only person, I believed, who ever came up short.

My father's family were farmers and soldiers. They'd relocated to Rawalpindi some years before he was born. Their Islam was uncomplicated but urgent, the kind you'd expect from folks drilled into discipline—as his family was, serially and generationally committed to the very young country's army. My father was still a child when the botched surgery called Partition was rushed by a criminally irresponsible British regime, retreating in ignominy and indifference; parts of his village were burned to the ground. Rampaging mobs claimed religion to justify their bloodlust, and their lust. Some women jumped to their deaths rather than face rape. Many were simply massacred. Madness reigned over the Indian subcontinent and did not subside for months. Some would say it has not, even now.

But his family survived. At what cost, I do not know; he almost never spoke of this time. His father pushed him and his siblings into the armed forces he himself had served. (My grandfather wore a British uniform, though.) Pakistan's meritocratic military was and remains an engine of social mobility. The army meant English, for example, the language of medical school, and medical school was his path out, first to England and then America. My father was an orthopedic surgeon who wished he could've been a chemist, as he infrequently lamented. Such glimpses of his true self were rare, and cherished. In this, he was the opposite of my mother, who was far more comfortable talking about herself, and talking in general. Not that this should come as any kind of surprise.

My mother's family was rather more intimidating, immersed as it was in our faith's richest traditions. My mother's grandfather and his father and their male ancestors *ad Arabium* were judges trained in applying interpretations of Shari'ah for the Muslim rulers of northern India and then during the British occupation. My mother was a radiation oncologist by training; she spent much of her career as a family doctor but never lost her inherited passion for literature, for music, for poetry. Her father had no sons who survived, but seven daughters who did—all educated, strong, independent, outspoken. I was spared the unfortunate and common association of patriarchy and piety. And parochialism. I was partly part of a family that appreciated, encouraged, and rewarded bookishness—which made life easier, since I was the kid who made a beeline for the library when the last bell rang, but also harder, because how do you define yourself against such an identity?

On what grounds? With what confidence?

None of the common clichés applied. My distant relatives practiced *habs-e dam*, a Muslim yoga. They learned multiple languages and traveled great distances; one distant ancestor journeyed to Mecca for pilgrimage by boat and by caravan through Yemen. He died on the return trip, his body buried at sea. We know, because his manuscript made it back and the incomplete travelogue was published. They did not need the West to discover enlightenment, nor to be saved from their own alleged barbarity. In fact they fought the Nazis, saving Europe from its own darkness. Many years later, I'd find my great-great-grandfather's books at Columbia's Butler Library. There are even Wikipedia entries devoted to some of my ancestors, honoring their contribution to Islam. The maternal line reached all the way back to Islam's founding generation.

In 656 the Prophet Muhammad's cousin, Ali, assumed the caliphate. Not everyone was onboard, however: Syria's governor, Muawiya,
believed the office should pass to him, given that his relative was the
previous caliph. To meet the challenge, Ali moved the capital from
Medina to southern Iraq. My family went with him, because they
were his family. We are his family. If you're wondering why we took
the allegedly Shi'a side, Sunnis supported Ali against Muawiya, too.
But boundaries that today seem uncrossable were hardly formed then,
and I suspect the progenitors of Sunni and Shi'a hardly differed in
most of their practice. The original Shi'a just had a stronger attach-
ment to Ali, and a gathering belief that he was not only supposed to
be caliph but something more than that. But all of that is secondary.

Several centuries passed in Iraq; the caliphate became a monar-
chic office, then a titular office, then irrelevant. In 1258 the Mongols
made a horrific mess of what was left, burning Baghdad to the ground,
trampling the last Abbasid caliph to death after wrapping him in a
fine rug. No exact count of the dead is available, but the numbers rise
to the genocidal. An entire world ended, a civilization nearly annihi-
lated. But our family survived, and many other Muslims did as well,
by fleeing to territories the Mongols were unable to subdue, largely
because their rulers were Muslims from the steppes of Inner Asia—
against them the Mongols had no tactical advantage. In our case
an admirably prescient ancestor made for the subcontinent around
1250, a journey long, bewildering, and dangerous. His proficiency in
the Qur'anic language meant that he, and his descendants after him,
would be much in demand.

Centuries later, Mongols who had converted to Islam conquered
South Asia—they brought gunpowder to a swordfight. These were
the Mughals (in colonial times, Moghuls). Among other gems, they
gave the world the Taj Mahal; they built what was then very possibly
the world's wealthiest empire, whose splendor humbled the mighty
Ottomans. What my family thought about all this, I cannot know—
fleeing Iraq before the Mongols came, only to end up in an India
ruled by Mongol descendants now proclaiming monotheism. The
family must have just continued its work, divining Islamic scriptures

for God's intents, serving as part of the bureaucratic backbone that stitched South Asia together and tied it to a global civilization. True to this heritage, my branch of this family helped found the first mosque in our corner of New England. We were pioneers, bringing Islam to virgin territories.

My purpose, it was assumed and implied and pronounced, was to carry this legacy, this unbroken fourteen-hundred-year-old chain, to the New World, migrating as our predecessors did, loyal to God, yes, but also to the *ummah*, the worldwide community of Muslims. When I was younger, there were one-point-something billion Muslims, a number so swollen and swelling it resembles the National Debt Clock; their fates, their fortunes were if not my responsibility then among my topmost concerns, and I felt it too. Not just obedience to God, but service to His people. Or at least that was the intention of my upbringing. Because, as Mike Tyson once put it, "Everyone has a plan. Until you punch them in the face."

· 3 ·

LINDA WAS A CHEERLEADER

ALL I'D KNOWN WAS LONGMEADOW, Massachusetts, the kind of bucolic paradise some Americans might be willing to invade countries and kill large numbers of people to be able to continue to enjoy.

Great and wizened trees provided ample shade. Kids like me could bike to any of the town's several shopping centers. The adults drove fine automobiles, parked in capacious garages. The schools were among the best in the region, and the region had some of the best schools in the world. Our place in this firmament was no less auspicious. We had a ranch home on Pinewood Drive: fully paid for, wonderfully landscaped, and truly unique—built by a Sephardic gentleman, the home included an interior courtyard with a rose garden, modeled on the Andalucía his ancestors were expelled from. It was the kind of home that for most folks would indicate a life that had met all expectations.

And when I was ten, it wasn't just lost. It was abandoned. For a house nobody needed, and no one had asked for. But my father wanted it, so he constructed it, and moved us into it. Every other winter, we'd visit Islamabad, my mother's home city. (Rawalpindi, where my father's taciturn family lived, was a half hour south.) In 1990 my mother, brother, and I went; we returned to find my father had purchased a great stretch of land across the border, in a small Connecticut town called Somers, where he'd build what could modestly be described as a palace, and priced to match. Eight bedrooms and as many bathrooms for three people, two of whom were married and ergo shared a bathroom and bedroom. (After four years of boarding school, my brother went away to college, then law school, then got married.) Three full and finished floors, two entire kitchens, a balcony stretching the length of the home that could have accommodated several dozen persons, and a swimming pool that contained three times as much water as a standard pool, which somehow turned into nine times as much time cleaning it. I know. Because I cleaned it.

There was also a granite Jacuzzi. I cleaned that too.

I entered a new school in the middle of fifth grade, right after Christmas break, and found my classmates more interested in their presents than in me. I hoped sixth grade would be my chance to reintroduce myself. But that summer my parents got a letter in the mail that changed my life. By denying me one. Students needed parental permission to be enrolled in sex education. Every single student got it. All of them. Except.

Not only did my parents never talk to me about girls, they made sure no one else ever would. I was deported to the library to study the solar system. For a doofy twelve-year-old who wore polos mismatched with pleated pants, prominent cinnamon-colored glasses, the kind of sneakers worn by people with tangible athleticism, and had on his opposite end great, thick hair that conformed to no known style and no barber's wishes, this was social homicide. Already timid, I was marked—in a town whose every inhabitant seemed to know every other—as the weird kid whose parents disapproved of sex, which sentiment was expressed in questions like, "Haroon, do you know what a penis is?" or, less charitably, "Is it because you don't have a penis?"

There was no right answer to these questions.

Shunned and widely boycotted, I had no choice but the Muslim bubble. We kept going to that same Massachusetts mosque, remarkable for its diverse congregation. Black Muslims, South Asians, of course, Lebanese, and Egyptians. Even Indonesians and Laotians. But the only "youth" there were either several years younger or older than me. In middle school, a two-year gap is a generational chasm. Because older kids didn't want to talk to me, I was left with kids younger than me, which cemented in my mind the feeling that I was a small child inside a slightly larger child's body.

For the rest of the time, I was on my own, in a bedroom big enough for two queen beds, and no chance of any girl ever being in either. I consumed books at a dizzying pace—everyone at the library fist-bumped me—and feasted on fantasy and science fiction and science. I loved physics. I wondered what became of the Moriquendi. I drew maps to make-believe kingdoms. I was oddly inclined to vexillology. I played Nintendo. I was a very effective player. Who played with himself. When our seventh-grade Spanish teacher asked us to pick Spanish names to go by, I was too shy to choose Mario, going instead with the first name on the list, Alejandro, which suggested a detached apathy I thought my peers might respect. By eighth grade, though, I had worked up the courage to ask for Mario. Some students chuckled, but then Mrs. Spanish Teacher went on to the next student and nothing happened. By which I mean nothing bad happened. I was ever so slightly emboldened. James, who owned every available New England Patriots jersey but apparently only owned Patriots jerseys, looked in my direction and smiled conspiratorially. He understood why I'd chosen Mario, and just like that I made friends. By being myself.

A year later I found myself in high school, doing more of that.

My parents would always walk into the family room whenever there was a mildly inappropriate moment on television, even if it was the only instance in the most innocuous program ever. For *Hook*, that'd be when Tinkerbell finally makes out with Peter Pan, which lasts only three seconds, but those are the exact three seconds when my mother walked by that very room out of thousands of square feet of options, or when my mother had just sat down on the couch to see what I was watching and cartoon Aladdin kissed animated Jasmine. In other words, video games weren't the only reason I had my own TV. Beyond Nintendo, I spent a lot of time upstairs, watching shows by myself. It was safer that way.

One afternoon, home after school, I caught the video for Green Day's new song, "Geek Stink Breath." Basically this consists of a graphic dental examination. Poor choice of visuals aside, the aural was infectious. A more unlikely candidate for the song Haroon couldn't get out of his head could not be proposed. I soon asked my mom to drive me to the nearest music shop—we had to go to cosmopolitan Enfield for those kinds of purchases—and unwrapped *Insomniac* before we even got out of the parking lot. Naturally, neither my upstanding mother nor her geeky adolescent child had any idea what Green Day was about, let alone what the band's name referred to. My eyes scanned the unfolded liner notes, a jagged white font set against an oily black paper that revealed every fingerprint, and alighted on the word that almost rhymed with "steam," the word that Billie Joe Armstrong raged into the microphone, which I had thitherto been unable to decipher: unmistakable, unreturnable, unbelievable, unmentionable, unspeakable.

Methamphetamine.

I wasn't precisely sure what this was, except that it was 200 percent haram. Mightily forbidden. I might've suffered a small cardiac event. *This* was what I liked?

I might have prayed to God right there and then that I'd be forgiven. But here's the thing. I don't think I had that much interest in being forgiven. Because the scandalous CD was not binned, tossed, or left to gather dust. Instead, I purchased Green Day's other CDs. I recorded their music videos. I couldn't get enough. I wanted to be the band. Two birds, as it turned out, with one stoner.

Our English teacher was flower-power counterculture, a very tall, very charming educator. I liked her deep kindness and reverent silliness, and so when she told me that people who wanted to write, or create, or simply read, were special, I needed to believe her because I found solace in words and calmness in books. The first day of each week, she'd ask us to write for ten minutes, and then looked for volunteers to read our work. One Monday I raised my hand to read an impromptu poem. With my mouth just inches off my desk—brown men can still turn red—I shared amateurish sentiments with kids I'd been around for years but never really got to know. And, as it turned out, vice versa. Somewhere in this piece I approvingly cited Green Day.

I was warmly thanked for my contribution, and we went on to grammar or whatever. After class I stopped by my locker, and Linda from English was right behind me. We'd been assigned lockers on the first day of high school, and kept those lockers until the last day of high school—the freshman wing would become the senior wing. For reasons alphabetical, Linda and her twin brother, Ted, who was never without a rumpled baseball cap, usually in some earthy, hempish color, had their lockers right before mine. I saw them every day of school. Ted would say hey. Every day. But Linda never acknowledged me. Not that I acknowledged her either; but while she probably didn't see me, I was afraid she'd see me. This time, though, I could sense she wasn't putting her books away in a hurry, as we always did, rushing between classes. Instead she was just standing there, waiting.

When I turned to face her I saw genuine curiosity.

"You listen to Green Day."

This was neither a question nor a statement. It was doubt seeking to resolve itself out loud.

But as I noticed for the first time her emerald eyes, my vocabulary all but abandoned me. "Yeah, uh, I like some of their stuff, I guess." A lie. I liked *all* their stuff. I had Green Day posters on the walls of my unvisited room.

"Huh." She nodded very slowly, like she didn't know if she could bring herself to believe me. "Well. That's cool."

Did I mention Linda was a cheerleader?

▨   ▨   ▨

It's one thing to while away the day imagining what life must have been like for Thranduil and Legolas—Islam might prefer I do better things with my time, but *The Lord of the Rings* didn't provoke a crisis of conscience. But what do you do when the things that make you feel good are the very things you absolutely must not do? That year, Haroon died; he was resurrected as someone else—he was still himself, as the movie *DodgeBall* put it, "in a legal sense," but in no other way. Girls acknowledged his zombie body. The music he listened to not only captured his angst, but escorted him by the hand into a world he'd always been beside, but was never able to penetrate— layers upon layers of force fields, robust invisible walls composed of dorkiness and difference, religion and restriction.

Up until then, for example, all forms of alcohol were only theoretically sinful. When would I be around it that I'd have to refuse it? Who would offer it to me that I would have to decline it on principle? And, of course, I'd not actually *want* to drink it. I assumed (and believed) that I wouldn't ever seek it out. I'd not only never talk to girls beyond perfunctory pleasantries, I wouldn't *want* to. I didn't even know Muslims would like talking to girls. We were phenotypically human, but fundamentally and genetically something else. Stronger. Lonelier. Not sexual, but with more babies. I fantasized, of course, but knew these variously elastic scenarios were forbidden, and until then impossible to act on. My parents never broached these topics either. Sunday-school instructors breezed over them, by which I mean never said a damned thing, and the parental death stares that accompanied moments of physical affection on television were clue enough about how I was supposed to feel.

It was an odd sensation to discover that one's body, which had never been much in one's control anyhow, was now gravitating toward physical objects it was supposed to be repelled by. In their defense, my parents were raised in a country where postpubescent men and women did not premaritally intermingle, at least not publicly, and certainly not casually. We might even say sororal forces, like powers of attorney for familial interests, had facilitated their marriage. Not that anyone went into that kind of detail. American popular culture's brash sexuality didn't just confuse them, it terrified them. Employing all the forces religious argument could muster, they led me to believe that in this regard the world outside was toxic and dangerous, an STD in this life and hellfire in the next. Now, of course, just because they frowned on it didn't mean they caused my interest; you do not have to deny a teenage boy a sexual outlet for him to be obsessed with sex. But because they did not talk about any of this, I had literally no idea what a relationship was, or how one worked.

They occupied a different way of being. I had to find my own.

The one thing my father regarded as highly as Islam was my report card. I would press my parents, over and over, to be allowed to apply to a prestigious prep school, like Andover and Exeter, a ticket to a great college and the career they believed (and I believed) I deserved; why, though, had my brother been sent away to august Deerfield Academy and I'd received no such vote of confidence? (My parents were also keen on Deerfield because it was gender-segregated—until his junior year.) But as my mother put it, "Even if we wanted to let you, you can't. You're too sick." She didn't want me out of her sight.

Then I found out about Yale University's summer program for high schoolers, which offered me the chance to earn college credits only ninety minutes away.

"I don't know," my mom admitted.

"But it's so close, and it's only for the summer."

They dithered. Until I sealed the deal. I turned to my father, deadly serious, speaking the language no Pakistani elder can refuse. "I'll have an Ivy League on my transcript, Abu."

·4·

JUDGE NONE
CHOOSE ONE

MY PARENTS GOT WHAT THEY WANTED. There would be two college courses from Yale on my eventual applications, and God willing a recommendation from a professor therefrom. I got what I wanted: space. I took Modern Social Theory, where I learned that religion was a hotly disputed category, and Introduction to Philosophy, which profiled the men—overwhelmingly men, all white, the supermajority Christian—who wrestled with some of the same questions I had subconsciously begun to address.

I judged our philosophy professor, who was in fact a graduate student who just needed extra cash, the most awesome person in the world. Every morning, he'd arrive with an iced coffee from a café deep in New Haven, which I wandered God knows how far to find, just so I could purchase my own, drink it, and ipso facto become him. It was expensive. His, I realized, was much lighter-looking than mine. Mine looked like shit. It tasted like shit too. After two sips—the second was for God and country—I dumped a nearly full plastic cup, plus lid and straw, into the garbage. Milk and sugar: where no man has gone before.

But this experience aside, I was changing. That summer merely made it easier to come to terms with it. I became a whole person, who began to feel like a man. I had a growth spurt. My body, which until then had seemed a collection of variously incompetent, frequently incompatible, and artificially unselected systems, layaway at the biology department, harmonized. These various systems not only agreed not to disagree, but to work together, high-fiving each other at every turn. I started going to the gym, reveling in my anonymity, copying the moves of other, more experienced users, torn up and raw the next day, the greatest feeling ever.

I found after just a few minutes of lifting weights that I looked like I'd been at it for years. This was like sunshine after a cloudy day, or, rather, spring after months of miserable winter. And I became likewise more brave. The style was grunge; the clothing attached to the music I listened to, the external embodiment of the attitude powering the sound. I'm not sure if I redefined myself sartorially because I wanted to, or because I thought this transformation would open doors thus far closed to me. Maybe I was just a South Asian American co-opting or submitting to the ideal of white adolescent rebellion, or maybe, as Harry Frankfurt unforgettably proposed, authenticity is bullshit.

First on my list was the toughest: JNCO jeans, which, those much younger or older than me should understand, are bell-bottoms on steroids; I added an assortment of necklaces, bracelets, rings. To this day, wearing jewelry on my wrist, or around my neck, feels strangely right. But having overheard my dad suggest that bodily injury was a fair punishment for earrings, I prudently passed. (I'd hoped to pierce the top of my ear.) When that summer ended, I returned home, the new clothes with me. I walked into high school with Airwalks, sneakers specific to skateboarders. I wasn't me anymore. I didn't explain. I let my ears burn while students stared. But I didn't go back, either.

Not that it was all mangoes and lassi.

Come the fall, I made sure to highlight my Yale experience on my college applications. I had a recommendation from a Yale professor! I met with an alumnus who was now a farmer! Yale rejected me! Even my brother's alma mater, the University of Pennsylvania, slammed the door in my face, and on April 1, 1998, too. *Every* Ivy I applied to rejected me. My dad was deeply disappointed, but my mother was far more concerned with my other failures. On my way to the garage, to head out for an evening, my mother would start to ask if "any girls would be there." It must have been the clothes. And the extracurriculars. I'd taught myself how to skateboard, learned how to stay mostly upright on a snowboard while going downhill at exciting velocities, and one April I even went surfing. Well, sort of.

We were in Vermont. The day was unusually warm. I stripped down to a T-shirt—calm down, I had snowpants on—and raced downhill. As I picked up speed, I saw well ahead of me a huge stretch of melted snow. At the very last moment, I kicked the front of my board up and surfed halfway across this enormous slush puddle, though of course I eventually slowed, stopped, and fell into gelid water.

Fortunately there was a lodge to dry off and recharge in.

Yes, I was loving it. All of it. But what I really wanted was a girlfriend, and I still didn't have the guts to try, not just because I thought liking girls was abnormal but because I was mortified: How could I possibly ask someone out? But that was part of the attraction (literally). If a girl liked me, then I could like me. I was okay.

Except with God, who'd be even more pissed off at me.

There are types of knowledge, Islam teaches, that Muslims might and should ascend through. My mind was paralyzed on the lowest rung: the kind of knowledge that doesn't translate into action. I had sufficient scholastic ammunition to call in theological airstrikes. I could kill anyone with God. My mind overflowed with proofs for His existence, the truthfulness of the Prophet Muhammad, the rightness of Islam. This, I'd been convinced, would help me leap from knowing about Islam to living as a Muslim. Except I never did. My religion was less a crutch than the broken bone. I had no crutch.

I might enjoy a burst of piety, a fit of seriousness and fidelity, praying on time and regularly, but these spells would rarely last more than a few days. Then, for weeks, if not months, I'd be on fumes— not only not praying, but actively avoiding any situation that would require me to pray. Trying to be a Muslim was worse than Sisyphean; instead of pushing the rock God gave us up the incline God made for us, which I'd tried to do for years to no effect, I sat useless on the ground, unmoving, while that giant stone ball grew bigger, heavier, more likely to crush me when my arms gave out as they always did, and each time it took longer to recover.

This was something of the soundtrack of my mind on any given day:

1. How could I complete the endless tasks Islam assigned me?
2. How could I make sure I was doing each of them for the right reasons every day?
3. And doing them in the right ways?

And, oh yeah,

4. How could I keep on the watch, the straight and narrow, not just for weeks or months but for *decades*, all to satisfy a God enough to not be burned alive endlessly or, ideally, even temporarily?

At some point you give up—or give in.

You must understand that Islam's God is awesome, in the original meaning of the word. "He" is formless, genderless, the original and essential Individual, undefined by time or space, though closer to us than anyone, including ourselves. He is not everywhere, nor is He in anything—the location in which He exists stands outside and apart from the universe(s) He created ex nihilo. Evil exists because He created a world in which it may, does, and will. He let Satan tempt Adam away from his originally upright foundation, his *fitra*; He indulges the devil's ongoing temper tantrum till the end of time. Therefore it was, is, and always would be His fault. Who the hell was He to not only so brazenly create me, unasked, but screw up the production of me—I had enough mutations for a family of four—and dump me in the middle of nowhere with no friends, and lastly append to all this

a fourteen-hundred-year-old revelation wh\
be incinerated for something as simple as wa\
What kind of religion forbids hugs?

At the heart of being Muslim is the exclusiv\
One, Unique, without partner or peer. This begins
the testimony of faith. Deny every deity before you
Deity. It wouldn't be an exaggeration to say Islam is \ \d with
God. It wouldn't be an exaggeration to say that I was too. I thought
about Him constantly. Just like I'd been raised to. Allah was the only
Allah I could believe in. And the last One I wanted to believe in.
Insofar as Allah is no watchmaker. Neither is He a creaky old bearded
man (that's usually the imam of the mosque) perched atop a cloud at
some distance from the Earth and perpetually at His wit's end (that's
a *New Yorker* cartoon).

The Qur'an says God created humanity to serve Him.[1] Hiccup:
God never asked if we wanted to be created. Or at least if I wanted to:
I don't presume to know how you feel. This basic oversight, this failure to simply ask us to click if we agree with the terms and conditions,
so tormented me that I finally raised it with a Sunday-school teacher.
"God knows us better than we know ourselves," he explained. "When
He gives us Islam, it's like a doctor prescribing medication."[2] Except
Islam, as I was told again and again, preached no original sin—we
began with fitra, with goodness. So why was I being ministered to
medicinally? Worse, no doctor I knew of would condemn me to dam-
nation if I refused his counsel, and I knew lots of doctors. Not to
mention the doctor didn't create me.

But to commit lèse-majesté? Compared to the mosque, with
its fire and brimstone, implied or declared damnations, sermons in
impassable and treacherous English, sure, high school seemed like
a candy shop (and alternative rock the confectioner). But would I—
could I—really become part of white America? You might be scratching your head and thinking: Why the hell not? I went to school with

---

1. Qur'an 51:56.
2. Figures a community of physicians would go there first.

ᴄe kids. I knew their parents. I wanted to date some of their sisters. I had begun to sneak out to bonfires with them. I stared in envy as they got drunk. But fleeing into whiteness would be abandoning *who* I was, and I don't just mean this religiously, because Islam is a religion, yes, but Islam is also a cultural identity, a heritage, an ethnic marker, a civilization, and sometimes more these things than faith.

In trying to define Islamophobia, many reach for racism. Now, Islam is not a race, except when it is. Islamophobia is like racism because Islam functions, for the Islamophobe, like race does for the racist—but for many Muslims, too, Islam functions like a kind of race. During my adolescence, hundreds of thousands of European Muslims were slaughtered by their fellow Europeans, tens of thousands raped, countless permanently exiled. Srebrenica—the first confirmed instance of genocide in Europe since World War II. Add in Omarska, the massacres in Goražde, the siege of Sarajevo. Serbian radicals moved on to Kosova, though having seen what happened to their neighbors, Albanians were ready to return fire. To me, the victims appeared indistinguishable from white Americans. They were more Western than me, by ancestry. Many of them weren't even religious. (And so what if they were?)

But as Muslims, they weren't just like me; they were in many senses inseparable from me. They were summarily executed, or violated and exiled, simply because they were Muslim. Renouncing my upbringing meant renouncing many other people like myself, coreligionists who were being killed for the very thing I was mooting leaving. Imagine a young Jewish boy, living in relative comfort and privilege, abandoning his faith while a continent away the Holocaust unfolded. Islam is not just what you believe; for most Muslims, who aren't recent converts, Islam is part of where they come from and *who* they come from.

But the tragedy facing the Bosnians only pushed me further along the path I was already on. I had little real idea of the mechanics of the war, and though I bought Bosnian president Alija Ali Izetbegovič's

Islam Between East and West, I hadn't yet read it. Rather, I absorbed the conflict from those around me.

I'd hear many uncles blaming the Bosnians for what was happening to them. If they were being killed so horrifically, and in such great numbers, it must be because God was angry with them. (And you wonder where I got the notion God had gone to war with me?) These Slavs, they weren't *really* Muslim. They were poorly disguised Communists. Look at how they dressed, anyhow. How they behaved. They danced and fornicated. If so, though, they were doing what I wished I could, and soon believed I should. Did they deserve to die so horribly and brutally for such? I heard from a Bosnian refugee a story I could not shake. Whether it was on television, or in one of the events our mosque sponsored to raise awareness of war crimes and urge community members to offer support, I cannot remember.

A squad of Serbs raided a Bosnian Muslim home sheltering three generations, including a grandfather confined to bed. They left him there to watch what unfolded. The young men were taken out and shot, which murders he heard. But his granddaughter was raped in the very room in which he lay helplessly. I do not know what happened thereafter to the woman, or to her grandfather. I imagine the criminals behind this act were never apprehended. But this is not the kind of story that leaves you easily. It forces you to confront a kind of mendaciousness that is hard to understand. Even though, as you may note, there are two Islams competing in this anecdote.

The Islam that taught us that the Bosnians were our brothers and sisters, an Islam that compelled fundraisers for refugees, or pushed us to stand in front of Springfield's City Hall and hold up signs in the pouring rain. An Islam that crossed colors and continents. But there was the other Islam of the men who believed that what was happening was the Divine's righteous wrath. For whatever reason I thought the second was really Islam. Because it's what people said in private, and not at the front of the mosque. Though if the Bosnians were being punished for their sins, what sin did this young woman bear? If the sin were the grandfather's, then why would God have the punishment taken out on his granddaughter instead of him?

The savage sexual assault of a young woman, still a teenager, probably the same age as me, in front of an invalid elder, was the legitimate comeuppance for an allegedly insufficiently pious people.

Who in the hell would want to believe in that?

On a nondescript New England evening, spent at a local Pakistani family's home, one of the uncles was again collectively condemning the *kafir* worldview, the wanton ways of the disbelieving world without, which left people to die alone. Islam, on the other hand, was about "family" and "community." But, I wanted to scream, "I am alone!" Right here, sitting in front of you, is a young almost-man who feels things that can only remain latent for so long. People die abroad, because they are Muslim, but a person is dying inside, because he is Muslim.

Not that they'd care. Or would know what to say. I had a year of high school left, and refused to waste it. Why spend all of my existence fighting against my most basic desires, when I was doing a pretty shit job of it anyway, for a personally unsatisfying and entirely marginal existence, after which I'd be lit on fire? If you're going to hell anyway, you might as well enjoy the ride. Some days later, over a sink full of dishes and a faucet at full blast, a thought would not leave me be. If I decided He didn't exist, then He didn't exist. If I pushed Him out of my head, I could do what I wanted. And so I did. I entertained the thought. I paused a moment to see if He might strike me down, but there was only water spraying over plates and pots and pans, the distant sound of my father's television, and the sense that a shadow that had long obscured me was now receding. I'd decided He didn't exist, and He didn't.

· 5 ·

CATHOLIC GIRLS

THE FIRST TIME I TRIED BEER, it was at a bonfire. I'd maneuvered a very large SUV through dense woods, headlights illuminating little besides brush and the haunted darkness beyond. Just when I was about to give up, and fully freak out about how the hell I was going to get out of there, I found a clearing and parked the Toyota my parents had loaned me. At which time I was all but mobbed by fellow students who greeted my newfound liberalism with the enthusiasm evangelists do a convert. Eric, with his Mohawk and long chains, handed me a can and invited me to partake. It was the worst thing I'd ever tasted, up to and including coffee. But I would not spoil the moment, so I discreetly emptied the can out on the ground beside me.

I had so many beers in this fashion that the next day, some students remarked on my stunning tolerance for alcohol. I tried other kinds of alcohol, too. Vodka, once or twice. Or thrice. Okay, more. There was one time, though—we'll get back to it later—when I had some kind of rum, and I loved it, but of course because I was not supposed to be drinking on that occasion, not just on Islamic or legal but even more purposeful grounds, I never found out what I was drinking. Many things in the world are inseparable from the kinds of people who do them. Opera is for rich old white people. They can keep it. While I continued to try alcohol largely because of the image it projected— sex, parties, not to mention a solid assist if not a slam-dunk over anxiety—there was no desire to smoke, either cigarettes or marijuana. Many of the kids who tried weed joined the laid-back, apathetic, aimless. Once I popped a pill that was some kind of hallucinogen. (I was awfully trusting.) I was terrified the whole night. One friend proposed cocaine. I was not that stupid. But that I was there to be asked—there was a method to my madness. It was not enough to disbelieve. I had to disabuse myself of faith. Mine was very much the atheism of a Sunni Muslim, me disbelieving in God like I'd been taught to practice Islam.

Not everything was so heavy. Some of the things I did were silly, maybe even endearing. I went to a hockey game in nearby Stafford; that had nothing to do with parental restrictions or religious mandates, mind you—my parents were happy my brother played and I attempted sports—but because of my own timidity. I went out to movies with friends, something withdrawn Haroon would never have done. (Two years earlier, I'd see *Star Trek Generations* with my mother. We watched Kirk die in a theater that got shut down soon thereafter, perhaps God's anger at the cinema for indulging such a disrespectful demise.) I went roller-skating with friends. Because I made friends. I had a life beyond my books, beyond my Nintendo, beyond my room. That life felt limitless at the time.

I even took Peter, a lanky Central European exchange student, to the Friendly's in Enfield for a greasy bacon double cheeseburger, the digestion of which was its own punishment. Peter watched my every bite wordlessly. He hadn't been raised with much sacredness; he was consequently unable to rebel against anything so great, so horrifying, so consuming as omniscience. I learned a lot more about myself that year, too. For one, part of me was a deeply superficial upperclassman—my parents raised us with a ferocious ambition, to do and conquer all (and I am so much better for it), but in this case it became the conviction that I could date any girl, no matter the alleged distance between her universe and my own. Plus I wanted the validation she provided. In combination: how can Haroon be a loser if he's dating a cheerleader? But part of me genuinely wanted someone to hold hands with, too. True to the culture that produced Bollywood, I was a soppy romantic at heart. There was more, too.

I was narcissistic: no one should leave me. And terrified: everyone will one day. And certain: I could not live without love. I felt shatteringly alone. Not just empty, but without the music, the clothes, the social circle, I felt excluded, disconnected, seeing shadows on the wall of a cave, life through a glass darkly. That sensation of being adrift while reality passed by just beyond could only be defeated by the immediacy of sensation, and the stronger the better. Tequila that warms the body. Hurtling down a mountain with the sound of snow underboard, balanced precariously, one wrong move and death. Or, in my case, broken wrists and a tailbone. (Not at once.) Dating sisters. (Alas, not at once.) But I'm getting well ahead of myself.

Carla first came to my attention in late March, shortly before graduation, which loomed over us like the end of the world. My good friend Jeremy and I were staying after school, walking the senior hallway when Carla stepped out of a classroom she shouldn't have been in. She looked right and left, like she was crossing the street, expecting vehicular traffic despite the gleaming linoleum. She waved to him, ignored me, and then proceeded to walk ahead of us. Even Jeremy, ever the embodiment of propriety, muttered an "Oh my goodness" before he noticed my staring and suggested I stop. Now, Jeremy had become a good friend, like James—although where James would always copresent with a Drew Bledsoe jersey and some iteration of a Red Sox cap, Jeremy believed in God and the Yankees.

Jeremy was a fervent Catholic, passionate about his religion, yes, but he danced and dated, and that threw me for a loop. When I admitted I was smitten by Carla's Italian genes, her stonewashed jeans, and her striped green tank top, he was only temporarily at a loss for words. "You like girls?"

My classmates had had me pegged not as homosexual but asexual. Who could blame them? Maybe they guessed Muslims reproduced parthenogenetically. Even if Jeremy didn't fully believe me, though, he promised to help me make the leap from fantasy to reality.

He was true to his word.

※   ※   ※

The first job I ever applied for was at a McDonald's. Had my mom and dad discovered this, they'd have been horrified: my priority should have been school. But I needed to pay for prom, so as I sat in that hard plastic chair, testifying to my aptitude for flipping burgers, guilt wasn't the first feeling that came to mind. After all, I'd tried to go along. I'd bought into it: *We* didn't drink. They did. *We* didn't dance. They did. *We* didn't date. They did. We did not like girls, never mind need them.

The hint of a future marriage was the most my parents provided me, a feeble hope they cast, infrequently and entirely insufficiently, in my direction, some sense that a part of my life, as yet inconceivable, might theoretically be enriched by companionship. An iron-clad Pakistani American Hegelianism. Thesis, antithesis, children. "When you are thirty-five," they told me, descriptively but also prescriptively, "you'll get married."

By then I'd be done with med school, the residency, the fellowship.

Nobody made eye contact during these unbelievably stilted conversations. In this, though, as I later discovered, my parents were unusual. Many South Asian families were far more comfortable with and eager to talk about weddings, if not marriage itself; though I found through future friends that most of their parents believed sexuality should still be channeled through marriage, they did not seem ashamed of the idea of intimacy. Husbands would talk about their regard for their wives. They would plan vacations together. They might hold hands. None of this was modeled for me, though. Like God, I was on my own.

Like Him, I decided to create something to keep me company.

Should some future historian seek to define American civilization by means of its greatest achievements, she should count among them the coming-of-age movie. I wanted my last months of high school to be *Ferris Bueller's Day Off*. Prom would be my riding the ball from *Take Me Home Tonight*. There are, after all, different ways of trying to live forever. I looked forward to life nostalgically, as if it were over before it had even begun. "Remember Haroon?" they'd say appreciatively. "Who snuck out to prom?" And with whom!

This imagining a decision as some third party would receive it was the outgrowth of my own youthful isolation, which was in turn the outcome of my sickliness. A fervid imagination created all kinds of scenarios to inhabit, test out, and follow through with, unrealizable possibilities preferable to lived realities. You see, I was always looking for stories without planning to, making them without making a big deal out of them. I understand now that these imaginings were a way out of otherwise indomitable nervousness and trepidation: stories weren't just a safe harbor from storms at sea but my armor and even my sword, a horse to ride into battle. To believe you can be with any girl in the world is less ridiculous when it's not you who are attempting to ask her out but someone else.

So somewhere along the way I decided I was a main character on a popular TV show; if I wanted to keep the show going, get advertisers to buy time, keep eyeballs glued to the screen, I'd have to act contrary to my ordinary instincts—to choose the adventure every time. You cannot imagine a more liberating fiction. Out of fantasy came reality.

On a Wednesday in early April, I was excused from school to attend Eid prayers at our West Springfield mosque—it was the second Eid, the festival to mark Abraham's almost sacrifice of his son. As per every year, we had to wake up painfully early so we'd not get stuck in the Outremer of the Islamic Center's parking lot and freeze to death walking to the mosque. Perhaps our obstinate Punjabiness demanded we wear *shalwar qamis* no matter its inappropriateness to the weather, but the effect was always the same. Your body went numb. Then your mind—though that was theology, not meteorology.

If Eid was one thing growing up, it was boring. But I'd get a hundred dollars, two crisp fifty-dollar bills, from my father, folded and passed from him to me like some kind of illicit exchange. My hundred bucks, it should be noted, helped pay for her corsage. Which meant she said yes.

Let me tell you how.

※   ※   ※

I was home by late afternoon and called Jeremy to find out what happened in school. Not that, as a senior, I really cared. As it turned out, because of Eid I'd missed everything. During eighth-period English, Mr. Malone's class, Carla had stopped by to deliver a message to her older sister, Maria, a senior like us. To call me crestfallen would have been an understatement. I was devastated. I'd missed seeing Carla? Carla with the wavy hair, which smelled like heaven, underneath which rivers flow? Carla with the mesmerizing sapphire eyes?

"Did she look hot like she always does?" I asked.

Jeremy answered elliptically. "You should ask her out before someone else does."

Just one thing. How?

I'd never talked to her, never acknowledged her, never so far as I could tell been noticed by her. But so badly did I want her that I thought I could cast my anxiety aside—I would be the superhero of some high school movie franchise. It should've been pretty easy too, considering that Maria had already told her of my interest.

Carla's locker was in the science wing, which is where I'd make the ask—I passed by her every day on the way to AP Biology. Except at the last minute I lost my nerve and hid in an empty classroom. A few minutes later, Carla's cousin Bradley walked in, thinking I had done the deed and was now celebrating in quiet triumph.

"Did you do it?" he asked, entirely rhetorically. He had a huge grin on his face. Until he saw me look down, ashamed.

"What the hell is wrong with you?" he may or may not have said. Bradley had nonverbal ways of communicating. We'd become fast friends because fate had put us together for seven out of eight classes both halves of senior year. On the one occasion we sort-of, kind-of got into a fight, he threw me into a pool. Which was his way of killing me softly, he being exponentially stronger than most of our high school put together.

Disgusted with my spinelessness, Bradley punched me. Hard. And then, to add insult to a gathering upper-body injury, he shoved me out the door. This meant I came into Carla's line of sight by flying out of an ostensibly vacant classroom, halfway across the hall, and nearly into the wall, before I could skid to any kind of stop. I tried not to think about how this looked. Her friends scattered at the sudden sight of me.

"Hey, Carla . . ." She turned to give me her full attention. That was not helpful either. "I was wondering if you—"

She was remarkably still. She had good posture. Also, while her gaze never faltered, I found it hard to maintain eye contact.

"Yes?"

She was formal, but not impolite. She knew what was going to happen. But she made no move to escape what may have been terrifying only for me.

"Would, uh . . . Want to go to the prom?" I'm not sure if I included "with me"; I may have simply inquired into her interest in the function generally.

"I'd love to." Then without turning her torso, demonstrating outstanding spatial awareness, she used her left hand to slam the locker shut and said she had to get to class.

I like to think I stood there like Peter Parker did when he first became aware of his spidery superpowers. I felt like a new man, who'd shed his skin. (Something spiders do not, for the record, do.) I was taller, better, braver, a cooler shade of brown. Sultan of all I surveyed. (All my subjects were in class, which is where I should've been.) High on myself, I spun around to tell Bradley the good news but ran into Mrs. D. of AP Biology instead. She'd been behind me during the entire exchange and was waiting either for the last stragglers to get to class or, more likely, to see how the prom invite worked out for me; it's not an exaggeration to say that the whole school had followed my recent personal revolution.

Mrs. D. practically gave me a black power salute. "Good work, Haroon!"

By the end of that day, the whole science department had separately congratulated me. I should, in honor of their sympathy and support, apologize for scoring a 2 on the actual AP Biology exam. In my defense, more important things were unfolding. My parents left town two weekends later, and with the phone freed—there were no cell phones back then—Carla and I talked and agreed we were dating. I had no idea what that meant: our two months together were my advanced placement in assimilation. How do dates work? (Ask friends.) Am I allowed to check her out because she's my girlfriend? (Answer didn't matter.) Holy crap, she's going out with me. (Holy crap, she's going out with me.)

One Saturday night in early May we went out to Friendly's. Carla's father told her (he meant me) not to be late. We talked well past her curfew over frothy chocolate milkshakes. She was wearing a blue sweater, though since this was a spring thing, I'm not sure why. She looked wonderful and adorable, so close and yet so far. It took everything in me not to reach for her. But I was mortified she'd reject me. It didn't occur to me that, in agreeing to date me, she was at least receptive to me kissing her. We pulled up to her house and I walked her to the side door, under the porch, one of those halfhearted basements, part underground and part above. (I sympathized with this bipolarity.) I hoped her father would not assault us (I meant me), so I tried to stay quiet though the driveway gravel crunched traitorously under my feet. It was the loudest sound I'd ever heard.

When she turned to face me in the pale lamplight of the doorway, ostensibly to say good night, I was so still she had to ask, "Is everything okay?"

I described how I saw our near future playing out. "I wanted to kiss you."

She went with it. She approached me gingerly, tentatively, the little rocks crackling under her shoes, but when she got close enough, she moved much more deliberately: she closed her eyes and accelerated toward me, tilting her head ever so slightly, so that my lips could find the way to hers all the faster. She got there first. I was kissed. Nothing could've prepared me for what it was, the wave of electric joy that began in my mouth and pushed everything else out of me. Rapture had come to lift me up and away.

I kissed her back, and a second later it was over.

She smiled and disappeared into her home.
Did she know I'd never even kissed a girl before?

If only there was a higher power to thank for this fantastic causation: Reject God, get girlfriend. Becoming, simultaneously, *the* boyfriend. Among my peers, I could now stand at least as tall as I was. I wasn't just one of them, but a very awesome version of them. Even as I made it up as I went along. Take Confirmation, which I dimly understood to be some kind of Catholic coming-of-age ritual, fast coming up for Carla.

James called the play. On the morning of the big day, we drove separately to a nearby pharmacy. He—not Catholic, but still Christian—approved a greeting card whose message gestured toward faith without collapsing into any explicit organized version of it. We were very proud of ourselves: Protestant New England Patriot helps Muslim atheist honor Catholic ritual. I bought and signed the card, an ecumenical gesture that explains, incidentally, why you're not reading *How to Be an Atheist*—for reasons few South Asian parents would like to hear.

James and I parted ways at the pharmacy—it's not like he was gonna come along, after all—and I made it to Carla's in great time. (The thought of joining them at church didn't enter my mind. It'd be another seven years before I'd even work up the courage to attend a Mass.) I knocked on the front door, card behind my back, my intention being to surprise her. She won that battle. She opened the door wearing barely anything at all. It was a slip, I think—diaphanous, waiting for the dress. I'd interrupted her. Not that any part of me was unduly distressed. She was so pleased by the card I handed to her that she gave me what may have been the greatest hug of my life. During which her father passed by in the hallway behind her. I frantically released her even as she held on to me.

He, however, said a casual hello and kept walking, unimpressed by the sight of us in what I'd call inappropriate embrace. He did not return several seconds later with shotgun, ax, or simply his bare hands. (Trust me: Mr. Carla could have killed me with his hand, the other maybe holding a beer, as my life ended in a bloodied teachable moment.) Carla let go; they had to be at church on time, and that was that. I walked across their lawn and into my car, too stunned to speak. My parents told me boys and girls didn't touch. Shaking hands was taboo; if even tolerated, it was only just that. You were expected to do so in a manner that indicated distaste. This girl's father, on the other hand, let his daughter hug a boy while wearing what to my eyes was astonishingly little—all things being equal, Muslims have more private parts—and, oh, all this while the family was on their way to church.

Who the hell were these people?

· 6 ·

HI, I AM NOT A CHRISTIAN

MANY WHO GO FROM THEISM TO ATHEISM, from religion to nonbelief, don't change as much as you (and they) think. The annoyingly fundamentalist believer becomes the irritatingly strident heretic, except there's no longer any theological basis to his rigidity. As such, they are—or he is; I'm thinking of Richard Dawkins here—even less rational than they were before. Which is just a way to say I've encountered several types of people who've fled from religion.

The historical atheist reviews the evidence for her religion and finds it wanting. She reads Bible criticism so devastating, for example, that she can never read the Bible, or attend her church, the same way again.

There's the empirical atheist, who had perhaps believed in a God of the gaps until the gaps were filled. She comes to believe that science explains enough, or better, or will get around to it eventually. God is the Answer she no longer believes in.

The moral atheist refuses to believe in a God who does not conform to her sense of right and wrong. If bad things happen in the world, and God does not stop them, then God is not. But that doesn't make any sense, does it?

There's another kind of empirical atheist, though. She finds the religious wanting. Not the object of her worship, but the worshippers themselves. She looks at the prayerful people who do what religion

asks them to and finds them to be lackluster human beings despite
their efforts. Or is it because of their efforts?

My atheism was born of frustration and exhaustion with the consequences of a religion I accepted as true but experienced, personally
and spiritually, as dissatisfying, if not choking. I chose not to believe
in God because, with Him out of the way, there was at last room for
me. My life became not just easier but genuinely really truly fun. The
problem with all this? I never seriously considered a Godless universe
convincing. I never found any atheist arguments persuasive. I knew
I was cheating. There's only so long you can suppress something that
you know is true—it's like forcing a buoyant object under water.
Eventually it'll resurface.

And smack you in the face on its way up.

The rush of seeing Carla, of feeling like I had accomplished something good with my little gesture on her day of Christian sacrament,
faded as I neared home. Nearly everyone we knew, like crew-cutted
Bradley with his overlarge muscles and Jeremy with his perfect faith,
was at church, while I was up in my room moping like a fraudulent
apostate. I knew I couldn't keep God out very much longer. I was
lying to myself.

I turned the image of her over and over in my mind. At the door.
Undressed. On their way to church. A plangent observation. In the
Muslim circles I'd traveled, my brief encounter with Carla would've
been treated, at best, as proof of Christian unseriousness. But it wasn't
that Carla's family didn't take God seriously. It's that their idea of
what God approved and disapproved of was different. Since I could
not *not* believe in God, perhaps the problem was not God, but Islam.
It was the first time I practically applied the theoretical arguments I'd
learned at Yale: though religions are comparable, they aren't meant
to be naïvely compared.

Which raised the question: If I was going to date Catholic girls,
why not become Catholic? But of course this book is not titled *How to
Be a Christian* either. Many Muslims dismiss the Trinity as halfhearted

monotheism; they judge Christianity wanting—by Islam's standards. They might say it's absurd that God should have to send and sacrifice His own Son to remedy a flaw in humanity He himself created in the first place, thereby taking some of the oomph out of the gesture, or that it's irrational to believe that God could be Son and Father at the same time. To the first, I have only to ask: What is the difference between sending one Son and choosing many prophets? Obviously the concept of repentance through Muhammad's model and salvation through Jesus's sacrifice are not the same, but I could only think of MD Uncle telling me God was the Great Doctor up above, prescribing us Islam.

To the second: I found the Trinity confusing, too, but that was not itself dispositive. God does not have to make sense to us. Rather, the more I studied Christianity, the more uncertain the provenance of the Trinity became—and that, in turn, threw the whole enterprise into question. The byzantine debates over whether Jesus was fully, partly, or simultaneously divine and human made me dizzy. But I was also learning that many concepts at the heart of modern Christianity emerged at least several decades after Jesus and, to make things worse, contradicted what the earliest Christians seemed to believe. Contemporary Christianity was not what Jesus had preached.

On top of this, the Bible itself had been carpet-bombed by critics: what was left were bits and pieces, reduced by skeptics to a treacherous topography. When some Christians claimed God inspired but did not directly author the Bible, well, that only had me wondering why we should even read it. The life of the Prophet Muhammad is rather well documented. History just unfolded differently. Christianity lived on the margins of Rome for decades; Muhammad's followers quickly gained political power and were able to direct the resources of whole empires to preserving and elaborating on their tradition. When I disagreed with Islam, I believed I was contesting the same texts Muhammad shared with his companions. When it came to Catholicism, contrarily, I could not feel certain that Jesus would have recognized the Church, let alone the Bible, which meant my embrace of them was self-serving: believing it to be true only because I wanted it to be true. As much as I wanted—no, *needed*—emotion, passion, camaraderie, community (and companionship) in my life, I also needed to feel that the beliefs I committed to seemed authentic to me. Even if I acceded to the Trinity, I still wouldn't know what kind of Christianity to practice. Catholic? Orthodox? Protestant? Mormon? (Yes, I read the Book of Mormon.) Not to mention: Jesus was a Jew and like Jews then and now, and Muslims then and now, wouldn't he have been a unitarian monotheist?—the evidence seemed to strongly suggest Jesus did not acknowledge anything Trinitarian.

But Christianity still offered what I did not find in Islam: warmth, kindness, gentleness, openness, an intimation that I might not be damned for my desires, say, before I even learned to drive. It may well have been that had I grown up with Catholicism, I'd have felt the same exasperation, because, after all, while our beliefs change, who we are rarely does. Half my high school went down into the muck with me. Jeremy, above all, was admirably patient with me even while I dug into his holy book and challenged his faith.

Take, for example, the question of Christ's resurrection, which Islam disputes, on the argument that Jesus was not crucified and as such did not, and has not yet, died. Speaking in the Bible about his impending execution, Jesus compares his "sign" to Jonah's.[1] A whale had swallowed but not killed Jonah, so while it *seemed* Jonah had died, he was yet alive. On the third day, Jonah returned, humbled and transformed. Maybe it appeared to others that he'd been resurrected. But only appeared. That was Jonah's sign.

Didn't this suggest, I challenged Jeremy, that Jesus did not die on the cross but only *appeared* to, which conclusion accorded with the Qur'an's perspective?

As for them saying, "We have killed the Messiah, Jesus the son of Mary, the messenger of God"—they did not kill him, and did not crucify him, but (another) was made to resemble him to

---

1. Matthew 16:1–4.

them. Those who differ over it are in doubt about it and have no knowledge but only speculation. Certainly they did not kill him! Rather God raised him to Himself—God is the Mighty, the Wise.[2]

I don't remember how this argument ever wound down. I do remember this much: Jeremy stayed with his faith, and I stayed without mine.

<hr />

2. Qur'an 4:157.

· 7 ·

WHICH OF THESE
TWO LAND CRUISERS
WILL YOU DENY?

I WOKE UP ONE MORNING to my alarm as per usual, but then my mother's angry voice as per unusual. She wasn't beckoning me downstairs. She was demanding I get downstairs immediately. Trying to play it cool, I told her I'd be down after showering. When I finally got to the kitchen, a pit in my stomach, it was to find my parents waiting in ambush.

My father fired first. "Why did you have a girl in your car yesterday?"

My eyes went wide. My mind went into overdrive, my face compensating by retreating into confusion, perhaps disbelief. "A girl?" As if I didn't know what one was. Perhaps if I forced them to define the female of the species, mere embarrassment would stop them from continuing their interrogation. (On reflection, this would have worked perfectly.)

As it turns out, someone in the Muslim community—the local *mukhabarat*—had snitched on me. This is what I got for driving around in a liability of a Land Cruiser, of which there were only two in town, the other belonging to the mosque president, whose family

49

was also the only other Muslim one in town. The two Land Cruisers were also the same color, beige with brown paneling. Since the mosque president's wife and my mother both headscarved, you can imagine the neighbors' confusion: "They all look the same to me." "So do their cars!" I decided to own it. Partway. I told my parents: "She needed a ride home."

And since offering a girl a ride home was already a trespass, maybe that and that alone was the reason for the momentary panic in my eyes. I folded an Eggo waffle in half and shoved most of it into my mouth, washing it down with a glass of chocolate milk. "It was nothing."

Calm down.

I'd been sloppy. So I went about erasing any signs of my actual life, with some cost to posterity. And my ego. Every senior was asked to propose a prophecy for another senior, the yearbook's Secret Santa. Jeremy must have taken off his Yankees cap, scratched his head, and concluded this'd be a riot: "Finding Islam doesn't work for him, Haroon dates a supermodel." Of course, since this was in fact published, I'd have to keep any yearbook at arm's length from my parents. When my parents asked me about yearbook photos—another letter in the mail—I had to move preemptively. "Yearbooks are stupid," I said, doing my best impression of a jaded teenager, permanently bored out of his mind. "Pictures are stupid."

On reflection I could've also pretended I'd become an extremist whose iconoclasm extended to portrait photographs. You live, you learn. But the yearbook editors were proactive; they assumed I'd merely forgotten to submit a proper headshot and substituted the worst possible snapshot, one in which I seemed to be in a rush to find the nearest bathroom. Any reader would wonder what kind of washed-out supermodel would resort to dating such an incontinent man. Underneath that was my senior quote, which I'd sent in well before life with Carla. Pearl Jam. With Nirvana and Green Day, they were my Trinity. Bradley had struggled with his, so I suggested a Chinese aphorism—something about lighting a candle instead of cursing the darkness.

I'd had to do the same.

McDonald's had never called back, so I found another job (one that'd be easier to hide—softening the blow of being rejected by a chain restaurant that sells foodlike product). It might have been unethical, and possibly illegal: I helped students write their theses. From scratch, or a rewrite. Technically I did not graduate high school once but several times. I profited from my bookishness, in order to pay for a life that tried desperately to escape from it.

I'd walk past Carla every morning, because the science wing was closest to the senior parking lot. My friends teased me for not making out with her; I, too, wondered why I held back, even as I knew. I was scared of putting my arms around her while kissing her. But there was an absence of opportunity too. Her friend Samantha presented one, by announcing a pool party at the end of May, which I knew I had to attend—I'd make my move then and there. But of course Sam's house had to be beside the mosque president's, which meant he might see my car, which, as noted, was also his car.

A huge risk to take two weeks before prom—but this new Haroon loved the edge.

Not enough, however, to drive over it. I asked my friend Jacob to be my ride.

Jacob was a bright kid who, sometime in the course of senior year, developed the habit of falling asleep during everything. He was bright enough to coast on his wits for a while, but the warning signs were there: judging by his snoozing, he deemed most of his life too unimportant to be present for. Also, he almost always wore oversize hand-knit sweaters, meaning he looked like his mother had purposefully gotten him lost inside himself. Also, in case you forgot, he was frequently asleep. But not when driving. Incidentally, Jacob's mom took a liking to me—she wasn't particularly religious but always asked me to find Jacob a nice Jewish girl, as if, as an adolescent kind of Muslim stranded in ostensibly Christian Connecticut, I had some special access to Jewish females that she lacked.

On the way to the party, naturally, Jacob's nose started bleed-
ing, so badly that we drove right past Samantha's and almost to the
Massachusetts border, in the apparent belief that the closer we got
to Canada the more likely the flow would be stanched. No luck. Jacob practically ran his mom's station wagon aground on a stranger's
lawn, and nearly did a faceplant on the grass as he sprinted toward
the biggest tree in the yard. It took me a moment to realize he was
repurposing leaves as napkins. Then we met the homeowner, who
had real napkins, which she happily shared after we explained why
one of our town's Semites was apparently washing his face with oak
leaves while the other was falling over laughing. This unfathomable
omen aside, I ended up that night exactly where I'd wanted to be:
On Samantha's pool deck. With Carla. Her smaller, firmer, more
beautiful legs, naked golden cream, pushing on mine, adrift inside
massive jeans. Beer had turned out to be an epic disappointment.
Bacon didn't matter. But this . . . My need displaced me. Blind children learn how to walk. They don't need to see anyone else to learn
how. It's deep instinct, buried well inside them, which in the right
time and place comes to the surface. Some force reached entirely
around my insecure, agitated, and cowardly impediment of a self and
shoved him to the floor. I had never felt so overcome. But here's the
thing: I could sense, with some radar I did not know I had, that she
wanted the same.

The energy hung in the air.

She was quiet. Too quiet. We were opposite ends of a magnet.
Fusion releases more energy than fission. Time seemed to stop. I'd just
reach over, put my arms around her, lock eyes with her . . . and watch
as her mom's station wagon pulled up. With equal and immediate
force we jumped away from each other. I walked Carla to her car,
dejected, with this meager consolation: as she made her way to the
backseat, she offered me her hand in silent and complicit apology. I
thought this meant she'd give me another shot. Or that I should take
more shots. My skinny fingers squeezed inside her smaller, softer, sub-
tler hand, held, cradled, safe there. There was so much in that grasp,
I fear I've spent my life trying only to return to that squeeze, the

promise inherent in it—that there was somewhere I would be held, that I could be with someone instead of just myself.

I led my parents to believe that on *the* Friday night, the first week of June, I'd sleep over at a (Muslim) friend's house in Agawam. This friend's mom conspired with me. So did everyone else. See: Letters in the mail. To leave school early on the day of prom, one had to have parental permission; most parents gave it. Mine? Do you have to ask? So the principal and vice principal winked at my departing a little earlier than the actual conclusion of the school day. I crossed state lines to my friend's home, showered and shaved, and returned to Somers in time for the evening's events. Jacob's neighbors were on vacation, so I parked my hulking SUV not merely in their backyard but under their deck. Having been caught once before, I'd not make the same mistake twice.

At Jacob's house, though, I finally relaxed. I was going to get away with this. We went into his backyard and posed for the camera. Back then you had to wait days for pictures to develop. You actually got to live in the moment, as opposed to waiting to look at yourself living it a few seconds later. The six of us—Jacob, Jeremy, and I, with our dates—were dressed to the nines. And the smiles we wore for the camera, belying what was around the corner. For reasons that will become obvious, I've no further pictures with Carla.

At prom, practically every student went out of his way to congratulate me, amazed I'd made it. More encouraged that I'd wanted to attend in the first place—everyone's belief system appreciates validation. And I wanted theirs. Maybe so that one day I wouldn't need it. Maybe soon. I'd gotten rejection letters but also admission letters. Between Boston University and New York University, I picked the latter. All good things must come to an end, Jean-Luc. I'd never see many of my classmates again. I'd never see this me again. It'd be like it never happened.

Carla and I slow danced to Sarah McLachlan's "Adia," which I cannot listen to even now without breaking out in goose bumps. I still ask myself, Who is this Adia? Why does she need to know we still haven't done anything wrong? Why was I receiving an Islamic meme here, of all places? "And Satan asked Adam, 'Shall I lead you to a Tree, and to a Kingdom that never decays?'"[1] The apple tastes better than it digests. But Islam's got no original sin. Adam's tempted by the desire to live forever. He falls, yes. But only in falling does he become the caliph he was meant to be.

Maybe we missed the point of the story all along.

We can do the wrong thing for the right reasons. Adam and Eve ate from the tree, but they repented. They were forgiven. They stuck together.

Time stopped for me in that slow dance; I felt poetry flow through me. I've learned in the years since that even when I'm driving, I've got to pull over whenever an idea enters my mind. You do what you have to, because you don't know if you ever can again. These moments vanish, like the world vanishes. The only constant is you. And Him. Jeremy and I saw each other once a year after graduation, for a number of years, but eventually we didn't even have that anymore. Shortly after I went to NYU, Jacob's mother became ever more insistent that I find her son a Jewish girl. Later I found out why: Jacob, who I haven't spoken to in years, became a Buddhist. Bradley and I nearly entirely lost touch. All that was still well ahead of us, though.

I was just a seventeen-year-old who wanted more than anything in the world to belong, to believe that there was a world he could just be inside and a part of, that he didn't need to analyze from without, prejudge, damn, doom, condemn, excommunicate, or be excommunicated from. If even for a night, let the stars circle me. The flared jeans, the metal necklaces, the occasional bracelets, the wallet hooked on a chain to my belt loop: these were the tribal markers of an amateur snowboarder, meant to validate me—by announcing that I was other than me. Sticking out to fit in. But those emblems couldn't tell you how badly I'd wanted this cheerleader.

---

1. Qur'an 20:10.

We can want what others want because they want it—and still want it for ourselves. Sometimes we're unable to point to where our desires begin and others' end. After prom we might have stopped at Friendly's, but I honestly can't remember. Carla wanted nothing to do with me. The last thing she did was chide me: You can't drink, you've got to drive. Away. Back. I did, around 4 a.m. The next afternoon, alone in an empty bedroom in someone else's house, Carla chose AOL Instant Messenger to shock and awe me. We should break up. Sure, I typed. Lied. Agreed. Died. I'd not expected this would end, even as I'd made plans to go away for college. We can hold two contradictory hopes in our head and still be devastated when one of them gives way. It's wanting to have your cake and eat it too.

But what the hell else would you do with cake?

I drove with my parents to New York the very night after prom, to see family. I sat broken and unspeaking in the backseat. My mom would pass away less than a decade later, done in by cancer. My father is still with us, another decade after that. But I could not admit to them, then or ever, that my end run around them had failed because I was, in the end, them. Carla and I never moved beyond that kiss; I'd been more Catholic than the Catholic girl. While I trembled even to meet her lips, she'd told me in casual detail what intimacies she would and would not be okay with. I'd nodded determinedly, as if this was a subject I'd long ago mastered. Like space travel. And yet for me, so new to relationships, so raised on the idea of marriage once and forever, dating was taboo, but I believed it was no different from marrying: once we were together, we would remain together. Terminology was technicality. So I was ruined like I couldn't believe. It's one thing not to go to prom, and another to be dumped the day after you've pulled off the greatest deception in your brief history.

If every person has one great test, then mine was—and may still be—parting. I'd learn I could deal with death. But I couldn't accept that God would let lives get entangled only to be yanked apart. How can you live forever and be parted forever? That's death. A real end without resurrection. A place where Islam can't go. Had Carla not broken up with me, could I have broken it off with her? Kahlil Gibran once said that "the deeper that sorrow carves into you, the more joy you can contain." From which I learned this lesson: the further you let a person into your soul, the longer it'll take her to leave. I couldn't have guessed then how much it'd hurt to give anyone anything of my heart, but I'd naïvely given all of mine, presumed the future existed while the present was still coming together.

I thought, against all logic, that we were bonded to each other. I had planned out the rest of my life as if we would be. I could not believe how crushed I was.

The following spring, I stopped by Carla's house to pick up Bradley—though he lived on the other side of town. Jeremy, who also lived a few miles away, was standing beside me. None of this memory makes much sense, but that's probably because all I was focused on, all I can really see so many years later, is Carla at the top of the stairs, putting dishes away. She might have waved. A year later, we ended up across from each other at a diner in Connecticut and shared where life had taken us. Jeremy laughed as he and I walked back to my car. "That was the longest conversation you ever had with her, Haroon."

"Maybe I should ask her out."

He snorted.

I never spoke to her, or even saw her, again.

Maybe we do not live one life, but many. Some overlap. Some are eras apart. Some never intersect. Maybe I tell myself this to keep the feelings away, because if I know they can unfold somewhere else, I do not need to know what they mean in this universe. My religion says a man should not be alone with a woman. But somebody should have told me a man should not feel so alone that he needs to be alone with a woman to feel like his life is worth living. Her smile, her lightness, her kindness, all of them a bond she provided to a universe I otherwise felt misplaced by. But what I missed most of all, in the months after the breakup, was her hand. From the first time she offered hers, at a roller-skating rink (a dance remix of Celine Dion's "My Heart Will Go On" was screaming out of the speakers), to the last, when we left the dance floor and I escorted her to our table—we'd just heard that same song, which had invaded the planet like the film it came from. "It may be you hate a thing and it is good for you." That'd be God. Beyond my desire for her was an awesome loneliness, a feeling of living in a nothing-place only briefly interrupted. Life bereft of a woman was no life at all. From time to time, this emptiness made the world stark and beautiful, but most of all it haunted me and pursued me. Something always comes from nothing. "With every difficulty there's relief." Him again.[2] It could be that this is me, or all of us. We stumble onto God in the blanks, the places we live in but don't ever really belong to, if only to be taught this hell of a mercy: we don't belong here.

---

2. Qur'an 2:26; 94:5

· 8 ·

AND SHAMS IS THE SUN

IN JULY, NEW YORK UNIVERSITY ordered us to freshman orientation. My father drove me down. I cannot recall what we spoke about, if anything; I was and still am mesmerized by the transition from northern Connecticut's corn and tobacco to skyscrapers and gridlock. I could not believe that the world's greatest city was just two hours away from my life and that wonderful, jarring, abrupt transformation, from the rest of America beyond Gotham to the singular craziness within, might be why I found it so hard to move away. Back then, I'd not have imagined I'd spend some half of my life in the five boroughs.

I was overwhelmed enough by one of them.

Incoming students were assigned dormitories at Weinstein Hall, which was almost kitty-corner from Washington Square Park, the heart of "campus." In my dismay over not getting into an Ivy, I'd dutifully picked the highest-ranked of the schools that had begrudgingly accepted me and so chose NYU. That was about all the research I'd done. So when we pulled up at University Place, I was stunned to find that there were no gates. No lawns. No paths for academic ambulation. NYU wasn't just in New York. It *was* New York.

"I didn't know there wasn't a campus," I said, forgetting my father was not just in the car but had been driving it for two hours. This was a man who crossed half the planet to come here and make a new life in a foreign land. Whose mother was illiterate, and whose son was in turn expected to be presidential material. Tiger Mom never met Punjabi parents. My father looked at me, confirming that I was the idiot he always feared me to be, but then seemed gravely wounded, realizing he was inseparable from my dumbness. I think he told me not to get AIDS as I stepped out of the car.

NYU had an academic plan, named for famous alumnus Samuel Morse, intended to give students a flavor of the humanities and a taste of the sciences. Just how much of the latter depended on how much you already knew. Gathered in a steeply sloping auditorium, dozens of us were left to suffer through a long, boring exam, testing our general knowledge. I was up high, in the back, when from way down below, a *desi* like me called out in desperation, "Does anyone have any idea how far the Earth is from the Sun?"

Seeing that the proctor had exited, I hollered back, "Ninety-three-million miles."

He stared at me in disbelief, but proceeded to write the answer down.

Haroon might not know what a penis is, but he knows everything about the solar system, up to and including Uranus.

His name was Shams, he was from Mississippi, and it was love at first sight. We were each astonished to find that there was another Muslim in the world—though, statistically speaking, this shouldn't have been surprising—who loved Rage Against the Machine, who thought girls in bell-bottoms were the haramest thing possible, who wanted to read the great books of our civilizations, who had the same questions, the same doubts, the same anxieties, who grew up in vanilla towns in which they were always at a remove. Speak, friend, and enter. Shams and I searched the NYU campus for the Islamic Center, which was found in Room 808 in the late Loeb Student Center. We reviewed the course catalogue side by side. (I had many interests, all of which seemed worth chasing: Economics. English. Physics.) And then those three days were over, and it was back to Holyoke, Mass., where I had a job as a junior assistant, a paralegal to a paralegal, a forty-five-minute drive from Somers. I'd lost Carla but also the world I'd tried so hard to be part of, and so briefly was. Everyone I knew was on his way out. I'd have two more months in an emptied New England. There's a reason *Ferris Bueller's Day Off* never shows you the day after.

While the credits rolled, and we adolescents went off alone, searching in different directions for that thing called adulthood, a phone call was received. My brother, who was then in law school, called from Saudi Arabia, where he'd scored a summer job with an American law firm that had a Jeddah office.

"I'm bored," he complained.

"That sucks," I said, commiserating. Because. "I am, too."

"Come to Saudi Arabia—we can do *umrah* together!"

Naturally my response to this couldn't be, "Well, seeing as I'm now kind of not really Muslim, I'm not sure I want to perform the minor pilgrimage to Mecca and then, as you suggested, pay my respects to the Prophet Muhammad in Medina." I hit instead on the financial impracticality of the proposition. "How am I to pay for a ticket across the planet?"

Saudi Arabia, however, is apparently so deadening your brother will pay to fly you there. Then what do you say? You reframe the opportunity.

Islam—or most Muslims, or maybe both—made me feel terrible. On the other hand, Christianity raised too many questions, and its accessibility declined as my Catholic friends disappeared. Maybe the problem was religion, and I just lacked the guts to own up to where I was heading. If God didn't move me in Mecca and Medina, then at least I'd know for sure. I was in a movie where the main character—me—abandoned ship and meant to swim to another, stranger shore, unsure if he could or would invent himself on the other side. Shams agreed: over Instant Messenger, he told me to make the most of it and go.

With only a few weeks to go before the big trip, I set myself to packing. That took all of half an afternoon. And then it was me, alone again, in my oversized room—which bed should I lie on while I waste away the evenings? One night I picked up Izetbegovič's *Islam Between East and West*. It seemed apropos, but maybe I was desperate. Instead of digesting the words, though, I was digested by them. Superficially it seemed like Izetbegovič was discussing my religion. But he wrote with an intensity, a fearlessness, and above all a sophistication I'd thought we qua Muslims were incapable of. There was real literature here, whole chapters on art, architecture, aesthetics, from the Western, European tradition.

He was Muslim and from the same place as me, broadly speaking.

But he talked of the Eastern Islamic tradition too. I found selections of poetry, a nod to the critical role verse plays in an Islamic ecumene that, I'd learn, stretched across even antagonistic empires, from Budapest to Bangkok. There was a snippet from a South Asian like myself, Muhammad Iqbal, quoting his *Javid Nama*, the Book of Eternity. Maybe Izetbegovič translated Iqbal's Persian and maybe he didn't. What mattered more was that his excerpt worked like a recommendation. If Izetbegovič was moved enough to reference Iqbal, then I'd have to seek Iqbal out. The bit Izetbegovič opened his book with didn't include the following of Iqbal's couplets, which I'd chance upon, and be astonished by, years later: "You can deny God," Iqbal warned, promised, conceded.

"But you cannot deny Muhammad."

· 9 ·

"ARE YOU THERE, MUHAMMAD? IT'S ME, GOD."

THE CENTER OF MECCA is the Ka'ba, a cubical temple built by Adam after his exile from Eden, then rebuilt by father Abraham and son Ishmael, and later the focus of one of Ishmael's descendants: Muhammad. Though Muslims do not pray to the Ka'ba, we face in its direction during *salat*, which means you must add, on top of sacred history, a demographically vigorous, linguistically various, jet-powered Muslim world. Mecca might be compared to Times Square, where every day is New Year's Eve and every call to prayer is the ball drop. Millions of pilgrims aren't just walking to the Great Mosque, but tumbling into it, pulled by the force of nature's God and gravity—Mecca lies in a valley—toward the fifty-foot-high house of nature's God.

Muhammad was born in Mecca, but driven from it about a dozen years after he began preaching Islam: in 610 he announced his first revelation, but by 622 he and the few who followed him, the first Muslims, made a secret, rushed exodus to Medina. About as far from Mecca as Washington, DC, is from New York, Medina lies on a flat, verdant plain—far more relaxed than Mecca and much greener (relatively speaking; this is, after all, Saudi Arabia). Medina has its own Great Mosque, at the southern end of which is a green dome-marks-the-spot: the tombs of the Prophet Muhammad, Abu Bakr (the first caliph, or successor, to Muhammad), Umar (the second caliph), and, some legends have it, an empty slot awaiting Jesus.

Abu Bakr had been Muhammad's best friend, and made the exodus with Muhammad personally, so it's no surprise he'd be buried beside the Prophet. But Umar became a Muslim on the day he planned to murder Muhammad, which gives his presence there a rather different valence. Umar had grown tired of Mecca's dithering before Islam's message (a challenge to Mecca's hierarchical, sexist, deeply economically exploitative norms) and wished to restore the privileges and priorities of the old guard. But Umar went one step further than most Meccans were ready to at the time. He coldly calculated: more Muslims, more problems. No Muhammad, zero problems. Could Umar have imagined, when he held his sword in his hand and swore to kill the Prophet, that he'd die some thirty years later helming a caliphate that included North Africa and Central Asia? Islam didn't turn him into a leader, a statesman, a strategist, a jurist, a manager of peoples. It *allowed* him to become one.

You can judge a leader by the quality of his followers. Weak leaders prefer mindless acolytes. But Muhammad won over a man of Umar's caliber, and in exchange Umar changed the whole world in Islam's name. What do you call a sin that makes a man a saint? Had Umar not set out to assassinate the last prophet of God, which as far as offenses go might be counted among the greater enormities, he would not have become Muslim. And just as contentiously, my family might not have, either: one year before Umar died, while he was still caliph, the first Muslims arrived in India, which became my family's refuge on fleeing Iraq. Sometimes the flaw in our character is the hole through which God enters.

Our first weekend in Saudi Arabia, we packed up my brother's Nissan and drove to Mecca. In our hotel—many are regularly demolished to make way for expansions of the mosque, so I don't know if this one is still standing—we changed into the obligatory white garments. We descended onto the plaza, and I faced for the first time the immense marbled hugeness of Mecca's Great Mosque, at the center of which, but invisible from where I stood, was the Ka'ba. The call to prayer rang just then, so in the crushing heat we hurried into a structure the scale of which, and pardon the Americanism, I can only compare to that of an alien vessel hovering over a major city in some science-fiction blockbuster. This one had landed.

On the way in, of course, my robes became undone and nearly fell off; my brother, mildly irritated with me but doing his best to hide it, came back and repaired my religious garments. The site of masses of people circumambulating the Ka'ba, which is how Muslims say *salam* to the structure, was deeply moving, and I too began orbiting the cube, merging into a mass of pilgrims from every part of the world.

It wasn't until the next weekend, however, that I saw my light on the road to Damascus, in Medina. Medina's Great Mosque is not quite as monumental as Mecca's, but I mean that only comparatively; it is still ludicrously enormous and far more elegant too, modeled after the Great Mosque of Córdoba.

On concluding our prayers in Medina's Great Mosque, my brother and I rushed to the tombs of the Prophet Muhammad and his two companions. We had only brief moments of reflection before Saudi police pushed us out: they needed to make way for the pilgrims behind us who wanted their brief moments of reverence. It was not enough time, of course. But as I exited the mosque, all but pushed out by the flow of crying, weeping, shell-shocked humanity trying to come to terms with where we were and who we'd just walked past, I thought not of God but His children. I remembered Carla, and her cousin Bradley, my friend and debate partner Jeremy, all of them Catholics. I thought less about where I was than where I might have ended up. Namely, not there.

Had I converted to Christianity, would I have made a pilgrimage to Rome instead? I'd have had no brother to go with. Probably my family would have turned on me. Absent Islam, I would never have visited Medina. Islam, you see, splits the difference between Judaism and Christianity. Like Jews, we do not believe Jesus was divine, that God is anything but One. Like Christians, we believe Jesus is the Messiah, and though we do not believe he was crucified, we do believe he was risen and will return at the end of time, to fill an unjust world with justice and live out his life and die like all other men do. Hence Jesus could be buried in the Prophet's mosque. But what of those who definitely were, Abu Bakr, Umar—and Muhammad? Medina gave me what Mecca did not and could not, and I will shortly tell you why.

In *1984*, George Orwell abruptly intrudes on his own narrative, inserting Emmanuel Goldstein's *The Theory and Practice of Oligarchical Collectivism* to give the reader a helpful background. Writers are usually counseled to avoid this kind of thing. Show, don't tell. I've no other choice, though. Outside Muhammad's massive ummah the Prophet is often mocked, rarely acknowledged, and above all ignored. In the West we say "Judeo-Christian," excising Islam from the tradition of which it is undeniably a part. So here is a little bit of that story, which you'll need to understand my own story.

The Middle East in the sixth century was dominated by the Eastern Roman Empire and the Sassanid Persian Empire. In the former, some were Jewish but most were Christian. On the Iranian Plateau, many were Zoroastrian. Muhammad's religion, Islam, would claim to be the restoration of all three. But Muhammad was born in Mecca, a city (by today's standards, a town) critical to these empires, though it didn't belong to either. Caravans of Asian spices and Indian silks caught a breath here before marching to northern powers. But Mecca was not any kind of capital, either. It might be called the alpha city of the Arabs: its real significance was religious.

According to Meccan lore, Hagar and her son, Ishmael, were present for the city's founding. By which I mean, they *were* Mecca's founding. And so Mecca had had pride of place for countless generations of Arabs; the story of Abraham and the presence of the Ka'ba, which Abraham had constructed with a teenage Ishmael, gave their home a status and symbolism far above any others. That story was deeply familiar to me: I'd grown up with it, and then I'd read about it, whether in Islamic sources or through the Bible in the weeks and months when I feverishly studied it. It goes something like this:

After decades of childlessness, Abraham at last had a son. No sooner was he so blessed than God commanded him to abandon the newborn infant and the child's mother in a land the book of Genesis calls Paran, which pre-Islamic Arabs believed meant the Hejaz. Alone and terrified in this remote, unfamiliar desert, Hagar searched desperately for water for baby Ishmael, all while having to watch her husband ride away, on God's command. Hagar's frantic running coincided with the bursting forth of a spring, called Zamzam, at Ishmael's feet. And with that, mother and child were saved. You may wonder: How can a mediocre stream save two humans who are in the middle of the harshest desert, never mind establish a critical node on the global trade network?

Birds, catching wind of the water, began circling overhead, at which time, just a short distance away, the Banu Jurhum were going God knows where. God, of course, knew where. The airborne avian commotion might've meant food or water, so the tribe dispatched investigators. Imagine their surprise at the report: "There's a woman, a baby; we have no idea what language they're speaking, and also lots of fresh water." They must have raced for that liquid gold, to stake a claim before anyone else. Probably the unlikely discovery gave them a sense that something of cosmic significance was happening.

When Ishmael was a young man, his father returned. Together they rebuilt Adam's Ka'ba, from which Abraham is said to have called out: "O humanity! Your Lord has established a house of worship—come to it!"[1] God caused the Prophet's voice to reach across the planet, a foreshadowing of Islam's belief in its own universality

---

1. Which story is found in Zaid Shakir's *Scattered Pictures: Reflections of an American Muslim*.

and the antiquity of that universality.[2] But then Mecca recedes. Isaac's descendants take up the torch—the children of Israel, including Jesus and John the Baptist. The baton is finally passed back to the Ishmaelites six centuries after Jesus: revelation's finishing line is in sight. Because while today the Ka'ba is starkly vacant inside, as was initially the case, for a long time it wasn't.

By the time of Muhammad's birth, around 570, the Ka'ba was filled with sundry idols, the gods and goddesses the Arabs had come to associate with their ultimate deity, al-Ilah, "the God" (contracted, it's "Allah," which just means capital-G God). In that Arabia, your lineage determined your fate. Polygynous marriages were common, contracted with little regard for a woman's wishes. Violence begat violence, the consequence of tribal codes demanding collective vengeance. It wasn't all harshness, though; the Arabs were a poetic people. They celebrated words. They celebrated the composers of words. They strove through words to preserve what the desert would inevitably wipe away. They valued bravery, chivalry, generosity, hospitality, and nobility. Although many Arabs were nomads, Mecca existed because of Zamzam's flow—and the continued reverence of the Ka'ba. Within Mecca, the dominant tribe was the Quraysh. They claimed Abrahamic descent and managed the *hajj*, the annual pilgrimage to the Ka'ba to honor Abraham's invitation—though not his monotheism. Most everyone was okay with the crowded polytheism that

---

2. On a recent trip to Jerusalem, a tour guide explained to my group that the city was sacred to Jews for reasons of David and Solomon (among others), for Christians because of Jesus, and for Muslims because of Muhammad's night journey from the Noble Sanctuary. I had to interrupt—Islam sees prior prophets and their followers as Muslims, believers in an earlier iteration of the same faith Muhammad was sent to renew and revitalize. Rather than see Islam as a descendant of Judaism, Zoroastrianism, and Christianity, Muslims see Judaism, Zoroastrianism, and Christianity as offshoots of a primal Islam. Since Muslims believe prophets were sent to all nations, some have made the case that Hinduism, Buddhism, and many other pre-Muhammadan religions may also be branches of the same primordial faith, which God first vouchsafed to Adam.

reigned in its stead. Muhammad, son of Abdullah, of the Quraysh, a descendant of Ishmael, was not. He was a *hanif*, one who yearned for the One.

Dissatisfied with his people's spiritual and ethical state, the young Muhammad would retreat to the mountains beyond Mecca and meditate. Not that Muhammad wasn't appreciated: he was widely trusted and reasonably prosperous. His employer, Khadija, a wealthy widow, was so impressed by his moral integrity that she proposed marriage, a gesture unusual even in our day. Muhammad said yes, and became the husband of a much older spouse. A wise choice: Khadija would become his primary support when he and then much of the rest of the world thought he'd gone mad. In Ramadan 610, to be precise.

As was his habit, Muhammad was alone in a cave, reflecting. Until he was not alone. A being appeared, commanding the merchant to recite. A terrified Muhammad said, "I cannot recite!"—Muhammad was illiterate. Each time Muhammad answered like that, though, he was painfully squeezed. (I think of it like pinching someone to confirm that they're not dreaming.) On the third try, his interlocutor interrupted with rhymed verse. "Recite in the name of Your Lord who created, created man from a clot—recite, your Lord is most generous, who taught by the pen, taught man what he did not know."

These verses were the first of the Qur'an, God's last revelation to humanity.[3]

Except Muhammad was not okay with this either.

What could this visitation mean except that he was possessed by some demon and that his whole life, as he knew it, was over? Muhammad fled from the cave. He lingered on the edge of the mountain, the horizon obscured by an impossibly large *thing* whose wings blotted out the sky. "I am Gabriel," it boomed, over and over. And then the part

---

3. The Qur'an is not arranged chronologically. These verses are located at the opening of the ninety-sixth chapter. Muslims believe the final ordering of the Qur'an was divinely ordained.

that changed the planet: "And you, Muhammad, are the messenger of God."

Muhammad arrived home shaken, shivering, leached of color. Khadija's reaction to what had transpired was, however, very different from her husband's. You're not mad, she reassured the love of her life. After all, she said, you're a man of character, an upstanding and gentle human being—what evil would ever come to you? Then comes the part no Muslim can recall without heartache, knowing what destiny awaited Khadija. With Muhammad still trembling, Khadija asked, "Is he still here?"

Meaning the Archangel, Gabriel. Muhammad said yes.

Then she inched closer to her husband. "Is he still here?"

Again yes.

Then she sat in his lap and asked, "Is he still there?"

He was not. He has modesty before a husband and wife, Khadija said, explaining how she'd made Gabriel leave. (I imagine her smiling at this little victory.) Therefore, she explained, he cannot be a devil. The good news: you're not mad.

The bad news: you're a prophet.

· 10 ·

A PLANET CALLED MEDINA

THE GREATEST STORIES HAVE humble beginnings. That's why we cannot forget them. Hagar, for all intents and purposes a single mom, dashing from one hill to another, looking for something, anything, that might save her son's life. Mary forced to leave her home and journey eastward, where she gave birth to Jesus alone. Islam began one last time in much the same way, with another woman holding fast against the world, though this was a different kind of love: a wife consoling an upright man, a wife who believes in her husband before he believes in himself. If Muhammad says Gabriel is there, I'll believe him—even if I can't see any such thing. Khadija took Muhammad to see her uncle, Waraqah, one of the few Christians in Mecca. He was sure Muhammad was a prophet, too, but warned Muhammad it'd be the same old, same old, so far as the other Meccans went. "Your people will attack and abuse you," he forecast, in so many words. It's the doom of most prophets to earn the scorn of their people. A rare few win their people over. Fewer still see such a spectacular turnaround as Muhammad did: in his life we find echoes of David and Solomon, of Joseph and Moses. The mission that began in love ended in love.

The love of an upright man for the people who wronged him.

Though it's hard to imagine that history now, with how modern Medina turned out. It's a huge city, bursting with humanity,

metropolitan but with a frontier feel. Medina has ancient roots, but
the contemporary landscape is young. There's an airport with flights
to other parts of the world; most major franchises and retail outlets
have their stores here, and there's even talk of light rail, high-speed
rail, and green-energy initiatives. Even the spirituality of the place
is inflected by modernity: how else can you explain the hundreds of
thousands of worshippers streaming in and out of a Great Mosque,
unbelievable in scale, beautiful in its execution, hard to get any full
sense of? After I was pushed past the tombs that day, I found myself
outside and on the plaza again, this time on the southern side, in
123-degree heat.

A temperature you do not ever forget. But it's not why I remember Medina. To deny God, I knew, was to suppress my reason—I could
be an atheist, but only at the cost of my conscience. But sitting there,
in a corner, up against what might have been a lamppost—frankly
it was so hot I don't remember—I had a more troubling realization.
To deny God was merely dishonest. To deny Muhammad was trea-
sonous. When I recalled my favorite stories from Muhammad's life,
there would be tears in my eyes. The mere mention of him put me on
a watery precipice. If I did not stay in Islam, if I opted out of my faith
or all faith altogether, what would happen to this man I loved, to
those tears in my eyes, to his effect on the world around him? Simple.

I'd be saying he was a liar. A fraud. A fake. And that wasn't just
enough, it was too much. Despite the fourteen hundred years that
separated us, we were not so different as the time between us might
imply. I believed in Muhammad though I'd never seen him. I believed he was there, behind a gilded screen, where everyone said he
was buried. In a culture dominated by merchants who'd leave their
homes for months on end and need to know their valuables would
be waiting for them right where they left them, all Mecca swore this:
Muhammad never lied. Never cheated. Never mocked. No one recalled him cursing, abusing, or dismissing anyone, no matter her station—or lack thereof.

If one day such a man says an angel has declared him a messenger of God, very much like Abraham, your common ancestor, what

do you do? The first Muslims picked Muhammad over their families, their careers, their reputations, their lives. At first they were largely of lower birth—according to the hierarchy of the time—but even converts higher up the chain accepted the religion's new order, attempting to treat one another as brothers and sisters in faith. Within a stratified, patriarchal, and classist society, Muhammad founded a community that cut across tribal boundaries, making women equal to men, and offering belonging beyond clan. While Mecca's elite ridiculed the entire project.

Because they could not impugn his character, these Meccans pronounced Islam genie-filled sorcery, the malevolent possession of an otherwise good man. What else could explain the poesy of the Qur'an—how had an unlettered man come up with something so unforgettably affecting? What else could explain the deep loyalty Muslims had to Muhammad, to their religion, to one another? Wherefrom their confidence, their willingness to stand against the longest odds? While the weakest Muslims suffered torture for believing in Muhammad, who for years could do nothing to protect them, still the last prophet told his followers they'd inherit Persia and Rome. Islam would reach all the corners of the world, he promised. And this rabble believed him, in that as in everything else. Within a hundred years, the children of the people who'd tried to stifle his message—and extinguish him—had left Arabia for lands unknown, gone and never to return, carrying monotheism and fighting for monotheists like themselves, Jews, and heterodox Christians.

There had and has never been an expansion like it. The Arabs possessed no technological or economic advantage, and no apparent demographic advantage, either. In Islam, the meek inherited the earth. A branch of Mecca's old elite soon seized the caliphate, the office invented after Muhammad died in 632, and moved the capital to Damascus after 661. In 750 a new dynasty, based in Baghdad, took over; Persian Muslims became key powerbrokers. The Mesopotamian caliphs began importing Turkic mercenaries, who seized power for themselves. While Islam began as an Arab religion, it didn't stay that way. It's rather clear it wasn't meant to, either.

■   ■   ■

One of the most loved early Muslims was an outsider, Bilal, an Abyssinian who'd been enslaved. His owner, Umayyah, was enraged by Bilal's conversion to Islam. That Bilal believed himself equal to his master, as Muhammad preached and Muslims wanted practiced, drove this aristocrat mad. For believing in his leveling religion, Bilal was daily whipped. He was also laid out in the desert sun, or had heavy rocks placed on his naked chest so he'd struggle for the slightest breath in searing heat. But Bilal refused to reject God. His repeated invocations—*ahad, ahad* . . . one, one—are reverently repeated by Muslims to this day. Before this, nothing in Bilal had stood out. In and through Islam, however? No amount of pain could wear him down. But short of killing him, which would mean a loss of his own property (and proof he could not compel his slaves to his will), there was nothing Umayyah could do: Bilal was unbendable. When therefore the Prophet's closest friend, Abu Bakr—buried beside the Prophet—offered to purchase Bilal, Umayyah swiftly accepted. Abu Bakr overpaid time and again for setting slaves free, an action Muhammad praised time and again. That meant Abu Bakr had money, but more importantly that he had tribal connections, protecting him as the persecutions intensified.

Many Meccans may've disliked Muhammad's message, but they'd always put family first.

So they unleashed their fury on the weakest links—those who had no powerful patrons—and Muhammad was unable to protect them. Muslims who wanted for prominent lineage were mutilated, sexually abused, murdered. By 616, a desperate Muhammad instructed his most vulnerable followers to seek the shelter of Abyssinia's Christian king. It still wasn't enough. The pressure on the first Muslims increased in proportion to their numbers, and the violence escalated. Fearing the worst—massacre—Muhammad journeyed to other cities, looking for refuges, but he was rebuffed time and again. On one occasion, he was hounded out of town and stoned.

But then a delegation from Medina, 250 miles north, showed up. This relatively wealthy oasis city was paralyzed by a three-sided feud: the Aws and Khazraj, who followed the traditional Arabian religion of the time, and several tribes that were also Arab but practiced Judaism. In the hopes of calming their feuding, the Aws and Khazraj accepted Islam as their faith and Muhammad as their leader. The Prophet had his safe haven.

Now he just had to get there.

With Abu Bakr, Muhammad fled under cover of night, hotly pursued by Meccans terrified by the implications of this exodus. After several tense days, Muhammad was reunited with his followers. He forged compacts between the arrived Meccan and local Medinese Muslims, and between the Muslims and the Jews, describing their Semitic partnership as one ummah of two faiths. And then he made preparations for battle. Muhammad's religion had long challenged aristocratic Mecca's glass and ordinary ceilings, but it had now become a threat to their way of life: the Prophet had gone from the persecuted leader of an unimpressive collection of marginalized converts to the governor of a city-state that lay astride Mecca's lifelines, the trade routes to Persia and Byzantium.

Several times Meccan armies marched on Medina. Muhammad did not start the conflict, but he proved more than capable of ending it. What other choice did Muhammad have? His community had nowhere else to go. But his inclination was always to peace. He didn't start by defending himself militarily—he'd tried for Abyssinia, for shelter elsewhere. There's no greater evidence of this than Hudaybiyyah.

In 628 Muhammad and a large host of Muslims set off to perform the hajj. Since Muhammad preached the restoration of Abraham's faith, it wasn't unexpected that he'd want to make the pilgrimage. But this move left the Meccans at a loss. Though they were large in number, the Muslims had made their way with only those weapons necessary to defend themselves on a long journey. Were the Meccans to let the

Muslims in, they'd give Muhammad's religion a boost they'd denied him for years. They had tried to kill him—would they now let him worship at Abraham's house?

But if they did not let him in, what would other Arabs think?

If the Meccans denied the Muslims, what would prevent them from denying anyone else? Damned if the Meccans did and damned if they didn't. But Muhammad stunned everyone, most of all his own flock. Though he had strength of argument and tribal custom on his side, Muhammad agreed to sit down with the Meccans, hammering out a treaty overwhelmingly to Islam's *disadvantage*. If any Meccan converted to Islam and fled to Medina in fear for his life, he'd be "returned," but if any Muslim fled to Mecca, he would not have to be. The Muslims even agreed to go back to Medina and return the coming year.

The Meccans congratulated themselves on a successful negotiation, while many Muslims fumed. There were rumblings of a mutiny. How could the Prophet of God give in? Did he not have right on his side? But the Treaty of Hudaybiyyah would be Mecca's doom. With war suspended across Arabia, people could safely visit Medina and hear the Messenger. More became Muslim in the next two years than had converted in the entire eighteen previous. In 629 the Muslims performed their pilgrimage as agreed. Bilal, with his strong and clear voice, climbed on top of the Ka'ba and sang the *adhan*, the call to prayer, making Abraham's cube a minaret once again, and Mecca's mountains the amplifiers, echoing with Islam's testimonials, sung out by a man who ten years before had been beaten for daring whisper as much.

In 630, two years into what was supposed to be a ten-year treaty, one of Mecca's allies attacked one of Muhammad's, abrogating the Treaty of Hudaybiyyah. By that time almost all of Arabia had converted. An army of over ten thousand converged on Mecca from all directions, bearing Medina's claim of vengeance, Muhammad's right to settle the score(s). In 616, for example, they'd exiled him and his family; his beloved Khadija perished in the wild, done in by old age and sanction. But Muhammad entered Mecca with his head cast so far downward he seemed fused to his mount. No different in poverty than in power.

The Prophet proclaimed amnesty, and this stunning kindness—the Meccans had, after all, expected to die—was the straw that broke Mecca's stubborn back. Two years later, a fever took Muhammad's life, but his religious vision had been achieved. Mecca converted to Islam, and Abraham's Ka'ba was—and till the present has remained—the empty house of an unrepresentable God. Revelation was finished. But as a civilization, Islam was just beginning. After Muhammad passed, his friend Abu Bakr was selected caliph. He ruled for two years before dying of natural causes. On his deathbed, he transferred power to Umar ibn al-Khattab, who ruled for ten years before being assassinated.[1] These were the two men buried beside Muhammad, both his fathers-in-law. One had been his best friend. The other was once his most implacable opponent. "Were you not enemies," the Qur'an asks, "but God made you brothers?"[2]

By unifying Arabia, though, the Muslims had concerned the Romans and Persians, whom we might describe as aggressively curious about the new polity. The Romans would send probing armies, and the Muslims too; allying with heterodox Christians and Jews, the young caliphate quickly seized much of the Levant and North Africa. The Persians, meanwhile, mustered a grand army in Iraq, which the Muslims unceremoniously demolished. Nobody in the Sassanid court could believe this was anything but a fluke, so even though the caliph Umar, having no desire to further provoke the Persian superpower, wanted to make a permanent boundary between what is now Iran and Iraq, the emperor and his generals determined to reassert their primacy.

1. The selection of Abu Bakr and thereafter Umar was supported by a sizable majority of Medinese and Meccan Muslims, though not all; over the following centuries, the debates over who should have succeeded Muhammad helped to create Sunni and Shi'a identities.
2. Qur'an 3:103.

Five years on, a Muslim army so badly defeated the Sassanids that the empire collapsed completely. Umar meticulously planned out the conquest of the Iranian Plateau, guiding strategy from afar, while a relative of his, Khalid ibn Walid, led from the front. About Umar we've heard a bit. Khalid had been Mecca's greatest commander, and then he converted, and he was still its greatest commander. Independent of Islam, the genius of these two men may never have been so realized, though it cannot be doubted—how else could you explain Umar's ability to govern a growing nation, or Khalid's strategic daring? Before Islam, Umar buried at least one daughter alive—a custom of tribal Arabs, who thusly expressed their preference for sons. After? Umar's daughter Hafsa, one of the Prophet's wives, was not only literate but held at the time of her husband's death the only complete copy of the Qur'an. (Much of Sunni Islam's legal tradition was transmitted through another of Muhammad's wives, Aisha, Abu Bakr's daughter.) Muhammad had effected a shocking transformation. He brought people to Islam by focusing on their good qualities, and gave them roles and responsibilities commensurate with their abilities. But these stories tell us how Islam came to be in the world. That does not mean they speak to us equally.

Many years after my unexpected pilgrimage to Saudi Arabia, I found myself leading a daylong course on Islam at an unconventional seminary. The seminarians were altogether wonderful, among the warmest and kindest folks I've ever met. Halfway through my teaching, however, a participant left me momentarily speechless. What was it, he wondered, that drew me to Islam? I was silent for a few moments, not having expected a personal question. I said the first thing that came to mind: a name.

Julaybib.

Julaybib was a Medinese man, probably Arab, whose name meant small or stunted. We don't know if Julaybib was his given name, or if he even had one. More bad news: His name was incomplete—there's no "son of" there, as per Arab custom, indicating Julaybib had no lineage. He was orphaned, stranded, unimportant. His name also suggests that he suffered from some kind of visible disability. He was a social outcast, mocked for his declared ugliness and derided for fraternizing with lesser classes, though of course who else would dare be seen with him?

When Muhammad arrived in Medina, Julaybib became Muslim too. But Muhammad's assumption of power wasn't a game of musical chairs at the top. Julaybib was not just taken under the Prophet's wing; Muhammad also approached a couple to consider Julaybib as their son-in-law. On account of Julaybib's many supposed shortcomings, the couple refused, but their daughter accepted him. Part of a younger generation, steeped in Islamic egalitarianism, she had fewer hang-ups. We don't know much about the marriage, except that it was apparently a happy one. And that it was soon over.

Soon after his marriage, Julaybib went out with Muhammad and several other Muslims on a raid against Meccan forces. After the enemy was defeated, Muhammad asked each man whom he'd lost, and those who had lost someone, answered. But the Prophet asked again, "Who have you lost?" Something was upsetting the mercy to all worlds. You could imagine there would have been an uncomfortable silence. Much looking into the sand, hoping it might whisper an answer. "I've lost someone," Muhammad cried, deeply pained. But who, they wondered, could Muhammad mean?

None besides Muhammad had noticed that Julaybib had not returned—in the face of war and death, blood and loss, who else would have?

They found his body surrounded by the bodies of several others, whom he'd died fighting off. Pointing to Julaybib's body, Muhammad exclaimed, "This man killed seven and then was killed?" Why wouldn't a man given a life, a family, a place in the world, not fight to the death to defend that dream, so that it would not perish from the earth? No one else had claimed Julaybib. So Muhammad prepared to bury Julaybib himself, and issued words that still shake me to my innermost. "He is of me," Muhammad said, declared, promised, "and I am of him."

Let me rewind. I knew Muhammad said this about Julaybib. But I did not repeat those words. Telling the seminarians this story in their cozy classroom, I could not repeat Muhammad's postmortem extension of his own lineage to a man denied any. I choked up on Muhammad's Spartan eulogy; these seminarians waited till I could resume. Years later, writing this, I tried very hard not to tear up, and I did not succeed. Months after that, editing it—the same. Who was Julaybib, after all, except a footnote? A man we'd preemptively judge utterly inconsequential to the grand alliances and events of the past—no Abu Bakr, no Umar, no founder of nations, no leader of armies, no wealthy trader, no great artist. For a kid who'd clocked surgeries almost from the day he was born, who was made fun of for being weird, different, dirty—"You're the same color as shit," they'd say, and I didn't have skin thick enough or white enough to shrug this off—was it any wonder I saw myself in Julaybib? Muhammad didn't have to care about Julaybib. He didn't have to give up his world, and everything (and everyone) he knew and cared for, for such a man. Let alone fight alongside him. Risk his life beside him. Bury him with his own hands. But he did.

It's said the Prophet Muhammad once told his followers that they were his companions, something like his apostles—a title that was no doubt a great honor. But those who believed in him without seeing him, he said, were his brothers and sisters. On that convection-oven Thursday afternoon, all of eighteen and rocking JNCO jeans and a Pearl Jam tag ironed onto my backpack, sitting outside the Prophet's tomb, I could sense what had just happened, or at least how heavy it was, how much it would anchor me and sustain me and circumscribe me. For it revealed me. I could deny God. Not easily, but I had. But to deny Muhammad? That, I would never do. Even if it meant burying parts of myself, the things I thought I wanted, the feelings I thought I needed, the relationships I hoped I could have. What begins in love must end in love. Muhammad was the first part of Islam I'd found that came from me. I was in fact still a Muslim. I had always been a Muslim. If one day I wanted to build a church, I had my rock.

·11·

THE FALAFEL PHILOSOPHY

WHEN I FINALLY MOVED into Weinstein Hall, where many freshmen
were dormed, I was confronted with such overwhelming diversity I
had no choice but to reduce it to manageable size. A few new friends
and I decided to go to the first desi dance party of the semester. I am
by familial origin Pakistani. Ethnically, though, I'm Punjabi.

It is an intimidating ancestry.

For if there's one thing Punjabis are famous for, it's the thump-
ing bhangra that provides the soundtrack for most South Asian weddings. Not just sound, but movement: spectacularly boisterous dances
accompany bone-rattling bass. I love(d) the music but couldn't make
my body do anything remotely publicly acceptable with it. Or any
other genre.

Ted, who'd had the locker next to mine for four years (his sister,
Linda, couldn't believe I liked Green Day), would say hey to me every day for each of those eight semesters. But after prom, Ted said,
"You danced like you had a stick up your ass," which was, I think, the
last thing he said to me, ever.

At least I tried dancing at prom.

Cf. the first South Asian party at NYU Fall '98. Our epic failure com-
menced with our almost Caucasian timing. With friends, Shams and

I ascended a hauntingly vacant staircase only to enter a vacant auditorium saturated by music so overpowering it settled in my skull as a migraine. By the end of the first hour, I'd left, having done nothing but observe an increasing number of cute girls flirt with not-me. Not-me also drank several glasses of unhelpfully unspiked fruit punch. Because I wasn't about to not dance at dance parties for the next four years, which is how the South Asian club had been advertised to me (viz, a club for clubbers), I decided to give the Islamic Center a closer look. Shams came along. He could dance. So maybe he just pitied me. But it was more than that.

After our visits to the Islamic Center at NYU, a little, L-shaped room that served as prayer space, meeting hall, social club, and dining room, we decided not only that we could take the IC to the next level but that we should and must. Inspired by the fact of each other's existence, we came to believe there must be many more like us out there. If we built it, they would come. It was a desire that more than overwhelmed me, consuming all my energy and enthusiasm. A decision that produced one Haroon, but prevented me from becoming other, possibly more interesting, and likely much happier, Haroons.

At the Islamic Center, Shams and I were quickly put to use, launching and editing a newsletter, Al-Falaq, or "Daybreak." Later I renamed it Aftab, or "Rays of light." (I had seasonal affective disorder.) At the last meeting of the school year, I dared to propose we produce a magazine: Blue, after the sky—open horizons and so forth—but this suggestion was greeted with blank stares and the chagrined clearing of throats. Ten minutes later, an outgoing senior nominated me for vice president. To have a more senior role in the organization had never crossed my mind. But I ran, I won, and won again; I'd be vice president for two years. I would come to be at the center of a burgeoning community and pushed my utmost to expand its reach, funding, and membership, meaning more eyes were on me, more attention, and more judgment. Maybe I was too stolid to track these feelings. Uncertain about my Islam, not a practicing Muslim, just a year out from a bout of amateurish atheism, already socially anxious and representing a rising Muslim institution? But wasn't it better to at least stay involved? On top of that, I was pretty good at the work—and while few others could, fewer would.

It wasn't like there was a ready crop of eager young leaders whom we could turn to. Whenever panic about my hidden impieties set in, which was rather often, I told myself: It's just a small community in a big Manhattan. It's just a few years. All this will fade. I anticipated I'd become a lawyer, on the theory that law and medicine were the only respectable professions available. (Also, my brother had chosen law, so there's my range of imagination. Blue indeed.) For all this light I wanted to shine, most of me remained obscured in shadow. Me, a lawyer? Living in suburbia? After freshman year, for example, I enrolled in the Summer Arabic Language Program at Middlebury College, up in a corner of Vermont where the outside world could not intrude. I'd learn the Arabic needed to understand my religion and enable our Islamic (Center) Revolution, and my parents were excited too, which was good because they were the ones footing the bill.

We were studying Arabic numbers that day—I don't mean the improvements on the clumsy Roman variety but number agreement in Arabic grammar. In Arabic, words can be singular, plural (which, unlike in English, means three or more), or a rarely used dual. Also unlike English ones, Arabic nouns are only pluralized if they describe a number between 3 and 10. That means you'd say "one star" and "three stars," but "twelve star," or even "one thousand and one star," because Edward Said. This all made sense to the class until someone asked about 11, which left our professor flustered—was it tied to 10 or did it make like 12?

He singled me out in no time. "Haroon, you have a Qur'an."

It may've been the first time I was religiously profiled. I raced to my room and panted back with a hardcover holy book, a dark-green edition that remains in my library. Professor Ben Amor flipped to the twelfth chapter, "Joseph," and asked me to recite the fourth verse, wherein Joseph tells his father Jacob ("Israel") of a dream. "O my father," Joseph relates, "I saw *eleven star*, the sun and the moon, and they prostrated to me," and the next words out of our professor's mouth sent a sciatic tingling down my legs.[1] "Did you all hear how eleven is inflected?" he asked the class, most of whom were not Muslim, did not have a Qur'an before them, and in general had no idea what the hell was happening.

Professor Ben Amor seemed stunned by the laws of Semitic physics—the holy book of his religion was *The Chicago Manual of Style* of his language, so that even now, fourteen hundred years on, should he have a question about grammar or usage, the Qur'an was a kind of final arbiter. He turned to the student who'd set this whole encounter in motion (who was, incidentally, entirely and hopelessly lost): "Eleven *star*," he said, pronouncing the Arabic as it had been vowelized in the Qur'an—singular in form, though plural in valence. "That's your answer."

Arabic has a continuity and consistency, dating back fourteen centuries, that most modern languages cannot claim; English, Spanish, and French didn't even exist when Arabic was an established language of high culture. I'd never had any kind of relationship to the Qur'an before, but now I wanted to belt it out, cry it, sing it, share it—at the end-of-summer variety show, I recited chapter 86, "The Night Star." To learn grammar was to appreciate the book's poesy, which in turn was to break open a once-inaccessible text. This wasn't just comprehending, though: it was falling in love. Even the shape of Arabic, spilling out in earnest strokes and zealous dashes and hyperactive dots, filled me with surprising warmth. I saw God in the cursive sparseness, the cracked and fragmented verses, the elliptical themes, jumping from story to lesson to consolation to consternation to contemplation.

He was there. In His book. Not in someone's mosque or a congregation but in the very enunciation of every letter. And it *was* poetry,

---

1. Most translate *kawkab* as "star," so I do, too—even though I suspect "planet" might be more accurate. Qur'an 11:4.

too: Good prose you cannot put down. Good poetry, on the other hand, makes you stop and look at the world all over again—like you never have before—every few lines. To read was to be refreshed. To recite was to be renewed. Exhaling the words was inhaling oxygen. A few students and I even woke up well before dawn—super early in Green Mountain July—to pray together. I found Muhammad in Medina and God in Vermont. Bright-eyed and bushy-tailed, overly full of my faith—and I'm sure they were used to this kind of response—I went to some of my professors and asked, "What about Friday prayers?"

"What about them?" (My grammar may also have been corrected in the course of this exchange.)

The director told me he'd make a room available, and even allow me to advertise services, on condition that I lead them or find someone else who could—this was a secular program. It was also a language-immersion program. Everything would have to be in Arabic; students enrolled in the program could not speak English, and I mean *any* English. Not for the last time, I found no one else who would consider leading Friday prayers, even as many of the students wanted to attend Friday prayers. I interpreted this to mean I should, and so I did. My sermons stand as the most clumsily phrased and possibly least inspiring in Islamic history, not surprising given my Arabic. "God is good. God is God. I like God. Do you know God? Pittsburgh is the most beautiful city in the world." By the sixth week I gave up and just recited Qur'an, because at least I knew that was grammatically correct. At nineteen, all but an imam. Thus I returned to NYU.

And was sucker punched. We were losing our adorable little L-shaped prayer space. A fancier student center was on the way. But we'd have no prayer space in my remaining three years, because previous sentence. New and returning students would be tossed into New York City with nowhere to pray, take a breather, or connect with fellow Saracens. I hadn't the least idea how the Muslim community had earned Loeb's eighth-floor prayer space in the first place, but now it was my problem. "With every difficulty," God says, "there is ease."[2] Not *after* the difficulty. At the same time. And why stop, after all, with a prayer space? I told Shams, whose parents that same summer had made him transfer to a college nearer to them and cheaper for them. "This means we can do what we've been talking about!" he said. "Not just at NYU, but at my school, too."

In my more recent travels across America, I find thriving Muslim communities, especially on college campuses. These often enjoy halal dining options, their own prayer spaces, sizable events budgets, solid relationships with various student organizations, female leadership—and perhaps most significantly, Muslim chaplains, women and men to whom students can turn for mature advice, pastoral care, institutional access, and religious expertise. Chaplains are a great development in American Islam, freeing students to focus on academics, student life, and new opportunities for personal and social growth.

They were foreign to my generation.

Many of our parents had built many of our first institutions, and we built upon them. But where we had to figure out how to do so, our parents, raised in Muslim circumstances, didn't. They were born into an Islam they carried here, and sometimes thoughtlessly reproduced. We, on the other hand, were determining what to keep and what to let go of. There were few we could look to—many who had the religious knowledge lacked the sophistication, generosity, and creativity to deal with a dynamic, progressive student body, while those who could be leaders had no mandate behind them. We had to find an authority to defend the decisions we'd make.

So Shams and I became Trojan horses. We read side by side, though he was back in Mississippi and I was still in Manhattan. We took courses in our respective philosophy departments, which had become our common major; we spent our free time discussing Muslim thinkers and issues in overwhelming detail, with the result that

2. Qur'an 94:5.

we felt more ready to understand whether our visions could be realized, should be amended, might be negative. Where these visions first came from, I do not know. Perhaps our parents, whose pieties copresented with insane professional ambition.

The self-starting syllabus opened with Islamist thinkers. Those who believed Islam had a clear role to play in politics. I'm glad we covered them, if only to confirm our feeling that they did not have much ground to stand on—Khomeini's Islamic Republicanism, for example, was just a Hegelian reaction to statist secularization. The shah enforced Westernization, so the clerics took power to enforce a remedial Islamization. Where the dialectic would next take Iran seemed obvious. We moved on to the Muslim Brotherhood and Jama'at-e-Islami. A generation of Muslims not too different from us, trying to take ownership of Islam from a religious establishment viewed, not fully falsely, as too content with the status quo.

Their solutions, though, were authoritarian; they used religion like Stalinists used Marx.

But we didn't find what we were looking for in Western philosophy, either.

I grew up on *Star Trek: The Next Generation*, which centered on Jean-Luc Picard, a Frenchman—played by a Briton, Patrick Stewart. Picard captained the flagship of a utopian United Federation of Planets, a kind of Communist United Nations. It was an exciting, challenging vision, but deeply secular. The rare characters whose worldviews were inflected by religion betrayed a telling bias. On a spinoff, *Star Trek: Voyager*, for example, the ship's First Officer, Chakotay, is a pious Native American. But there were no human characters, on all of *Star Trek*, who might be identified as Christians.

The white people were objective, neutral, transcendent; they were ciphers for a nonlocal universality. Even today you can flip on a news channel and encounter several "experts" on the Middle East who know next to nothing about it. Perhaps if they're lucky they've accidentally ingested falafel. But they're *allowed* to be experts, because they're (usually) white males. What I mean to say is, certain people are assumed capable of rising above not just their own but all particularities, for they presumedly possess none. Everything about them is universal. I once attended a lecture by a so-called public intellectual who leaned agnostic in his sentiments, and was grossly Islamophobic in his beliefs, despite knowing almost nothing about Islam. Thanks to my major, and this was the greatest gift my philosophy professors gave me (and a ringing endorsement for a robust humanities education for all), I could see the emperor wore no clothes. For he, a secular European, hailed from a subcontinent that faced deep challenges.[3] For example: declining fertility and a hostility to the immigrants necessary to remedy that. Would he argue Europe's beliefs similarly responsible for Europe's state? Could a brown Muslim man stand up there and make the same dismissive, contemptuous remarks about Europe that he was making about all Islam and, if not, *why* not? Not that my intention is to empower a parallel blockheadedness. But let's pretend.

Europe has realized a far less harmful way of life than its recent past would have suggested possible: quite pacific, positively communal, and in many ways ideal—an earthbound, incipient United Federation of Planets—except that the attraction of this way of life must be tempered. Latter-day Europe is calmly, respectfully, but incontrovertibly diminishing. And this applies to either side of the Iron Curtain. If that speaker's logic was that the problems of the Middle East world should be laid at Islam's door, then where should we have deposited Europe's? But don't misunderstand me. I'd never presume to argue that all of Europe is reducible to x, y, or z, let alone that any culture or region of the world can be definitively pronounced upon as lacking. Except that was what this speaker was doing to Islam, and only because no one talked back.

---

3. South Asia is far more diverse and populous than Europe, with borders more easily demarcated than Europe's, yet the former is considered a subcontinent and the latter a continent.

In my philosophy department we concentrated our attention on the brilliant and the parochial. Their worldviews were not just unaware of other kinds of learning, but dismissive of their own backyards. Of God and faith, little to nothing was ever mentioned. The intensity with which Shams and I confronted religion in our lives could not be satisfyingly addressed, and yet we'd chosen philosophy in the belief that it might. The only thinker on offer who spoke to any of this was Nietzsche, and he was squeezed in with Schopenhauer and Hegel. While I admired the wit and force of Nietzsche's convictions, his perspective did not speak to me, either. Was I really going to take this superman business seriously when I could not bring myself to correct my waiter if he got my order wrong? And Nietzsche *loathed* Christianity, which I'd thought about joining—which is to say, there was no room in anything of what I'd been learning for Carla's generous family, or Jeremy's admirable piety. Many of these thinkers explicitly condescended to everyday America in the way they implicitly condescended to Islam. To appreciate, then, while still a very young man, that an entire tradition cannot see most of the world while presuming to represent it, opine on it, define it, and therefore effectively circumscribe it, was embarrassingly empowering. Motivating. Freeing. But aggravating. I'd have to spend my life responding to this blinkered nonsense.

Or I could offer my own ideas.

If these Western philosophers were allowed to look to Paris and London for inspiration, couldn't I look to Somers and Sarajevo, to Western and Muslim thinkers—and to those who were both, like Izetbegovič? Answer didn't matter.

From Abu Hamid al-Ghazali, I learned that you could fall apart and that the end of your world was not the end of the world. Only in his twenties, this medieval philosopher and theologian chaired a whole university, accomplishing things most scholars only dream of. His book knowledge, though, did not suffice for him, and when he realized his inability to make his religious beliefs become religious actions,

the rug was all but ripped out from under him. An Augustinian memoir, *Deliverance from Error*, revealed the paralyzing effect of reason's
inadequacies. The only ground for religious knowledge was intuitive,
experiential, empirical—not learning, but becoming. That is to say,
knowing something is not becoming something, let alone being that
thing. You can master religion (or at least appear to) but not be the
least bit religious. Islam required self-transformation, which would
only happen—to borrow a Foucauldian language—through a technology of the self, a set of practices by which we improve ourselves
even as we measure ourselves. This newer older Ghazali went wandering, seeking after teachers, trying to learn how to be a Muslim. By
the end of his life he'd produced a magisterial forty-volume work, *The
Revival of the Religious Sciences*, which still has few peers.

But knowing you need to do something is still not doing
that thing.

The Sunni scholar Jalal ad-Din Rumi, too, had a crisis of faith
and found refuge in Sufism, that same technology of self that Ghazali
had sought to master. But Rumi expressed his insights in poetry that
could reach the hoi polloi as well as the higher-ups. And then Rumi
led me to Muhammad Iqbal—and Iqbal led me back to Rumi. A
merry-go-round of Muslim. I entered a web of footnotes, dog whis-
tles, citations, subtle asides, likes and retweets, obvious jabs and
counterpunches, conversations that spanned continents as swiftly
as they did the centuries. Rumi's most famous work, the *Masnavi*,
opens: "Listen to the ney, because it tells a story / It complains of its
separation."[4] In Persian, the last bit reads "*shikayat mi konad*"—"it
complains of its separation"—by which he meant our ongoing exile from God and from the garden, from our original abode. Iqbal
used a related word to title one of his most famous poems: *Shikwa*,
or "Complaint."

Muhammad Iqbal was born in 1877, twenty years after preco-
lonial India's last gasp, the First War of Independence. Muslim and

---

4. A *ney* is a kind of flute, and one of the oldest instruments in the world. The
ney is hollow but, when filled with breath, produces music.

Hindu sepoys in the British East India Company's employ had re-
volted in the name of the last Mughal emperor, Bahadur Shah Zafar.
Which is why he was last; the resistance, in need of a symbol to rally
their supporters, chose the only ruler whose name could command
widespread allegiance. Zafar didn't have much say in this nomina-
tion, though in fairness he hadn't had much say in anything. He just
happened to have an important last name. The revolt was put down
with great bloodshed, and the British inaugurated the Raj—direct
colonial occupation. The once-mighty Mughal line was done away
with, hanged from trees, otherwise killed, or, in Zafar's case, deported
to Burma to spend the last of his days. This left Constantinople, the
seat of the Ottoman ostensible caliph, the last independent Muslim
sovereignty of appreciable power.

But its future, too, looked bleak.

From 1908 through 1913, much of the Balkans was lost. In 1911,
Libya. The subsequent massacres and huge refugee flows outward,
the ethnic cleansing of many of Europe's indigenous Muslims, were
an immediate cause of Iqbal's *Shikwa*, a furious protest of God's plan
for the world.[5] So far as I'd known, no Muslim—other than myself
and in my heart—had dared to question God's management of anything. That Iqbal did when he did, and in Islam's name, was all the
more bewildering.

In 1905 Iqbal went to England and Germany to study law and
philosophy, at a time when the number of Western-educated Muslims—worldwide—could fit into a modern American mosque, many
of which are bursting with overly credentialed professionals. While
studying in Europe, Iqbal nearly became an atheist. It's hard for
Americans, in a world so shaped by Americanness, to imagine just
how traumatic these years must have been, but let us try. The institutions and symbols Iqbal's people had so long been dependent on
were violently ripped from them, trampled underfoot, or emptied of
all plausibility. The effect of these experiences can be heard in an

5. See Andrew Wachtel's *The Balkans in World History* and Justin McCarthy's
Death and Exile: The Ethnic Cleansing of Ottoman Muslims, 1822–1921.

epistolary confession addressed to a woman whom Iqbal may've been
madly and futilely besotted by:

> As a human being I have a right to happiness; if society or na-
> ture [culture] deny that to me I defy both. The only cure is that
> I should leave this wretched country forever, or take refuge in
> liquor, which makes suicide easier. These dead barren leaves of
> books cannot yield happiness.

Another scholar, another breakdown. What was it with Islam
and insanity? I didn't have any sense of Muslim humanism, say Ibn
'Abbad's dark night of the soul, but I knew suicide was categorically
forbidden, a failing for and of kuffar.[6] How did a quote unquote good
Muslim get away with this?[7] "I have got sufficient fire in my soul
to burn them up," Iqbal continued, speaking of those dead barren
leaves, "and all social conventions as well." It was bad enough he
didn't belong in Europe, but after three years abroad, India became
a foreign country too.[8] I was seduced by his unapologetic fury, while
his rage at the present circumstances of his fellow Muslims struck a
chord. But more than that, his urgency spoke to me. I, too, felt it,
that fathomless, almost indomitable compulsion to do something, to
be something, to accomplish something. To leave a mark. To be that
mark. Before I left.

---

6. See George Makdisi's *The Rise of Humanism in Classical Islam and the Christian West*, and Hamid Dabashi's *The World of Persian Literary Humanism*. Most
great scholars of Islam were often poets and polymaths; the idea of a narrow
focus on law or religion is a more recent—and unfortunate—development.
7. Mustansir Mir provides a strong introduction to Iqbal, *Iqbal: Makers of
Islamic Civilization*, and to his poetry, *Tulip in the Desert: A Selection of Muhammad Iqbal's Poetry*. See also Naveeda Khan's *Muslim Becoming: Aspiration
and Skepticism in Pakistan* and Farzana Shaikh's *Community and Consensus in
Islam*. Ayesha Jalal has written an indispensable history of the movement to
establish Pakistan, *The Sole Spokesman: Jinnah, the Muslim League, and the
Demand for Pakistan*, which provides valuable context.
8. This and the previous quote are from *Iqbal: Poet-Philosopher of Pakistan*,
edited by Hafeez Malik.

At the center of Iqbal's philosophy is *khudi*, a term that originally meant selfishness. (The root, "khv," is present in the Persian word for God, *Khuda*, and in English as "sui"-cide.) Iqbal asked Muslims to revisit the definition of "khudi," or rather, by force of personality and argument, he forevermore forced them to. Through him, "khudi" began to mean self-fullness, a robust and vigorous individuality, the original and necessary form of which existed as the Divine "I"— Khuda—and the contingent form in "us." Rather, actually, *as* us. Iqbal believed we are selves, though more potentially than actually. Selflessness, the ideal of many Sufis, had led Islam astray, replacing an empowering monotheism based on a real relationship between a real individual and her Creator with a pantheistic and neo-Platonic miasma. Too many Sufis, Iqbal argued, believed that *only* God existed. Selfhood, and the wider world, were myths which suborned apathy. Our separateness from the world and from each other was not just real, Iqbal argued, but critical: until and unless we accepted our unique selves, our separateness, we could neither respect our selves nor anyone else, nor act (and this was perhaps his greatest concern) with purpose in the world.

He found the idea that we are all one, or that God is in all of us, to be the height of dangerous delusion. For how can you act in the world if you believe that neither you nor the world really exists? Why would you do anything if you believed the world was just a manifestation of God, a distraction from some higher plane, instead of a preparation for the calling of that next dimension? Our purpose in life, as Iqbal saw it, was to become full of our selves, more completely and courageously individuated. And why did he want us to become individuated? Because Iqbal refused to accept the world as it was. He demanded that Muslims rise again. He refused to accept that Islam was a spent force.

Once you'd mastered your lower self, reining in your impulses, whims, and baser desires, Iqbal argued that what was left of you was enduring, even immortal, but unique too and meant to be. Islam was not the automation of Homo sapiens by ritual indoctrination. It was a technology of the self that produced persons who were not controlled by the world, but bended the world to their will, a will so great and so grand, perfected in the person of Muhammad, the ultimate human self, that God Himself would grant, in the world to come, whatever that self wanted—which could include, too, what you yourself wanted. How can you be worthy of paradise, of eternal reward, if you aren't even real? This frame, Iqbal argued, explained Islam's historical successes, because it was once how Muslims saw themselves.

And those successes explained subsequent Muslim failures. For, Iqbal argued, Muslim triumphs brought a young and impressionable ummah into contact with the formidable legacy of Hellenic philosophy, which, Iqbal lamented, preached the illusory character of the self, the oneness of all being, and thus renditioned moral agency and robust autonomy.[9] Deluded by such philosophy, and estranged from its vigorous spirituality, the Muslim world began to fall. But not only could it rise, but it would—the fires of khudi still smoldered. This from a man so tormented by his alienation from the world as it was that he felt he must either destroy himself or redesign the planet. There were no other acceptable choices.

In an age when persons of color were reflexively judged inferior, Iqbal dared to learn from the West, as well as from Hindu religion, culture, and philosophy, and of course from Islam—and then to speak back to them, critically, creatively, coherently. This accomplishment under such magnificent cultural and political duress suggests the strength of his personality. But what gave him the permission, the confidence, the conviction to reclaim religion from the *ulama*, the scholarly class? How did a man with a Western education, with no beard, with a law degree, who loved German philosophy, receive the title Allama, "the *vastly* learned"? Critical to Iqbal's legitimacy within the Muslim community was his insistence that his lifelong project of reconstruction was a restoration of Islam, not a reinvention of it.

---

9. We would be wrong to assume that only the Christian West traced its intellectual heritage to Greece. As many Muslims once saw it, the Hellenic legacy was their own as well. The Ottomans even called themselves Emperors of Rome.

Rather than say, to be cliché, that Islam needed a reformation, Iqbal believed Islam was an ongoing reformation. Iqbal might mine Western ideas and thinkers, but doing so was not crude borrowing or plagiarism, neither substantively nor procedurally. Islam, Iqbal argued, was genetically dynamic: it was meant to be purposeful movement in a world fated to change. Iqbal not only went back to Islam's sources but also demanded every generation of Muslims separately and together do the same. Iqbal took Muslim societies, ideas, and practices, and compared and contrasted these with Islam's sources, which Sunni Muslims would contend are primarily the Qur'an and the life of the Prophet. Then Iqbal urged us to reflect honestly on the results of such comparison and contrast.

I found ample evidence of this approach in Islam's founding generation. Frequently one of Muhammad's companions would encounter a new situation, which would not just remind her of a specific verse of the Qur'an or some of Muhammad's words, but enable her to see it anew. "It was as if I was hearing those words for the first time!"[10] That I might begin to do this for myself seemed outrageous at first, and then unlikely, and at long last, inevitable. For Shams and I were beginning to approach our religion with some measure of informed confidence. We dedicated ourselves to constructing a world outside us that could reflect the conclusions we were coming

---

10. When the Prophet Muhammad died, Umar refused to believe it. It was left to Abu Bakr to rally the community; he is Sunni Islam's first caliph because he perceived the full consequences of Muhammad's death. It was Abu Bakr who reminded Umar of a Qur'anic verse that declared Muhammad was just a man, that he would die, and asked if, when that happened, you would "turn back on your heels?" (3:144). When Umar heard this—though of course he'd heard it countless times—he said he finally understood it. Abu Bakr's subsequent speech to the gathered community, "that whosoever worshipped Muhammad, know that Muhammad is dead," but "whoever worshipped God, know that God Lives and cannot die," eloquently reflects the reasons for which Medina pledged itself to him. He alone best understood that the community would now have to decide its own affairs, without a conclusive arbiter.

to within us. And it didn't matter that I was in New York and Shams was in Mississippi. Because Islam was universal in intention, it was localizable in practice.

Until encountering these three thinkers, Ghazali, Rumi, and Iqbal, I'd equated interpretations of sources with the sources themselves. What someone told me God meant by a certain passage was what God meant by it. No longer. The Qur'an not only could be applied to the world even as it provided me serenity and purpose, but it should. Would have to. Just as Islam is regularly judged by secular epistemologies, I wondered if, say, Rumi's ontology could become the foundation for an alternative means of knowing—and doing—and critiquing. If Iqbal's vision of khudi could be used as a mechanism for understanding life, even or especially my own life. If we could draw nourishment from other embodiments of faith and belief. I set my mind not only to encouraging serious Muslim engagements with our tradition but also providing the space and resources for so doing. Others should be blown away just as I was.

The Islamic Center at NYU was to be the launchpad of that project, not just because it was there, but because I believed it could be that place. Whenever we'd increase the size of our prayer space, the congregation would fast catch up, and soon enough threaten violation of the fire code. We didn't have to make people want to go to the mosque; we just had to build a mosque people wanted to go to. The Catholic Church at NYU offered us a temporary prayer space. We booked rooms and halls across campus, like any other club. But unlike any other club. What in freshman year had been a small community with potential had become, by my third year, the busiest club on campus by number of activities—out of tens of thousands of students. Destiny. Convergence. We wildly exceeded our own expectations—we had jazzy advertising, fun events, and a special buzz to our name. We made being Muslim something cool. I was excited and terrified. I suppose I'd built my own personal roller coaster.

· 12 ·

YOU THINK YOU NEED TO GET MARRIED

WHEN I FIRST GOT TO NEW YORK, the sheer density of people was intimidating to the point of debilitating. I so feared boarding a subway train, you'd have thought I'd been asked to jump off a plane without a parachute. When the train arrived in the station, and there were too many people inside, a subjective calculation I performed in my head as the train was still coming to a stop, I retreated. But not only was I afraid of being around the people *on* the train; I was petrified what people on the platform would think if I did *not* board.

Everyone fears something. My fear stemmed from the certainty that I was being laughed at, that I was inadequate in constitution as well as appearance—I moved like an ungainly child through a world of assured adults. My involvement with the Islamic Center was escalating despite this discomfort. Or because of it. Perhaps the work helped to overcome my existential stage fright—if God's calling you, that's a kind of Xanax—or perhaps it was compensatory. If I do this work, and it matters, then the voices in my head don't matter.

So long as I'm doing God's work.

A gang of us had come together, the right mix of people, at the right place, at the right time, to turn something small into something great. To take one example: between the start of my freshman and end of my junior years, student attendance at Friday prayer services nearly quintupled. I habitually dry-heaved in the bathroom ten minutes beforehand. Still I did it. The work for the Islamic Center, including the sermons, and the dry-heaving because of them. Time and time again. I got up to speak, presented, directed, organized, liaised. As painful as it was to step in front of an audience, it was thereafter wonderful to receive their applause.

I was doing good, so I was good. They liked me. So I should like me. And I would, until I forgot they liked me, or remembered they had no reason to like me.

But that wasn't the only reason.

Given the choice between those who were supposedly qualified to give sermons, out of whose mouths might emanate embarrassing or infuriating things (allegedly words, sentences, and occasionally what seemed to be, but only on superficial examination, ideas, and still more rarely conclusions, never mind takeaway points), and the students who worked to redefine our Muslim community, we picked the latter, i.e., us. If you have to select between the outwardly qualified, who leave you humiliated, and everyday kids who at least live in their community, go with the kids. A certain common sense. Our own.

Iqbal hadn't waited for someone to tell him he could challenge received opinion. I'd first sermonized at Middlebury, which meant I gave my first sermons at NYU the following fall, when I was all of nineteen. Sure, some of the folks in attendance told me I had to dress like a specific kind of Arab to give a sermon or have a beard yea long, but then I remembered the kinds of speeches they liked, which used to be delivered from our *minbar*, and then I marveled that nobody had thought it important to tell me, for example, not to (1) make wildly racist generalizations or (2) talk for more than twice the allotted time or (3) declare all Muslims liars or (4) present analogies that make sense only in a universe where Thomas Friedman is compensated or (5) whine about how badly you need to get married because (6) the sisters are tempting you with form-fitting jeans, and oh yeah (7) you need to get married.

Because these things happened. Sometimes in the same thirty-/ sixty-/ninety-minute (God help us) block of time. I was already sick and tired of small-minded Muslims who held our communities back just because they accepted mediocrity. Who confused their Islam for Islam. Give them room, and soon enough they'll set a partition across it. Beardedness, I induced, was not a qualification for any office. The person who knows the most Qur'an is not by that fact alone the best person to handle alumni relations. Worse, why was it only in Muslim institutions that the grounds for expertise were so ridiculous—why should the qualifications for public relations or website design include visible indicators of piety? And how did you know that piety was genuine? (I could pretend as well as anyone, after all.)

We received a great deal of criticism for our decisions, of course. But many of the people who told me the things we were doing were wrong—that we were too liberal, too progressive, too secular, and, my absolute favorite, too American—would never play by those same rules in their own lives. They wanted their kids to go to Harvard, not an Islamic seminary no one had heard of. They expected the best for themselves, except when it came to religion, at which point they suddenly became content with total crap. Imams who spoke English as well as anti-immigrant white-supremacist bigots; speeches that were coeternal with God. We had bigger fish to fry.

We wanted to be more than just another student club. At the core of our vision for the Islamic Center would be a new kind of imam, a human Triboro Bridge connecting us with the university and the city. With a full-time Muslim chaplain, as we conceived and called the position, the Islamic Center would grow into an umbrella organization affiliated with the university but independently funded, overseeing but not dictating to affiliated student clubs. Very consciously, our model was Hillel. I'd visit the Jewish students' organizations, their facilities, their events, and wondered: Why didn't we have anything like this?

I knew enough of Islamic history to know we were capable not just of reinvention but sophistication. We didn't dedicate the time and seriousness, didn't bring to the task the thoughtfulness and obvious strategy, that we needed to—that's why our institutions had thus far performed so poorly. There was a nationwide network of Jewish student organizations, well financed and pluralistic; why couldn't there be a Muslim equivalent—with NYU as Sector 001? Why not reach out to clubs with whom we had shared interests, or overlaps in membership—black student unions, Pakistani associations, and the like? Why were we interested in excluding rather than in finding points of inclusion?

Our strength was our numbers. We should have played to our strengths. There were other decisions, too, which might have been as significant. The most important of which was the redressing of a persistent gender imbalance. We created a two-person vice presidency, one seat reserved for men and the other for women, just to guarantee that women would always have a seat at the table. Affirmative action until equality became second nature. And since the vice presidency was often a step to the presidency, this would help put female leadership forward. Indeed, the president after me, Saira, had been vice president during my senior year. There were people who told me communities run by women would never prosper. Like the many male-dominated Muslim regimes worldwide that they had abandoned?

But racing ahead produced friction, which culminated in a small, and small-minded, campaign by several old-school Muslims who did not want me to run for president of the Islamic Center in my senior year. They'd decided I was behind an anonymous e-mail prank of a sexist nature (I was not) and tried to force me out. People I assumed I could trust revealed a pathetic, spiteful side. Former friends hacked into my computer and left me voice-mail messages reminding me I was "unfit" to be a Muslim leader, based on said tempest in a teapot. Since I knew we were on the verge of something special, I persevered. I was going to help change the ummah, even if a subset of the ummah didn't want me to. Every journey has its potholes and its assholes.

Today you might know them as trolls. They were loud, and mostly irrelevant.

Instead of contributing, they criticized anyone who tried—anything. As it turned out, the people behind the prank were the very same ones telling me I should not be president. Like the politicians who fund extremists and then announce that we must withhold democracy because the extremists might come to power. (You think people suddenly act out of superior motivations because they have more resources?) But I made my peace with it all. These students didn't want to go where many of us were going. If they really wanted to, I told some of them, they could start their own Muslim center. We, on the other hand, were going to become an institution. A hub, not a club. I had no clear idea how, but that's the platform I ran on. Hope and change. Expansion and inclusion. Growth and the requisite enthusiasm to go with it—more of more.

The same woman who'd nominated me for vice president three years before told me she thought someone else could do a better job. And she had a point: there were a lot of outstanding people in the Islamic Center. But I won, and had an excellent board elected to work with me. They included Saira, who had entered the Islamic Center in charge of the newsletter—somehow our Ring of Power—but soon grew well beyond that role. As an outstanding business-school student, our female vice president could apply what she'd been learning to the Islamic Center. We bowed to her wisdom. Others, too: Junayd, also from NYU's strong business school, took over our charitable activities—our outreach efforts expanded in scope and sophistication. A physics major, our male vice president, Ishaq, took charge of religious activities, making sure we were always ready to accommodate the ever-larger crowds that showed up for Friday prayers. No mean feat, since that meant juggling room bookings, predicting attendance, and running the one regular function that would make or break our reputation. An arts major, Moses, handled advertising, design, logos, branding.

We needed a consistent look, and he did it: his logo is still used today. When we brainstormed a tagline, I suggested the ICNYU was what a great Muslim community should feel like, and one of our sophomores cut that down to bite-size splendor: what community should feel like. It felt good. It felt amazing. It felt special.

It also felt hypocritical.

While I knew that leadership skills and piety were not eternally entangled, I was not honest about the state of my Islam, either. I kept telling myself the duplicity was unavoidable. First off, why did I need to tell everyone my business? Second, there must be other people out there like me. If I wanted to pray every once in a while in a place that felt like my own, shouldn't every other Muslim deserve the chance to, too? An Islamic Center of second third fourth chances. But I wasn't just someone out there, I was the guy giving sermons, or leading everyday prayers, who people looked to, by default, to answer questions, because after all I'd sought and gained the position of president. There were once again two Haroons. The me for public consumption—who felt like things were going remarkably well, who *wanted* to be in the public eye, who *needed* the attention—and the me who behaved, shall we say, nontraditionally. The reasons I wasn't dating, for example, were nonreligious—nobody said yes. Not even once.

But at least, by then, it had become easier to ask. The Islamic Center had transformed me. If I could extemporize in front of dozens, certainly I could ask someone to coffee, tea, or a movie. Wasn't life about taking shots? "It's something," as Matt Franklin's dad tells him in *Take Me Home Tonight*, one of America's greatest achievements, "just to hear the gun go off."

First year of Arabic, Shams suggested I ask out a fellow freshman, Rania. I chickened out, but we'd become friends in the meanwhile. She was active in student life too, and being that she was Tunisian and Muslim, we had many occasions to work together. She was smart. Funny. Passionate. We cared about the same causes. We attended some of the same classes. We sometimes sat down to lunch together. Hell, I don't know—maybe we would've been perfect for each other.

I'll never know. At the close of junior year, I sent Rania—name, of course, changed to reduce my embarrassment—a bouquet of flowers. The attached card included only two verses of poetry. (My own, without attribution.)

A few days later I invited her to an open-mic night on campus. I was going to read the whole poem, of which I'd sent her a couplet. Do you know what it's like to read a poem to your crush to a room full of people who aren't your crush? Because I do. She canceled last minute. Undeterred, I dragged her to a Starbucks later that week, where I sat her down, unfolded my poem, and proceeded to pronounce my desire in a private audience. Halfway through what I still consider one of my life's high points, her boyfriend walked in. He recognized me, and said hello; he'd attended some of our Friday prayer services, where I gave the sermon.

A credit to my studiousness, I, also president-elect of the Islamic Center, understood in her lucid Arabic there on Broadway all the reasons she could not go out with me, all of which were standing in line ordering two coffees, one for him and one for her. He, like me, being Pakistani. He, unlike me, not Arabophone. I walked all the way back to my dorm on Lafayette, down Broadway, through SoHo, and past Chinatown, crying part of the way. When I was in third grade, there was a dark-skinned girl who sat a few desks down from me; I was in love with her. She was Italian, I was South Asian, but we were the only visibly unwhite kids in the class. One day, Patrick, destined to be the county's next alpha male, announced his belief that she wanted to kiss him. She protested that this was not the case. Prove it, Patrick said, and he upped the ante, challenging her to kiss every guy (on the cheek). Which she did, all of them excepting me. Apparently she was a self-hating shade of mocha cappuccino. In all my twenty years, I'd kissed or been kissed by one girl. *Ahad, ahad.*

Three weeks after being elected president of the Islamic Center—and that same day professing my love for Rania to Rania and her expressing astonishment that I liked her and then anger because her boyfriend had claimed credit for the flowers but no that was not enough to win her over—I was on a flight to Egypt. More Arabizing.

But rather than *A New Hope*, I got *The Empire Strikes Back*. Then, during the break between our first and second months of class, I flew to Tel Aviv and took a *sherut* to Jerusalem. I thought Islam's third-holiest city would affect me like Mecca and Medina had. *The Revenge of the Sith*.

·13·

BETWEEN THE DOME
OF THE ROCK AND
A HARD PLACE

WHEN OUR EL AL FLIGHT landed in Tel Aviv, all the passengers were to deplane onto a waiting bus, to be ferried across the tarmac to the terminal. All the passengers but four, that is. There was the one bus bound for the main terminal, and a second—which, long, ungainly thing, looked like an accordion that had mated with a caterpillar—that had the task of taking the three Palestinians and myself, an honorary Palestinian, for further questioning. In the time we had together, we shared names and traded bios. Like me, they were students—studying in Egypt. Unlike me, they called this place home. Unlike me, they had a harder time getting in. For I was Muslim but also—and this confounded one Israeli soldier after another—American.

Before even reaching passport control, I was interrogated by two women who were very interested in determining if I was callous or dangerous. These were the facts they had to play with: I'd turned twenty-one a month before. I was single. I'd arrived via Cairo, where I'd already been studying for a month, and after this trip, I'd go back for another month. I was studying Arabic. I was of Pakistani descent, and roomed, in Cairo, with Haris, an Indian Muslim raised in Saudi

Arabia, who was at NYU on a student visa. This most interested them, not just in Tel Aviv, but back in Egypt where the flight originated. For before I had even made it to the ticket counter, two men and a woman pulled me aside for questioning, which began and ended with my naming my friends. Sorry, Bradley, Jeremy, Jacob, and James.

I needed white names.

Several hours later I was judged nonthreatening enough to enter. The Lonely Planet guide to Israel hadn't bothered to include a section for traveling while indigenous or sharing the religion of the indigenous.

A shared taxi drove several of us forty-five minutes across a gorgeous landscape, most remarkable for its tininess—with all the attention Palestine and Israel receive in American press, I assumed the region was vast, so I didn't expect the journey between Tel Aviv and Jerusalem to take less than an hour. I'd asked the driver to find me a hotel in Jerusalem, which he did, not far from a Sbarro that, weeks later, would be targeted by a suicide bomber. I had never been to a place that made me feel more preternaturally uncomfortable. Many inhabitants were refugees who'd found a safe haven at the cost of expelling or suppressing that haven's native population, a desperate conflict that any reasonable person would have seen coming from a century ago. I was dropped off at an unusually narrow hotel, squeezed between two buildings that looked resentful at having been separated. The hallway was dominated by a rich maroon rug, and the reception desk looked like a ticket counter you might find at a bus stop. All I had time to do was drop my stuff off, because security delays had almost cost me my goal: a visit to the Old City, where I'd join Friday prayer services at the Noble Sanctuary—you might know it as the Temple Mount—which includes the Farthest Mosque, al-Aqsa, and the Dome of the Rock. When I finally arrived at the Sanctuary, there must have been several hundred thousand people there. If not for the occupation, there probably would have been millions. There for the same reason as me.

※   ※   ※

In 619, at the lowest point in his mission, Muhammad was carried overnight from Mecca to Jerusalem.[1] At the far edge of the Noble Sanctuary, Muhammad led every one of the prophets in prayer—one of the most powerful images of Muslim universalism, because prophets were sent to all peoples. Muhammad also came to the large rock, now covered over by one of the most beautiful buildings in the world, and from there he ascended into heaven. Which has still more significance. For Muhammad approached God's throne, leaving even the angels behind; none of creation had ever been permitted such proximity. In the intimacy of the Divine audience, Muhammad was informed that Muslims should perform *salat* fifty times a day. On his return, Muhammad shared word of the assignment with Moses, who urged Muhammad to talk God down to a more reasonable number. They went back and forth, Muhammad to God, back to Moses, back to God, until five prayers were agreed on. Moses insisted that even this was overly much, but Muhammad couldn't bring himself to return for another reduction. (I'm with Moses on this one.) Every time Muslims pray, something of Jerusalem stirs within our hearts. It was from Jerusalem that Muhammad went up to God, after all, not Mecca or Medina. And each prostration—when the Muslim touches her forehead to the floor—is deemed a reproduction of Muhammad's ascent, the closest she can get to God. The favored way of beseeching Him, it represents the humbling of the self, but also Islam's refusal to sunder external form from internal condition. You can understand the deep desire to be there.

I had made it in time to join Friday prayers. Mind you, most young men—my age, for example—weren't permitted in, and most

---

1. Fuller details of Jerusalem's significance in Islamic sacred and secular history can be found in Kanan Makiya's *The Rock: A Tale of Seventh-Century Jerusalem*. Muhammad Iqbal's *Javid Nama* belongs to a genre of literature that takes the Prophet's night journey and ascension as inspiration—some have argued that this genre is the origin point of Dante's *Divine Comedy*.

every time I returned there during that trip, I had to argue my way in. But what I found behind checkpoints and past interrogations made it nearly impossible to leave. Many places matter. Rarer is that place that feels deeply, truly holy. In the face of immense limitations on their freedoms, Palestinians had created here a religiosity that breathed through ancient stones. It felt like God was here, in a way I've rarely felt God. Was it in spite of the tragedy of Palestine, or because of it? It was a summer of intifada. And yet no Palestinian storeowner or restaurateur or taxi driver ever took my money.

"You are a guest in our home."

Their home. Where they were prisoners or refugees or second-class citizens.

There are many places where Muslims oppress other Muslims. Consider the history of the Kurds, as one example. Governments that do not allow their citizens to freely assemble, speak their minds, or even move about the country. Saudi Arabia, astonishingly, will not let women drive. Muhammad's first wife, Khadija, was his employer. A later wife commanded an army in battle, and yet a restriction on women motoring is declared Islamic. There are also many places where Muslims oppress people of other faiths. But these are harder for many Muslims to confront, because they involve a kind of self-critique that no people find easy to pursue. It's the same reason many Americans might get whipped up into outrage over something occurring in Saudi Arabia, neglecting that we have funded and armed and defended no other Muslim regime so strongly. Complicity has a funny effect on morality. But that doesn't mean the Palestinians haven't been wronged. The difference is how it's played out.

Uighurs are persecuted by China, and Chechens brutalized by Russia, and Kashmiris' homeland occupied by India, though none of these register in quite the same way. Partly it's religious—Srinagar is not in the Qur'an, nor is Urumqi a sacred city. Partly it has to do with the outsize attention Israel receives in American media, claims to sharing our values—if, of course, by "our values" you mean values we've tried very hard to abandon. It is also the lopsidedness of the conflict, which is frequently reported entirely backwardly in much of American media. However, it's not only that. Who, really, is surprised by the crushing underfoot of small minorities by vastly larger states? What chance did Crimea's Tatars have against Stalin, or the Rohingya on the fringes of Myanmar?

What boggles the Muslim mind, what represents to it, again and again, how far Muslim civilization has fallen, is the fact that a tiny state can occupy some of its holiest places and no productive action can be taken. That tempts some Muslims to ugly anti-Semitism—Israel must have far more power than we can see!—and others to impotent fury and rage. If Palestine is occupied, what does that say about those who seem to be able to summon nothing but indignation? What is it about modern Muslims that made us so unable to live up to our ancestors' achievements, or our contemporaries of other backgrounds? To be Muslim is to be the stunted descendant of giants, to live in the ruin of your own civilization.

Seeing young men slammed to the ground for not answering a question quickly enough, a family uprooted from its home to make room for someone from somewhere else entirely, prompts a young man to ask why even if there may be tens of millions more like him, collectively they could do nothing. It is a question many Muslims feel, though they may be afraid to voice it, for fear of blasphemy: If Islam is so great, why are Muslims doing so badly? Maybe that's why so many Islamic extremists find it so easy to kill fellow Muslims. Yet to feel more keenly my own impotence was not among my reasons for going to Jerusalem. My Meccan and Medinese experience, three years earlier, promised better. But I was older this time around, much more politically conscious, and the obvious contours of the conflict were impossible to set aside. In fact Jerusalem just amplified what I'd been feeling in Egypt ever since arriving there. I'd gone to Cairo because I had exhausted all options for Arabic study at NYU, and believed that another summer dedicated to God's language would inspire me in the way Middlebury had. History doesn't repeat itself, though, except as tragedy, farce, or fiction. In Cairo, I could construct no consistent spiritual practice, not even surrounded by mosques and muezzins. But why? I wasn't lazy. I was an active writer, a good student; I took part in student life, maybe more than I should've, and otherwise kept myself busy. When my anxiety ebbed, I'd work out; I read books religiously and watched movies superstitiously. Religion was the one part of my life where all discipline disappeared.

Back in Cairo, one night stands out.

Haris and I ventured to Hardee's for what undergraduates call dinner. There in that little outpost of America was a piece of Egypt irresistible. A cream sweater, an elegant counterpoint to her stretchy black pants. Haris, who had joined me in this excursion to Africa from NYU, was upset with my wussy voyeurism and pushed me (literally) to talk to her. But some force kept me glued to my garishly fluorescent plastic seat. My mind could conjure a thousand reasons for what might go wrong, anyhow:

A male relative might see and kill me.

She might say no.

She might laugh and say no.

She might say no and laugh.

Her friends might laugh.

Her brother might laugh and then kill me.

And so I left, hamburgers in bag, bag in hand, my other hand holding on to no one else. The roads were sporadically lit, drowned in pollution, overrun by cars parked wherever space could be imagined. When they're in motion, it's worse. Cairenes have an extraordinarily high opinion of their driving. I needed what they had. Walking the Avenue of the League of Arab States, I was again that ungainly, uncoordinated, unpopular almost-adolescent. Cars honked so we could avoid them, little vehicles strained by the numbers of passengers inside, their headlights mere ornaments, pedestrians the bonus points in a video game of someone's cruel design. All I had accomplished was forgotten, or belittled: After all, who am I if I cannot talk to a woman? Who would I be if I was not trapped inside of me?

I sulked back into our apartment in a mood so sour I could only come to terms with what had (not) happened by deciding I was a character in a novel. One I'd have to write to redeem myself. By the time I'd slipped out of my sandals I entirely hated this pusillanimous excuse for a protagonist, who'd talk all day and plan all night about Islamic Centers, new prayer spaces, professional chaplaincies and Muslim philosophies, locked inside himself and unable to find the key. He was neither Muslim nor not: unable to submit to God, unable to repudiate God, an either and or, an in-between. Haris and I moved into our "two-bedroom, two-bathroom, fully furnished" apartment a month after the spring semester ended, but the second bedroom lacked air conditioning and a functioning ceiling fan, was arguably actively haunted, and the second bathroom was so small I could not sit on the toilet and close the door. The other bedroom, with air conditioning, had two mattresses, each against opposite sides of the wall, and a busted TV. We had a massive dining table but only two dining chairs, whose appeal could be summarized thusly: if each nation exceeds in at least one thing, then in Egypt that one thing is not design.

It was not the kind of apartment you wanted to come home to. Our living room, for example, was a rectangle of linoleum tiles the color, and occasionally the texture, of rust; the walls were the color of lemon juice; the only furniture was two lawn chairs, kidnapped from an American summer barbecue and left to rot in the stale Cairo heat. We had a balcony that looked out on the apartment of some government apparatchik, probably a cousin of Mubarak whose principal qualifications for office were his lack of ambition and slightness of scruple. Haris proceeded to take his second shower of the day and meanwhile I broke down. I don't know what else to call it. Perhaps dissociation. I was so angry with myself for not talking to the Hardee's girl, for being once more stuck inside of me, that the furiousness won out and expelled me from me. At least I was no longer trapped.

But no longer embodied, either. I felt myself float out of and away from myself, gawking at my wimpy useless form, standing pointlessly in the middle of a miserable apartment. Egypt was a deep disappointment: a country with so much potential, not just stuck, but sliding backwards. But who was I to have thought I could fix Muslims, or repair Islam, when I could not even overhaul myself? I wasn't going to save the Muslim world through my pathetic efforts at NYU. I *was* the Muslim world. Afraid. Frozen. I could not move forward. I was not even inside of me. So I did what all revivalists do. I thought to go back. That wouldn't be what *I* would do, mind you, but it could be what another version of me might do. What we would do together, old Haroon and new. We ignored Haris showering, parked my feet into their sandals, snubbed the antiquated elevator—it was big enough for almost one person—and bounded down the unlit stairwell, through a lobby that would elsewhere pass for a loading dock, and down the Avenue of Plentiful Rainfall, outrunning the aged Japanese compacts that kept this capital in perpetual gridlock.

There she'd be, midnight tights and drooping vanilla full-sleeve, and we'd approach. Say something. Anything. If even she turned us down, or a male relative (perhaps a sniper) took aim at our body, at least we'd have a story. For which she'd have to be there, mind you. Who'd wait at Hardee's for over an hour? We stood outside glass doors, covered in grime and dripping sweat, panting while mumbling curses, discomfiting the customers. I was just one Haroon, again. The failure, debating how I'd make Haris understand why I'd gone out and that I'd missed her, which should've been obvious well in advance. Or I could say I went to a mosque, but he'd never believe that. Eventually, exhausted, I found a place to rest on the corner of a street where the traffic would not die no matter how late it got. So many Muslims, it hit me, and yet so little changed. Whoever said there is strength in numbers didn't meet modern Islam. We were an inversely proportional civilization. When we were few, we were bold. Now that we were many, we were all but moribund. The only way I could think of making sense of this was by writing.

I would write a novel. And I did. I needed to.

When you write fiction, you conjure characters. If it's good fiction, you must see them set free. I wasn't bold enough to, and created ciphers instead of actual personalities, ideas instead of individuals, placeholders for concepts instead of people with jagged edges and multipolar internal geopolitics. Revealing more than I'd like to admit to. *The Order of Light* was about an unnamed Arabic student in Egypt who gets lost one night in Cairo (true) after failing to talk to a woman who'd caught his eye (true), and even fails in trying to find her later (true), and hours later ends up at a mosque full of crabby Kurds, adherents of a suspicious Sufi order that seemed to espouse outrageous beliefs about the end times. I modeled the mosque on a real one I found while wandering deep in Old Cairo, but the Kurds and everything after was fictive.

The Kurds claim they're descendants of Saladin's army, which liberated Jerusalem in 1187. Their ancestors had been instructed to hide their Sufi order in Cairo until certain prophesied events occurred, at which point they would have to reveal themselves in such a manner as to save the world from a grave doom. The order's leader, Rojet, eventually lit himself on fire before a McDonald's on the Avenue of the League of Arab States, sparking a popular revolution across the Near East, democracy, Islamist power, then disaster. The point was to tell a story about after people have had too much. The status quo was unsustainable. But what would follow? All that frustration had to go somewhere; it'd be directed out as much as in.

Suicide as regicide, down with the dictator and down with the people who let themselves be dictated to. Implosion and explosion, an energy radiating outward in devastating human waves, smashing apart what was outside while it broke apart what was inside. My conceit—spoilers until the end of this paragraph—was that the main character was simply a younger Rojet, the man who'd abluted with petroleum, the bane of modern Islam, before spontaneously combusting and burning down a block of stores in a corner of Cairo whose money came from its corruption. And yet I did not think these suicides were faithless. They were acts of devotion to God, sins that produced saints, like the man who wanted to kill the Prophet ended by serving the Prophet. If there is any consolation, I called the Arab Spring, including the arrival of political Islam into power and the violence thereafter.

But writing about suicide? I conceived of these self-immolations as nakedly Abrahamic; in the Muslim tradition, the young Abraham, not yet a prophet, smashes his people's idols to reveal their inconsequence and harmlessness. Unimpressed by this argument for radical monotheism, his people cast him into a bonfire, but God intervenes to seal Abraham off from the heat. He was in the fire, but not on fire. I wanted to bring this tradition to my time, to speak timeless values in a contexted place: What would it mean to cut the idol down, when the idol is now the self, man who has deified himself into the measure of all things? Would there be a self after, like Iqbal promised? Or would nothing remain, because there was nothing there all along? But to kill oneself thusly, no matter how reverently, would still be sinful—it would demand the same bonfire Abraham landed in. There comes a point when sin can only lead to sin, and faith as well to sin. Was the course of the modern world simply incompatible with Islam, whose time had passed? Such a time would have to come to pass. Every great idea fades.

I could not otherwise explain why the Muslim world performed so poorly, or Islam affected me so unevenly. The two were one in my mind. I should have been able to force myself to wake up to pray *fajr*. I did not know why I could not compel myself to pray five times a day when I was in a place overflowing with mosques, with minaret alarm clocks ready to remind me in case I had forgotten. I didn't know why I would rather be in TGI Friday's flirting with the waitress than in the mosque studying the life of the Prophet. I should have simply been able to *become* Muslim. I should have pushed myself into obedience and, once there, settled down. And if I could not so reinvent myself, then what did that suggest about me? Light a fire and throw myself in. Die before dying, as the Sufi poets would say. If God willed, you'd live.

■   ■   ■

Two days before we left for New York, while my roommate was severely ill with a blood infection and could barely lift himself from the bed, our landlady showed up with the remaining furniture. Two months late, or Muslim Standard Time. She was proud of herself. Chairs for the vast flanks of the dining table, plus unimaginably ugly sofas and tables for the sitting room. Whether rich or poor, Egyptians had realized an admirable utopia of embarrassing tackiness: I once saw a man exit a Mercedes limousine wearing a purple suit and green tie. This was upper-class Cairo, the razor-thin topmost slice of the heart of the world we were about to be told was the greatest threat to America and Western civilization since the Soviet Union. Before leaving, I'd begun to contemplate walking away from the Islamic Center, hoping to go somewhere else or at least be someone else. I was tired of every thing having to mean everything. New York was big enough, NYU was vast enough, to contain other possibilities. But the Prophet warned us a time would come when holding on to Islam would be like holding on to hot coals. Whenever I heard this story, I used to wonder who'd purposefully burn himself. As it turns out: someone who thought he had to. Or someone who was made to.

Haris and I reconnected as soon as we had set ourselves up in Manhattan. He was downtown, but I was on the Upper East Side, in my first private apartment, shared with two friends, one I'd made at Middlebury. My first class was Persian, which I selected because (1) there were no Arabic courses left and (2) I thought I'd be less likely to meet my future wife in Hebrew. In that, I appeared to be right. On the first day of Persian, I noticed Hafsa—and on the second day, she must've noticed that I'd sat next to her. But all we'd exchanged were pleasantries. With butterflies in my stomach, I could hardly sleep and woke up every morning earlier than I needed to, desperate to make sure I'd make it to class in time to get the seat next to hers.

When I got out of the subway the next Tuesday, though, folks were congregating in the street, right off the curb, looking against traffic, their necks tilted at forty-five-degree angles. No one spoke.

Until spoken to. A plane, someone told me, had flown into the tower. I assumed he meant a private plane. A terrible, horrible, but fully accidental accident. Thinking no more of it, I went to class—and found out, minutes later, just what had happened. Our professor, who'd suffered the shah's authoritarianism and then Khomeini's, let everyone except the Muslims and Middle Easterners leave. He shook his head. He was afraid. Not just because our nation had been attacked. But by whom. Be careful as you make plans to find your ways home, travel in groups, accept that it would never be September 10th again.

On the way up the stairs and out of the building, I asked Hafsa if she needed help getting home. She hesitated, then looked me up and down and said, "Nobody knows I'm Muslim." I was brown, bearded, and president of the Islamic Center at NYU, whose community was one of the biggest in proximity to a mass murder that'd be claimed in our name. She left, the professor began smoking on the sidewalk, and we all trembled as we stared up at the smoke that had devoured that perfect blue sky.

Where there were once two towers, now there were none. Then there were police cars—endless sirens. The city was on lockdown. Frightened and confused students filled Washington Square Park, classes ended, but the trains stopped, cell-phone service was down, every television endlessly replaying a moment of catastrophe. We heard Cleveland, Pittsburgh, Denver, and Seattle had also been attacked by jetliners. Car bombs had gone off in the nation's capital. I knew, instantly, that this could only be al-Qaeda's doing. Somewhere near the Ultraviolet Café I saw Junayd, purely by chance. We decided we should round up as many of our students as we could. We rushed to our temporary prayer space, inside NYU's Catholic Center, expecting to find Muslims, but instead we found an Orthodox Jew.

"What are you doing here?" I asked. We knew each other but, as I wanted to subtly communicate, on this day he would probably not want to be found in a mosque.

"I figured if someone needed to get home, and wanted someone to walk her, I could come along. A hijab might provoke rage right now. Alongside a Jewish man, perhaps less so."

On that day out of all days, he thought of us.

Before, the gaze of an omniscient God compelled me. Thereafter, the omnipresent eyes of a surveillance state would not leave me be. There would be nowhere we could go where we would not be asked to apologize. Many like me would come to regret wasting the time when we could have chosen to be different people. But those days were gone, never to come back. I could not now walk away from the Islamic Center. I would never be able to.

·14·

WAKE ME UP WHEN SEPTEMBER ENDS

MY COUNTRY HAD BEEN ATTACKED. In my religion's name. To slow those who not only believed in but pursued the goal of civilizational war, whatever hesitations I had about my place in the world would have to be pushed aside. And they were—though not without the cost every suppression exacts. There was much we could have done differently. But a lot, so much, too much, was done right; it remains astonishing to me that in the year of the worst such attack in American history, the Islamic Center at NYU was the most active student institution on campus (again). We won awards. We had spectacular turnout. More students became Muslim that year than any previous. We were on fire. I was alight. Though my legs might be shaking, my stomach quivering, my clothes inappropriate to the occasion or I was simply the most junior and least qualified person speaking, still I was there.

Representing the Islamic Center became my life. I perceived my place in the community, and the crisis in our country, as fate working its ways; because I was relatively well read in Islamic history and because, in no small part thanks to my upbringing, I could hold my own at many of the events I was called to, I felt called. I did not give out, give in, or seek to absolve myself of the burdens of the moment.

But don't misunderstand me. I was no rabbi, priest, pastor, professor. I was a kid in way over his head. Reporters I'd never met stuck microphones in my face and rattled off listicles before the Internet invented them: Islam, jihad, Shari'ah, suicide bombing, polygamy, Iraq, Pakistan, Afghanistan, Taliban, terrorism, Palestine, explain, explain, explain! Now! Now! Now! You had eight seconds and, oh yeah, if you fuck it up, you might give added momentum to the hawks eager to use 9/11 as a global casus belli. It was their story of what had happened, and why, versus no story.

We weren't in any position to offer our own. But we would be.

My friends and fellow NYU Islamic Centerists went above and beyond what anyone could've expected, but our biggest accomplishment grew out of my admission of my own unpreparedness for the role I was thrust into. Not to mention many of our senior leaders were seniors, and a lot of our institutional memory would graduate with them. This was, I realized, why so many Muslim organizations failed to get off the ground. Individuals masquerading as institutions, the problem becoming obvious when inescapably that person declines, fades, passes on, or merely moves on. Or is crushed by his work.

That semester, I took my second-to-last philosophy requirement, Philosophy of Language. I couldn't get myself to focus, skipped most of the lectures for obligations I felt I had no choice but to attend to, and by the end of the semester found myself with a paper due in twenty-four hours, on top of pending media requests to explain whether Islam and therefore Muslims were not compelled to war with the West. I e-mailed a friend from class, Michael, and asked to read his paper. Then I rather amateurishly rewrote it. I got an e-mail from the professor the very next day, asking to see me in his office. Michael must have received the same. He had us sit across from him—Michael hadn't the faintest idea why he had been called in—and the professor read from my paper, then Michael's.

Before he got three sentences into Michael's, I said, "I did it." I turned to Michael. "This had nothing to do with him."

I got a zero (for the paper)—I finished with a C- overall. My low-est grade in four years. Fall 2001 was the only semester I didn't make dean's list. I'd been working diligently to achieve a great GPA—for what exactly I don't know—and now that wasn't happening. The Islamic Center was hurting me. There was no career here, no pay-check, no ticket to graduate school. But if I learned any lessons, they were small ones. During my last semester, I took a course on Czech literature. It was the only class I took for me and me alone, that had nothing to do with imposed professional ambition, perceived reli-gious obligation, or identity politics. Who knew I'd find something that echoed within me. A part of the world that was Western, like me, but experienced the treachery of modernity, like me. Most Slavs could not imagine that the world had only one direction, that history and national identity were domestic partners, that everything turns out okay. It was also my last final ever. I remember walking to the Astor Place 6 in the rain. What, I wondered, if I went to graduate school and studied Czech, maybe Russian and Hungarian?

I fancied a musty home on a bucolic campus, lined with book-shelves, snow outside and me inside, a fire that still didn't keep me warm enough, always reading or writing, studying or teaching. I could detach myself from being forced to be a Muslim, from always being called on to defend, explain, and analyze, from the civilizational choices on offer. That same spring, though, Israeli forces assaulted Jenin. Thousands of New Yorkers came out to protest in solidarity—many in rallies I helped to organize—but the American right decided out of conviction or deception to conflate al-Qaeda with all Islam, and their narrative was beginning to win. I might've hoped that after 9/11 we would go back to normal, that no one could do anything as senseless and supercilious as invade Iraq on no grounds whatso-ever, but that's what happened. America would plunge herself into a permanent, escalating emergency, trapped by Islam. Just like I was. Prague was a pipe dream. I'd never wake up from September.

I tried to make the most of it.

■   ■   ■

Despite our rather rushed and inauspicious introduction, my crush on Hafsa had become almost unbearable. Conscious of my epic fail with Rania, I asked a friend, Imran, about Hafsa—did she have a boyfriend, who was she, did she have a boyfriend, what was she all about, also boyfriend? I'd have guessed Hafsa was South American, but that made no sense given her name—and the fact that she was taking Persian. (If you're wondering why I didn't just ask her, I will remind you we're talking about me.) Imran all but delivered me a dossier. "She's half-Japanese and half-American, and she converted," he volunteered. Literally all of this information was wrong, but I admire Imran's unblinking conviction in its veracity and would like to add that he is today an attorney specializing in reviewing death-penalty cases for false convictions.

Hafsa was actually Turkish. She conquered me like her ancestors had mine. The first time I asked her to join me for anything, or what you might call a date, we walked to Figaro's, a café right off MacDougal. She joined me at my events and bolstered me when I felt worn out or insufficient to the task. Come her birthday that fall, I invited her to dinner (Persepolis) and a movie (*Monsters, Inc.*). I got her a card that shared how happy I was to have met her, a tentative and tepid attempt at expressing my affection in the most inoffensive terms. But over dinner she told me how glad she was that we were friends, which I took to mean she didn't share my feelings—although, why then was she out with you and only you on her birthday, dumbass?—and so I threw the card into the first garbage can we passed. We walked from the Upper East Side to Grand Central. Three days later, online, wimpily and wussily, I confessed that I liked her. She asked if that wasn't obvious already.

I set myself to making it up to her (and me), so on Valentine's Day, when she wore a black shirt and gray slacks—she was petite, and she looked a little lost inside her outfit—I took her out for dinner and handed her a bound volume of the poems I'd written her, the e-mails I'd sent her, each of which contained a clue that led to the next, the last of which said, simply, honestly, deeply, "I love you." I don't remember the name of the restaurant, the neighborhood, nothing really except her looking at me, a blur of diners beside and behind us, her eyes wet and filling, unable to say, until a few hours later, that of course she felt the same way, and so it was done. Because I did love her. Insanely. At no point did I ask her to marry me. It went without saying. My relationship would be a hybrid of arranged marriage, as my parents had, and the liberal social order I coexisted alongside—I wanted to fall in love, but the first time was the only time; once lightning struck, you captured it and bottled yourselves up ever after.

Nobody told me wedlock took work, nor did I ever think to ask myself: How well do I know me? Are we ready for this? What is it going to take? I assumed that because Hafsa and I were together now, we'd always be—that this would end with marriage. Emphasis on end. We met, we fell in love, we said we were in love, so now there was nothing more left to do. After all, Muslims didn't divorce. Separate. Selfishly pursue their own selfish passions. I don't mean I had doubts about her or about us. Everyone who knew us knew we were head over heels for each other. I mean, rather, that you can only be successful in a relationship when you have the courage to express yourself, and you can only express yourself when you know what you want to say. How could I do that, considering I had barely scratched my own surface? Or really cared about myself very much either?

Which is just a way to say I took Hafsa for granted. Myself too. I made no plans for my life after college, assuming that I'd just go to law school and it'd all just work itself out—kind of like marriage, now that I think about it. The real worry on my mind was still the Islamic Center. I was the bastard child of the uncles I so disdained, expending all my energy on community life and none on their bourgeois preoccupations.

The Islamic Center needed someone who could represent the community, advocate for it, defend it, but most of all push it forward, because it could not end here. Not on my watch. Not just with a successful response to terrorism. That's the campaign we set ourselves to, "Mission: Masjid," inseparable from the broader effort to secure a permanent prayer space on campus, to make sure American Islam would have a home for the kind of Muslim I could be, had I had the courage to admit to it. I called on Shams and he answered. He wrote up a three-page document advocating for our cause, printed at a local Staples on creamy résumé paper, bound and topped off with a black back and transparent cover. I thought this the zenith of professionalism. The proposal concerned the necessity, viability, and benefits of a "Muslim chaplain," of which, I believe, there was only one anywhere else in the country at the time, at Georgetown University.

I went, backpack very much attached to me, to the office of a senior university official, a woman whose stunning workspace occupied the rarefied top floor of NYU's library. It occurred to me that there were levels of power and influence I hadn't the slightest idea of. I was shown in, very painfully aware of my ungainly backpack straps flapping around, shaking like my quivering legs, which at least were hidden inside jeans (yes, I wore jeans), and tentatively offered her our proposal. Unexpectedly, she asked me to sit down, which I did, like an idiot, with my backpack still on. This formidable woman proceeded to flip through the proposal—admittedly, there wasn't that much content—while I sat there hopeful that Garamond was the right font and fearful that I might vomit from sheer nervousness and, if so, whether I should volunteer that this was one more reason why we needed a chaplain. After a few minutes, she tossed the proposal to the side of her desk and stared through me as if I was just another window in her office. Or perhaps she was thinking about the towers. "I think religion's caused far more harm than good," she pronounced, "but I'm happy to look this over." She meant my religion.

What could I say to that? Invite her to Friday prayers? I (superfluously) summarized the proposal, thanked her for her time, shook her hand, and left, certain we'd hit the wall. But she read it. I know, because she e-mailed me soon after to say she was impressed.

Before September 11, 2001, when you faced south down Thompson Street, you'd see the twin towers. To your immediate left was NYU's modest Catholic Center, where our Muslim community had been offered a temporary space. Today, there's a new World Trade Center. In place of the Catholic Center is the Center for Academic and Spiritual Life, with an odd casting over the outside, and a noncommittally modern interior. The CASL includes the Islamic Center's full-time prayer space, as well as a much larger room for the hundreds who show up for Friday prayers. It's ours, but by the time of its completion it was already too small. Though that's a small price to pay. And we paid. Money. For the view alone, the Islamic Center's might be the neatest Muslim prayer space in North America. Through a wall of glass windows, you take in the refurbished Washington Square Park and, through the famous arch, down Fifth Avenue, the twinkling nighttime lights that look like so much sidereal eye-candy, all the way up to and including the Empire State Building.

I don't think I'm prouder of any other project I've been part of. Not in my whole life. I helped build a growing community, defended it at its most vulnerable—when our city, our country, our sense of ourselves, and even my religion were attacked—and kept on, establishing a fixture on Gotham's religious landscape. My hope was that the Islamic Center would grow from there, on its own energies, into an institution that could never be identified with or reduced to any one person. But here's the catch: I don't know if I should be proud. Even as I am honored by my role in the development of such a place, I cannot ever imagine doing the same again, precisely because it feels fraudulent. I did not pray regularly. I was going out on dates. I was not what I thought a Muslim could be, or should be. And I held myself up all that time as an *Islamic* leader. I was giving Friday sermons.

I did so, of course, because we had few if any other available preachers, and I usually spoke in broad, general terms—Islam as a worldview, so on and so forth, staying away from topics that'd render me baldly hypocritical—but there I was all the same, at the front of the mosque, standing tall. Should I have held back because my Islam was not up to some externally imposed standard? Should I have sat on the sidelines instead? Even after September 11th? I liked what I did. Kind of. I was *good* at what I did. Really. I don't know who else would've suffered a thousand interviews, spoken to hundreds of journalists, juggled so many requests, written up funding proposals and long-term vision statements.

I was front and center when most everyone else wanted to run away.

In *A First-Rate Madness*, Nassir Ghaemi argues that the mentally ill thrive in crisis. Perhaps there's something about their constitution that produces an enviable limpidity of purpose; a lifetime of struggling with one's inner demons steels oneself for other kinds of challenges. When they are roused to action, Ghaemi insists, they are exhausting opponents. They calculate the odds against them with sobriety and restraint. Their pessimism is their courage—they have always faced grimness within, and so when the world is darkness without, they alone are prepared, because they alone have lived through lightlessness. The problem is that the world is not an emergency. So what do these same do when the storm breaks and sunshine returns?

They might make life a permanent emergency. Or they might fall apart.

I got to do both.

·15·

MAKE IT LOOK LIKE YOU'RE WORKING

I SUFFERED MY FIRST PANIC ATTACK in law school. It was also the worst panic attack I'd ever experience, probably because at the time, I didn't know what panic attacks were. I figured the world was ending. I rushed to my standard-issue dorm bathroom, did *wudu* (the watery purification we splish and splash through before *salat*), and prayed like a man who had foreknowledge of his death. But worshipping didn't reduce the agony in the least. I could barely breathe. I crawled off the prayer mat and pushed myself up against my musty furniture. I begged God through tears and gasps to let the world end faster.

Sometimes on entering or exiting the dorm, I'd see a petite blond on the steps. She'd smile at me, but I never worked up the courage to smile back. Which was unfortunate given that I knew no one at Cardozo Law and spoke to next to no one except for awkward small talk. I'd made no effort to befriend, engage, or even sit in the same areas as my fellow students. I'd maybe go to class, feel a surge of excitement— This time I'll do the reading and be prepared come tomorrow!—but a few hours later I'd have boomeranged back to my deadening apartment. Soon I stopped trying altogether. Two years prior, mind you, I'd been riding high.

As the last semester wound down, things were looking up. I was personally honored, and the Islamic Center collectively honored, for showing leadership in the aftermath of the attacks. Junayd, one of my closest friends, was elected the men's vice president of the Islamic Center; Saira, I was thrilled, became president. She was the first woman to run the club in a very long time. My purpose in creating a two-person vice presidency had paid off—Saira had been the women's vice president the year before. The "Mission: Masjid" campaign was taking its first steps. It looked like we'd have a chaplain, and a permanent prayer space, soon. After graduating, and because it seemed appropriate, I interned at the Organization of the Islamic Conference (now the Organization of Islamic Cooperation). But then, nothing.

Not for want of some effort. That same spring, I'd applied for all kinds of jobs, including at a Muslim school where, on the day of my interview, the largely Palestinian students decided my name sounded like Sharon—as in Ariel—and called me that for the rest of the morning. After the interview, I waited for a phone call: nothing. None of my other interviews panned out either. For all I'd done, I had no skills anyone wanted. Or, rather, that I knew how to describe. By early August then, with nothing else available, I moved back in with my parents. It kind of made sense. I was planning to go to law school anyway, so I applied to work, this time as a paralegal, at the same firm I worked for after high school. How's that for a sad-sack circumambulation?

Right after my internship at the OIC had ended, and a few days before I was scheduled to move out of our Upper East Side apartment, that Muslim school finally called to let me know I got the job. But I was scared of moving into my own apartment, had already committed to that law firm in Massachusetts, and my mother was unwell—we'd soon find out she had cancer—so it seemed better, safer, easier, righter to leave. I gave up, in other words, and returned to Somers. Now that I was no longer the center of everyone's attention, I entirely deflated. Now that there was no one calling on me, I had no answers. I spent the year living at home, assigned to an office in

Springfield, Massachusetts. I applied to law school, even though the LSAT repulsed me, and bested me. I seriously thought that the only other option beyond law—a career, remember, that had occurred to me only because my brother had chosen it—was homelessness or, as my father might have suggested, becoming a garbage man.

And law school, as you can imagine, ended predictably enough: the panic attack should have told you that. I dropped out, not even a semester in, and the only thing I'd earned was (1) the hefty tab of a wasted semester and (2) the cost of the year and a half it had taken me to realize law was not what I wanted to do, plus (3) moving back to Somers, *again*, to live with my parents, *again*, this time without (4) knowing what the hell I wanted to do. Thinking, in fact, that there was literally nothing I *could* do. I'd be home all day and every evening, staring at the walls. Sometimes I'd see James, say to watch a football game. Me and Jeremy would maybe watch a movie, usually sci-fi, the geek glue all that bonded us. But mostly I was on my own. And miserable. The only thing that somewhat alleviated my growing terror was movement.

When I could, I drove. I drove to get away. From me, yes, but also from everyone who reminded me of what I'd done to me. I'd blast the radio, which boosted the manic episodes I'd confuse for purpose, punch the pedal and let it fall back, the way only Bavarian engineering allows. Everyone else I knew was on the prescribed career track. The highway to South Asian salvation. Everyone else was a five-times-a-day praying God-is-a-doctor Muslim professional who was also an MD doctor. While they climbed the ladder, getting married, buying houses, making babies to fill those houses, where was I? Promise and potential, but other folks also saw those ahead . . . until they didn't. We haven't even gotten to what might've been the worst of it: Hafsa was in New York, waiting on me to ask her father for her hand, but I'd nothing I could go to him with. No savings, no career, not even ambition.

I didn't want what others wanted, but I'd no idea what I *did* want. Which explains my fondness for speed. In the months after Cardozo the dosage had to be regularly upped: 110 miles per hour. Then 120.

There were places where these scalar quantities were legal, though not New England. Which is where it occurred to me for the first time. With Connecticut forests limning the edges of the windshield, white dashes the length of cars clicking by, one after another until only muscle memory and muscular tires kept me pinned to the road, my fingers curled around a hand-stitched black leather wheel, the gauges glowing orange against the dark, I spied three concrete pillars holding up an overpass not far ahead. If I floored it, I could collide with them in seconds.

It'd be the fastest I would ever go. I'd leave the world like I should have lived in it.

Going places.

I reached out to my mother's friend the very next day, telling her I needed to talk.

We talked for hours in a dining room with fire-engine-red high-backed chairs and a checkerboard marble floor—she and her husband had wanted to be stylish once, a very long time ago. She was the first person to want to know how I felt, inside, which question left me entirely at a loss for words. I'd spent a year at NYU handling all kinds of heated queries about Islam, radicalism, the Near East, building an organization in the face of enormous pressure, planning out multimillion-dollar fund-raising campaigns. I could use words to enrage or calm a crowd. But to describe what was going on with me?

The best analogy I could find was to the weather.

"You know how, in summer, you feel a storm coming? When I was a kid, and I knew a downpour was coming, I'd pedal home as fast as I could so I wouldn't get stuck, you know, in the rain . . ."

Maybe she knew where I was going with this. But she needed me to say it.

"I feel those clouds coming every few days." A black, driving, pounding rain, a monsoon that made it impossible to see even a few feet in front of me, vertical waves of water that cut me off from everyone and everything around me, nothing but liquid walls falling, eroding, flooding, consuming, swallowing, the world disappearing into gray-blue curtains unceasing.

"But do they make you *feel?*"

"Sometimes, when my stomach gets really bad," I ventured, "I have to take painkillers. Serious ones." Though she knew. She was not just a psychologist but a psychiatrist, the only one I knew. She'd finished medical school with my mom. They remained the best of friends. "As bad as that pain gets, like I'm doubled over in pain, I still don't cry. But some nights I come home and it hurts so much I just start bawling and I can't stop."

I become the thunderstorm.

"How bad does it get?"

"There are days where I don't want to do anything, and then there are days where there's so much energy inside me I feel like I'm going to explode unless I lift, or drive, or write, something, anything, to release the pressure. Sometimes I write for hours and I don't know why except if I don't, I feel like I'll die from what's happening inside me."

It had been years since I drank, and even though she suggested a little alcohol could help with my nerves, if used moderately and responsibly, there was too much Islam in me, or on me, to make that any kind of option. And I had a wife de facto if not de jure, so even though the idea of talking to a woman I found attractive immediately blew the storm clouds away, I couldn't do that either. She believed Lamictal would make up the difference, which is what she told me when she called the next day, and said: "You're bipolar."

Later amended to bipolar II. Like I got promoted. To tell another soul, beyond the privacy of doctor-patient confidentiality, would've meant admitting to an illness that was not just embarrassing to allegedly have, but that I did not or should not have believed in. I'm not entirely sure where I'd gotten this idea, except I felt very strongly that Muslims were not supposed to have these problems. If Muslims did, I'd inferred, it was because their belief in God wasn't strong enough. Which was my own interpretation of her diagnosis. I hardly prayed, I wasn't really religious otherwise, and even if the last few

years God had gone easy on me, physiologically, I'd no reason to expect a permanent truce.

She was far less eschatological. She pushed, so I was pulled. I
tried the pills until I felt the unpleasant side effects. A few weeks
later, another Muslim doctor I'd gone to see for a routine checkup
told my mother about the Lamictal and the ensuing conversation
was so unpleasant I decided never to go back to any doctors. I told
my mother I was off the drugs, because I was. The problem wasn't internal, I decided. I needed to change my circumstances. For whatever
else I had to say about the Muslim world, its charming madness, its
vibrant chaos, always captivated me. So I'd go back.

This time even closer to home.

I went to the City of Islam.

I went with my mom, who had decided, as her own illness pro-
gressed, to spend time with her sisters, almost all of whom were in the
Islamabad-Rawalpindi Twin Cities Metropolitan Area. This made for
an immediate improvement in her mood. Maybe because she'd been
sick, but even before the diagnosis, she'd been isolated in Somers.
She and I both. My mother was happy in Pakistan, and I was happy,
too. I had a chance to live in the place I was from, to sink back into
the soil my roots dug deep into, to see where my family came from
and not as a tourist. To develop a connection to Pakistan that was
mine. And it was about Pakistan, but more than Pakistan. I took language classes, first at a language center and then with tutors. Urdu,
Shahmukhi Punjabi, Persian. I loved the languages like I loved Arabic, not, though, because they gave me access to God but to this
glorious Indo-Islamic complex of stunning brilliance, generous cos-
mopolitanism, immense achievement—and it was mine now too. I
could read Iqbal in the original. I could read the people he read. And
then I'd pass it on, just like I'd taken what I'd known and used it to
build a community at NYU—the same, but different.

I'd become a professor and teach what I loved learning. Texts unconventional enough to satisfy. A career bourgeois enough to be acceptable. Given my passion for Iqbal, for Pakistan, for the history of
Islam in this corner of the world, it seemed logical to eschew Middle

Eastern studies in favor of the rarified air of South Asian studies. Also, I learned how to drive on the wrong side of the road (it feels better with your left hand on the gearshift). I only hit one car, and that was jostling for pole position. We left Islamabad in April—my mother and I both back to Somers; me, only temporarily. I had plans, but I was desperate not to fuck it up all over again.

I decided to give myself a year off, in order to produce the strongest graduate-school application possible. First I needed to rock my GREs. Verbal was one thing, but I hired a math tutor—the prodigy also known as Jeremy, who'd in the interim become a math teacher—to ensure my overall score was high. Second, I rented a studio near Rittenhouse Square in Philadelphia and took Gurmukhi Punjabi/Urdu/Persian at the University of Pennsylvania, intent on my language skills being top-notch. I sent off my applications that fall, ecstatic. So-called bipolarity, I concluded, was simply dissatisfaction with insufficient and inappropriate aspiration. I'd go to a great school. I'd learn, educate, write. My parents were supportive—though when I told my father I'd turned down Harvard, I understood the expression someone who regrets his whole life makes.

And then I began to fuck it up all over again.

It came down to a three-way tie between Chicago, Penn, and Columbia. (Fact: Not how three-ways go.) Penn had its advantages: I already lived in Philly, and knew the professors, the department, the neighborhoods. I went to Chicago in February just to see how it felt. Bone-chillingly cold, if you need to know. I stayed in a dorm with leaky windows, and I imagined this was how a true scholar lived, shivering and vulnerable, barely warmed by hot tea or coffee—I was now fluent in milk and sugar—dedicated not to his comfort but to the world's books, to knowledge, to deepening our understanding of the world. The campus was also gorgeous. The school *felt* another order of smarter. The academics were more serious. Even the most gorgeous girls wore glasses. But Chicago was far; my family and especially Hafsa were in and around New York (and Hafsa was waiting anyhow), and anyway I already knew New York. I went with Columbia when everything in me said go to Chicago.

Find a way. Make it work. I chickened out, in other words.

Even my meetings with Columbia professors had been slapdash and aggravating—several forgot to show up, and in one instance, the professor wasn't even in the city on the day of our scheduled appointment. Too, all three schools had offered roughly similar stipends, but while Philadelphia was affordable, and Chicago very affordable, the cost of living in New York was obscene. Instead I told myself I could make up the difference doing work for the Muslim community in New York. I didn't choose the school that spoke to me but the one that other people would have told me was the right choice. But I was still excited about the future. Even though my novel about Cairo and the Kurds and an Arab Spring and Middle Eastern conflagration was published and then disappeared, having barely made a dent in the universe—a few thousand were sold—still, it was something. The high that came from the courage to abandon law school and pursue graduate studies—to forge my own path—drove the darkness farther down than it'd gone in a long time. I interpreted this as a lasting victory.

Between graduation from NYU and my starting at Columbia, Hafsa and I had had three years apart. We were still in love. But our relationship felt like it was on cruise control, like this is what we've been doing and this is what we'll keep doing, and we can keep our eyes off the road and hands away from the wheel, because why would the road ever change? When I met anyone comely, though, my mind immediately spun a story about the two of us together. I never came to terms with these longings even as Hafsa and I talked matrimonially. Was I somehow unfaithful? Bored? Dissatisfied? There was Priti, a college freshman who ran track. Once I walked her back to her dorm room because she felt ill. "I have to puke," she said, and I asked, "What can I do?" She said she would run home, and she dashed down the street. We had about as much in common as Carla from high school did with me.

At Penn I took Persian and, of course, on the first day of class met Mehak. She was at Temple, subjecting herself to sociology. I was enraged that she was engaged. Relieved too. I decided that because I too was otherwise engaged that we would be friends. So we became great friends. In a fit I bought Andrew Solomon's *The Noonday Demon*, the story of the author's struggle with a debilitating depression; I hadn't even gotten ten pages in before feeling I should go to the top deck of my building and jump off. But I told Mehak, not Hafsa. Didn't just text her; I called her. She instructed me to drop the book instead and I did. She invited me to see a movie instead and we did, in West Philly, on the far end of the Penn campus, that very same afternoon. I think it was *Kingdom of Heaven*, but maybe I just made that up.

After the movie, Mehak urged me to see a doctor, and I did, again a psychiatrist who was also a psychologist. I'd never just talked to anyone before. In fact, only a few days before all this, I was sitting in my apartment, watching a segment about mental illness on the news and thinking to myself what a load of horseshit. The very next day I was feeling so stir-crazy, so near to putting my head through the wall to shut off all the voices in my head, that I went and spent two hundred dollars at the Puma store. This wonderful doctor, whose last name had to be Goodman, got me back on medication as well. I didn't have the guts to tell Hafsa, not about my friendship with Mehak, obviously, but about how serious my psychiatric condition was. Hell, I could barely tell myself.

I don't even know how we decided to get married.

I was coming back to New York, and I'd have access to student housing, and she was going to start law school—at Cardozo, in fact, just like me (she would graduate, though; minor detail)—and so I took her to see my parents. We'd waited long enough. My mother gave Hafsa her own ring, which gesture touched me to no end. My parents came down to see her parents. My father asked her father for her hand. His voice was shaking. I'd never heard my father's voice do anything but boom. But just as things appeared to be coming together for Hafsa and me, in that we were starting to follow the trajectory we assumed we should, they were also starting to come apart. Most of it was my fault.

Like many modern Muslims, steeped in some kind of neo-Islamist miasma, I was taught that religion and culture were two different and exclusive things, and that the more of one you had, the less of the other. This is not only very stupid, but explains why so much of religious Muslim life is so godawful boring, and so much of our contemporary literature is literally childish: we are afraid to think complicated thoughts, for fear that any kind of nuance is only a gateway drug to heretical atheism. At the time, however, it meant I wasn't only dismissive of Hafsa's culture, but threatened by it. After all, I should have had religion, but I had no real religious practice; I didn't want to have culture, because that was the alleged opposite of religion; but I really didn't have culture either.

It's one thing to raise children and tell them to hold off getting married until they're ready to settle down. If you don't even tell them what it means to be committed or, how about this, that sexual desire is normal, or that attraction is common, you're just leading them into disaster. My parents made it very clear to us, by never saying anything at all, that we would have to find our own life partners, but because dating was also manifestly and self-evidently haram, I don't know what we were supposed to do. This isn't a *desi* thing either. Most South Asians are more in love with weddings than marriage. Or each other.

Hafsa and I began arguing, sometimes fiercely; she wanted things done her family's way and I, well, as I said, I had no idea what to do, except I felt railroaded in the process, no thanks to the absence of any alternative models I could appeal to as against her own. Over Christmas break we decided on an April engagement party and a late-summer wedding. But very soon after I had come back to Columbia from vacation, I was called to Somers. My mother was in the hospital, trying to yank out the IVs. We'll never know how conscious she was, how much of her was left. "Let me go," she demanded. "Let me go." But it was worse than that. We made her go.

·16·

THE GRAVEDIGGER SAID

MY MOTHER WAS ONE of a very small number of women studying to become doctors when there were only two medical schools in all Pakistan; on top of that, her education was paid for by the Adamjee family, which issued scholarships to deserving students. After their marriage, she joined my father in Kingston upon Hull, where he was already working (as an orthopedic surgeon). In the early 1970s they moved to Brooklyn, where she completed her residency—in radiation oncology. But she never got to practice. My father scored a job in western Massachusetts, and that same year, I was born—so sick that she had no choice but to abandon the career she'd worked so hard to prepare for.

About a year after she died, my father and I went to Pakistan. One of my uncles made the odd decision to accost him. Us. America. "You thought," he fumed, "that by going to America, you would be saved."

Myths of greater wealth. Promises of prosperity. Roads paved with gold. The man continued, fearless, biting, spiteful. "The medicine here is no worse than the medicine there. You didn't have to leave Pakistan, you see?"

I still wonder if she wasn't exposed, during her residency, to something radioactive, which'd explain my having lost the genetic lottery despite a brother, born several years earlier, who is superbly healthy—and a father built like an ox. When my mother died, on Valentine's Day, her four younger sisters and two older sisters were flourishing, and all of them are still alive today, more than a decade on. That uncle, however, was right: Pakistani medicine was the same as American medicine. He died without warning that same year. Nobody saw it coming.

I'd come home once a month from Penn to see my mom, who seemed to be getting better. By the next fall, my first semester at Columbia, she was back to her routine, teaching classes on Islam in her spare time. Over Christmas break, I even dropped her off at a small house that could only be reached by a one-way tunnel through a sad little shadow of a mountain. I waited until she was done, two hours later—the benefits of a well-financed public library system keeping me company—having shared her family's learning, our bookish inheritance, with housewives, also dragged, uplifted, otherwise transported to strange new lands, eager to learn about their faith, and excited to have someone to learn from. They didn't have a choice in their marriages either. Neither, I suppose, did their husbands. But it's not like the wives chose the destinations.

But in late January, after I'd gone back to Columbia for my second semester, and Hafsa and I had begun arguing over the wedding, my mother was taken to the hospital by ambulance. I took the first bus up. My brother met me in Hartford, and we drove over to St. Francis Hospital together. She was propped up on a bed, an IV attached, but other than that minor detail, it could've been any other afternoon. We talked about books, the ones she'd read, the ones I was reading. She asked me if I still wanted to write. She asked how Hafsa was. She asked about my health. She was always asking about my health. When it was obvious she was worn out, I drove to the nearest Starbucks, drank some very strong chai, and caught up on homework. I was studying the history of Buddhist India.

And then I felt an ominous scratching at the back of my throat. If everything happens for a reason, then tell me the reason. Because the right thing to do was go home. Immediately. My mom wasn't just at risk directly. If I made my brother or father sick, they'd pass the illness on to her, and she was in no shape to fight anything off. As per my usual, this would be no everyday cold or flu. I felt so terrible when I emerged at Port Authority—which looks now like I felt then—that I took a cab uptown. For the next few days, my mother and I spoke over the phone regularly, me telling her that, as soon as I got better, I was coming right back, and she telling me to wait. I only wonder now if she knew, even then.

Lying in bed, I decided I'd order a CD set, one we'd spoken about back at the hospital—her room had a CD player, so it seemed like a good choice. It was a new recording of a very old poem in praise of the Prophet Muhammad, the *Burda*, widely believed to have healing powers. (Muhammad Iqbal turned to it when he was in poor health.) When I announced the gift, though, she pushed back, in a surprisingly robust voice. "I won't be able to listen to it, Haroon." She sighed and the tiredness resurfaced. "You should return it and save your money."

Puzzled, I asked, "Don't you have a CD player?"

"They changed my room," she explained.

"Well," I offered, "you can just play it at home when you get discharged."

But she repeated herself. "I won't be able to."

It didn't matter that I'd gotten sick. I could have still been there, with her, because she knew. And she still didn't tell me to come back. Maybe she was afraid I'd think I caused it. That I'd feel guilty. I still don't know.

While she was visited by a stream of aunts uncles cousins friends colleagues, tended to by doctors nurses, I was barely able to lift myself out of bed. My temperature soared to over 102. I slept and slept and when I didn't I stared at the ceiling wishing I could. By Sunday morning, the fever lifted enough that I could handle a shower; while shaving afterwards, though, I noticed my eye. Just when I thought I'd be able to go see her—she'd be discharged from the hospital later that same day—I had to hold back. But at least she sounded better on our daily telephonic check-in. I must not have, though.

She pressed me on my health, and I reluctantly revealed that I'd gotten some kind of eye infection; the whites were now ochre. She called back around 6 p.m. to tell me she'd spoken with an ophthalmologist and called in a prescription at Hartley Pharmacy. Consider the circumstances. My sickness had literally derailed her life, and yet the last thing we talked about was . . . my sickness. What follows next I learned from my father, because my mother and I never spoke again. Abu left Ami in the study, where she was resting. He saw her in the kitchen, around 8 p.m., warming herself some porridge. She said she was going to bed. He went to his room so she wouldn't be disturbed.

Had she called for him, for any of us, in the hours that followed? She was apparently up for dawn prayers, because her prayer rug was unfolded on the floor, though when my father came to check in on her early that morning, she was lying down in bed, raising her hands to her ears in the way Muslims begin prayers. Had she been trying to pray since dawn, or was she trying to pray now, knowing that it'd soon be over, that the curtain would be lifted?

The doctors had released her with a clean bill of health. They missed, we all missed, a certain something in her last blood test, an indicator that her liver was failing. This would torment my father in a way it could neither my brother nor I; we were not doctors, we could not ask what we'd overlooked. An ambulance raced her back to the hospital, and I was on my way to Hartford again. "One more thing," my brother said, on the phone, the soft traffic of a hospital in the background, hushed conversations, intercom announcements, sporadic beeps and bells, his voice drained. "Bring your Qur'an." In their haste, they'd forgotten their own. I brought my dark-green Middlebury edition. I saw in a dream, Joseph says to Jacob, "Eleven star, the sun and the moon."

My mother held on long enough for me to arrive. She was uncon-
scious, but alive. And then God began turning off the lights. One
organ after another failed. She being the glue that held the family
together, her dying prompted our first fundamental dividing. Should
we force her to stay, or should we encourage her to go? *"Mujhe jane
do,"* she'd cried—"Let me go"—yanking at the tubes, tearing at the
wires. Go where? Back home? Onward to God? I believe she kept
me away because she always kept me away, like she didn't let me go
to boarding school, because I was sick. Maybe she didn't think I was
strong enough.

I'd never seen my father like this before, hesitant, pale, quivering.
He wanted to keep her on life support; he and her doctor agreed.
My brother, myself, and the only brown doctor disputed this. We
conferred in the hallway and realized that we might have to make a
decision to countermand our father. Her liver was done. Her kidneys
soon too. Sometimes you don't have the time to come to terms with
the loss. You're asked right then and there to deal. We persuaded
my father, or maybe it's more accurate to say that after some time,
he couldn't put up any further resistance. They pulled the plugs. As
my brother recited the thirty-sixth chapter, the heart of the Qur'an,
a chapter called "Y. S.," she passed. There was a hint of a smile on
her face, which visibly relaxed, the swelling abated, as she died, even
as her heart-rate monitor screamed, panicked, hyperventilated. Flat-
line. The last of the chimes we'd ever hear, the final act my mother
acquired for this world. Maybe that's what she'd been asking, fore-
telling, anticipatorily requesting. Maybe someone better was calling
her and she preferred His company. It was Saint Valentine's Day. Two
days before, a snowstorm had blanketed New England. Two days after
she died, the weather was unseasonably warm. Frozen ground turned
soggy. As digging goes, the gravedigger said, it was easy.

We lowered her body, wrapped in a white shroud, into the grave.
Her body was turned to face Mecca, and planks of wood were fitted
over, beginning at the feet, locked into a small indent that had been
produced for that purpose. But the last few planks could not be lowered from above. They required someone to be down there, over her

body, feet on the ground. I was volunteered. I should've been aghast. But I've never known, before or since, the peace I was consumed by down there, the two of us but not only the two of us. The last planks put down and secured, hands descended to pull me up and, with my foot against the dirt, I was lifted out. Hundreds of people came to pray. And then they were gone.

I went to her room that same night, where she'd sew or read, and I prayed. Through the three windows, each as tall as me, there was forest, and beyond that, the Springfield skyline, even Hartford's tallest buildings. Did she sit here and wonder why life had brought her here? Did she wonder what her life was for? Did she blame him, or Him, or me? Did she accept that she'd die much earlier than anyone she knew? Did she really die like I saw her die, at peace with herself and the world? What did it mean that her last act in the world, repeated until her body could not sustain her soul, was to try to pray? Did she even know she couldn't get beyond that movement, or was she stuck, like a pious broken record? I'd joke that my dad was the last man, who'd endured things few of us moderns could be expected to survive, let alone so stoically. He is still with us. But he's not the same.

When a friend suggested my father remarry, an elderly widow also alone, he refused. He was still in love with my mother, though it wasn't any kind of love we moderns would recognize. That way of living is endangered—arranged marriages aren't anything we can come to terms with, but that doesn't mean it didn't suffice for him. There are different kinds of love and I only began to see it then, but not entirely, fully, completely. We show we care in different ways. When, six years later, my divorce was destroying me, a friend of mine, an engineer, took me for coffee. Marriages fail like buildings, he said. Some break down gradually. Erosion. Lack of maintenance. But some, he said, contain a defect, a flaw, which might remain hidden, but which causes a spectacular collapse. Sudden, shocking, violent, unbelievably hurtful. Isn't life like that? I said. Is it better to know you're dying, or just die?

■   ■   ■

My father's home was too big, and too far from everyone else's, and too much of a burden to pay for—the building of it had already begun to crush him financially, well before my mother became sick. He relocated for a while to Pakistan, trying to reconnect with his family. Which meant I had lost much of mine. To lose one's mother, of course, and then the home that you knew her in. So long as that home was there, if even in the background, I felt moored. Thereafter I began to live in the knowledge that any project is temporary, any achievement is fleeting. It was a heavier mental burden than I thought it'd be.

A few months later, Hafsa and I had our engagement ceremony, a cauldron of frustrated relatives and raised voices. Interruptions. Shouting matches. Everyone wanted his own way of doing things, and no one could find a resolution. A lot of this was my anger over my mother's death and my father's departure. But by the end of that same summer, we were married all the same. Shams spoke at the wedding. My friend Ali, who would ask me to promise him, one night six years in the future, not to rashly take my own life, nonalcoholically toasted the Pan-Islamic spirit of the moment. And then we moved into a precious campus apartment.

Before we could set to work on our partnership, though, Hafsa disappeared into the black hole that is law school and I resumed Columbia, having fallen very far behind because I took so much time off after my mother had passed. Hafsa and I argued a lot those months, bad blood over the way the wedding had gone, and then on top of that the anxieties and stresses of school(s). It was all so different from how it had been when we first met, from the adventures we'd had. Though her family was always awfully nice to me, I felt out of place among them—and fully placeless without them. The cultural gaps were vast. Muslimness did not imply sameness. Her brother-in-law, Mahmud, and I became good friends, possibly because we had the most in common—his father was very religious, and probably would've loved my father (had he not then been in Pakistan), and Mahmud's struggles to come to terms with that upbringing meant he channeled his Muslim identity into commitments like I did.

But I was not married to Mahmud.

Hafsa and I could still talk as if we'd known each other forever, finish each other's sentences, laugh at each other's jokes. But I withdrew from her, probably not deliberately but all the same irrevocably. The key to a good marriage, as I can tell you because mine went supernova, is honesty. The ability to be truthful to your partner, and to have a partner you can be truthful to, matters. But how can you be open with your spouse when you cannot be open with yourself? When you do not even know what is happening to yourself? The downs became so severe I'd shut myself in my apartment, turn off the lights, and sit in darkness for days—on one occasion I watched TV for twelve straight hours because I could not open my front door let alone face the hallway. Even the highs were a little lower. I saw psychiatrists and took the medications they dished out, but every time they asked me how I felt, I stiff-upper-lipped it. What was happening, I suspected, was a product of ungratefulness, not anything substantive, systemic, ingrained.

I met with one psychologist twice a week for three years, and never told her any of the things that truly haunted me. That I could not bring myself to pray, so I was going to hell; that God wanted me one way, and I wanted to be another, and so either God hated me or God didn't care about me. That though I was supposed to be happy with my wife, I'd develop crushes on other women, and the surge briefly kindled some spark of life in a dying inside. That when I was younger something happened to me. That someone close to me asked me to do something that left me deeply ashamed. That even the memory of it made me flinch and my mind sped away. To other topics. New chapters. A different paragraph.

But I could say none of these things. I could not admit any of these things. There was a cork inside of me: all the things people told me I should be were keeping most of me down. Some months into our marriage, I went back to drinking. This time not to fit in or have fun, but only to reverse my descent, to bring me back up when I got too down. One Long Island iced tea produced a really great rewrite of a short story I'd been working on. But every glass only made me feel guiltier. There was no chance I'd cheat on my wife. I didn't know what else to do, so I chased after what I'd made at NYU, at the cost of paying attention to Columbia. If I could not worship God, I would work for God. I'd earn some needed cash, too, and this was helpful, but not the primary motivator.

I became the Islamic Center's director of public relations. I took the sermons I once delivered on campus and brought them to the rest of the nation and even other parts of the planet. The applause, the attention, the hopping and skipping across the country, the commitment to a cause greater than myself, which genuinely mattered to me, these tipped me out of depression, even into mania. I became a professional Muslim. But I was not as young and naïve as I once was. I was older, and married, with serious expenses. I felt used and abused by communities that would expect me to fly from one coast to another, or take a week out of my schedule, but pay me hardly enough to cover any part of my rent. Yet I kept going. I would come home worn down, depressed, but three days later I was packing for another trip. The irony: so that I would not kill myself, I nearly killed myself, and then I nearly killed myself anyway.

· 17 ·

THE LATE, GREAT
MOSQUE OF CÓRDOBA

FOR A GOOD TEN YEARS, from the end of high school and through our first year of marriage, I had been on a spectacular run. Cancún was the harbinger: Hafsa and I decided to go to Mexico for our honeymoon, postponed until the winter, after we were done with our first semesters. By day two I felt ill. By day six I was hospitalized. By day seven I was well enough to see some nice things and think, "Wow, this place is awesome. I should really visit sometime." We scanned some Mayan ruins, floated through a Venetian-themed shopping mall, and the next day we flew home. The following December, on the edge of 2007, it began.

Whatever it was.

Whatever I ate made me spectacularly ill. Not eating, of course, also made me unwell. The very thing I needed to keep me alive was destroying me. Nor did this malady submit to any logic, let alone any diagnosis. A particular food might be tolerable for a few weeks and then inexplicably became the source of epic gastric distress—even the morphine family could hardly do it for me. An hour in, and I was back to writhing in pain. When I explained to one doctor that more than a quarter of me—fifty pounds—had vanished in twelve months, he told me it was a great thing to lose weight. I wanted to punch him in the face and tell him that what didn't kill him made him stronger.

It's nearly impossible for me to convey how devastating this was except by telling you about my hands. I could feel my bones scratching at my skin, the thin epithelial layer, stretched taut over my innards, daily becoming more diaphanous. I was sure my bones would soon rip through. Blood, tendon, ruin. I'd become inverted, skeleton without and strands of skin within, neither living nor dying, just going gaunter, some kind of Gollum, which scenario sometimes became so vivid I'd become nauseous, or on better days be merely overcome by a melancholy singularity that swallowed all hope and light. I could do nothing, go nowhere, talk to no one, and find comfort in nothing. My only recourse was to stuff my hands into my pockets where I couldn't see them, or I'd blast the music on my iPod so loud I couldn't hear myself screaming at me. "I'm fucking dying." "I'm ugly." "I'm a skinny, weak, unwanted child." "I'm going to die alone, unaccomplished and unwanted." I went to hospitals in Maryland, Connecticut, Texas, and later Turkey and the Emirates, and, of course, Mexico, and the more honest doctors would admit cluelessness. My only consolation seemed to be that I might be cited in an article somewhere. I was going to live my life a dependent freak, helpless and useless.

Depression is defeated ambition turned inward. All that fire inside me, the desire to do so many things, had nowhere else to go. Then I lost another ten pounds. There was gravity, but no bottom. My etiology was a familiar theology.

The Muslim's most pedestrian actions are supposed to begin with "Rahman" and "Rahim," two of God's names, meaning "Compassionate" and "Merciful." These don't just denote those qualities, though they do that, too. They *are* Him. It's as if you were to be known by multiple first names, all of which described you, all of which were you. He was al-Ilah, yes, but He was also Merciful and Compassionate. Most Arabic words descend from trilateral roots, out of which are formed semantic clusters; terms of related meaning sound alike, like the progeny of a forgotten ancestor, their primary root letters always in the same order, slotted into slightly different patterns. The trinity from which we derive Rahman and Rahim, *R*, *H*, and *M*, began with the word for "womb," and evolved from there, a surprisingly maternal touch. RaHMan. RaHiM. But to me, God did not seem in the least bit caring.

He seemed vindictive.

Why else would He strike me with an illness beyond anyone's comprehension? Was it a feedback loop from heaven on high, me angry at Him, Him against me? But then, He started it, didn't He? What in me deserved, from before I had any agency, autonomy, accomplishment, or error to my name, such perduring illness? I was obsessed with my inability to correspond to God's will, and outraged by that will too, for I suffered it. God hated me, but had chosen to kill me slowly. Since He gave me life, though, I guess He got to choose how to murder me. Isn't that what death is? God's assassination of His own creation. Those different atheisms again. One comes from moral frustration—I cannot believe God would let such things happen, so I cannot believe there is a God. If He is not Rahman, then He is not. Except, of course, many terrible things are true. I always believed in Allah. I just didn't believe in Rahman or Rahim.

Then it got worse.

I was on the Long Island Railroad when I felt an unusually sharp pain in my stomach. Rather than do something different (like, I don't know, consult me), my body decided to divert blood from all other sectors, such as and including my brain, or at least this is what a doctor hypothesized several hours later. Two syncopal episodes, one after the other. Panicked passengers dragged me onto a nearby chair and alerted the conductor, so an ambulance would be waiting. It is beyond embarrassing to be wheeled through all of Penn Station—the nation's ugliest transit point—bared for the world to see. Two days in the cardiac ward did not lead to a determination of what was wrong, except that my resting heart rate resembled a nearly dead man's. Hafsa cried out of helplessness. Where others are prohibited salt, my cardiologist cheered me in the liberal application thereof.

Anything to up the bpm. This, too, was thrown in to round out the conversation: "Maybe you should get a pacemaker?"

Near Miami I almost collapsed due to unbearable pain originating from where else but my midsection. Naturally this happened while we were boarding a plane, and I practically collapsed onto the floor of the jetway. I closed my eyes and tried not to think of the almost inestimable shame of being wheeled out the length of the airport via stretcher, past practically every gate, for as fate would have it we were at the farthest one; I was utterly horrified to be so on display. The second time as Michigander farce: seven days later exactly, I was rudely awoken by a sensation of internal rupture so severe I all but threw myself onto the floor, drowning in sweat, my heart pounding so hard I thought it might burst. I rolled onto my back, looked up at the ceiling, and asked God if this was it. I thought myself the measure of self-reliance when, after I managed to crawl to the nightstand, I ordered myself a taxi.

A few months later, in November and back home, I spent three days in the hospital with the same kind of pain. But if I pretended this wasn't happening, then this wasn't happening. My mind was all I had. Always had, at least. My body was flaky; God gave me, made me, put me into, a damaged vessel, closer to a cadaver, but in that span of senior year, and then college, it had been mine, it worked, it did what my mind told it to, and look at the things I had done! And now He was snatching it back, by which I mean breaking it and taking it. That, I could not stomach. Literally. If I was going to die, I'd rather die having done something. I was determined to see Muslim communities reach their potential, even apparently at the cost of killing myself. I don't mean so abstractly but genuinely. I'd thrown caution and myself to the wind.

Even if I didn't get sick, if I, say, survived the trip there and back, an ever unlikelier proposition, I knew I'd been used. Chantelle, a South Carolinian airline pilot I met on a flight to Georgia—she was sitting next to me because she was on vacation, not wantonly neglecting the plane—said she thought we all prostituted ourselves in different ways. I don't know about that, but on the subsequent cab ride to my modest hotel, something of a touristic log cabin, I saw some truth in her words. I'd agree to go speak at almost any venue, never get much money, if any, in return, and then repeat the process. While circumscribed. Not just financially, but thematically, substantively. I would lecture and prod and provoke, sure, but I couldn't say all of what I was feeling, or much of what I was thinking, because I was afraid I'd burst the bubble in which I lived. I was a poorly compensated half-truth.

Whether my talk was well received did not matter. Most communities, strapped for cash—especially the ones whose board members drove sedans that cost way more than my annual salary—offered meager reimbursement, and rarely if ever maybe a rental car. I would be deposited in a suburban hotel far from everything, for however much time remained until my speech or my flight. What was there to do? Wander hotel hallways that seemed to reflect an architect's disinterest in our need for orientation? Go outside and hang out in the parking lot with other people's borrowed American sedans? So I remained in the rectangular coffin of my hotel room and asked myself questions only the angel of death is meant to. If I was lucky I might not have a panic attack.

The inevitable response to engaging so many, feeling briefly of some flickering cosmic significance, then finding myself deposited in a lifeless, carceral, overly air-conditioned cellblock, staring out windows impossible to defenestrate therefrom. Someone else made the room. Someone else stayed overnight before me. Someone else would clean up after me. It'd be like I was never there. The end was the beginning was the hospitality industry. I'd hit thirty-two states by thirty-three. If you think that's the worst of it, though, you'd be wrong. Even as I hopscotched across the country, I was a freelance journalist, a website editor, running my own consulting firm, of course performing public relations for the Islamic Center at NYU, and, last and often least, pursuing the PhD that once had me excited enough to turn my entire life around.

Why? Because I believed there'd be one gig somewhere around the bend that would fix it, whatever was wrong, that would deliver

me salary and benefits, preoccupation or occupation, something, anything, everything, a final end to a perennial problem, a feeling of
purpose imposed from without because it could not be found within.
And then I found something close to it.

My brother-in-law, Mahmud, was a manager at an increasingly inter-
nationally regarded travel agency. He was very good at his job, but
he'd hit a wall. His mostly Muslim customers would go to Mecca,
Medina, and, increasingly, Jerusalem, too, as if they'd suddenly remembered their American citizenship. Then they'd visit family in
Bangladesh, or Sudan, or Morocco. But lately even those visits were
declining—the longer they'd been living here in America, after all.
While ordinary vacations didn't appeal to these clients (they weren't
designed for them), what were North American Muslims, with many
resources but no options, to do?

Western *and* Muslim. Fortunately there was a rich, largely un-
heralded confluence of the two. Mahmud handled the logistics,
marketing and money, airlines and hotels, designed to appeal to this
underserved upwardly mobile demographic. I'd design the itinerary
and the tours, delivering lectures on sites I picked out in advance,
noting what merited our time and what didn't. We'd commence with
Spain's fabulous legacy, because after all who doesn't want to go to
Spain? From there we'd expand to Turkey and Bosnia and, eventually, I hoped, Albania, Bulgaria, Sicily, Portugal, and Russia, places
whose histories belonged to us as Muslims. Our excursions would be
fun. They'd be a chance to meet people, maybe that special someone.
But you'd learn. You'd come back inspired. And I'd do well as well.
The reimbursement was a great improvement on nearly all my prior
engagements.

We traveled with well-to-do customers; I got free vacations and
stayed in fancy lodgings. Plus I was making good money. I could
also talk about Islam without letting people hold me up as a religious leader, which I'd never claimed to be but never contested
very strongly either. (What was I going to do, scream, "No, I am

a nonpracticing reprobate"?) Now I'd explore and involve people in the histories, legacies, and unknown stories that so captured me, other kinds of Islam and other kinds of faith, that resonated with me, nourished me, inspired me. At most I gave a few hours of lectures a day, and the rest of the time I had to myself. Suffice it to say I'd rather be unemployed in Spain than employed in America. Each city is a little world unto itself, charming, genial, storied, resonant, like a song you don't mind losing yourself in, Granada most of all. I'd insist to every customer that, whether your experience of a Muslim megalopolis is Karachi or Cairo, Istanbul or Teheran, Granada will surprise you with its familiarity—it has that Pan-Islamic smell, the congenial crowdedness. It is a place that retains a residue of some prior people. Nicotine and gasoline.

You've never been there but immediately you feel you belong.

It remains, in a way, a part of a heritage you didn't know the breadth of.

But each of these trips had an upside-down. What'd happen if I got sick? What'd happen if my customers had to watch me being taken to a hospital? How would I even begin to explain to the doctors, in my rudimentary Spanish, what was wrong with me? Even if I held up healthwise?

By the turn of the eleventh century, Spain was Muslim-majority. Its indigenous population had voluntarily Arabized and Islamized; it was not ethnically Arab, of course, but it was largely Muslim. It is neither now. We were touring the death camps of a brilliant civilization. Less museum, if you will, and more mausoleum. We had no choice but to face a slow-motion holocaust; most of Spain's Jews were wiped out or expelled relatively quickly, while the much larger Muslim population was whittled down over many decades. The last case of a Spaniard practicing Islam—a crime before the Inquisition—was prosecuted in 1728, though the last Muslim kingdom fell in 1492.

By the time the second trip came around, nearly a year after the first, in what'd be my final excursion to Iberia as a tour guide, other parts of my life had changed. Mahmud didn't go with me, because Hafsa wouldn't. In the fall of our fourth year married, she began to walk away even in the middle of ordinary evenings. Sometimes I'd find her in a corner, quietly crying. My beautiful wife, heartbroken. It was the same thing I was feeling. Which feeling I refused to share with her. In fact the only feeling I subsequently had for her was anger.

Feelings are fucked up that way.

I believed she had no right to be upset (with me) because I was already upset (with her) and I hadn't shown it, admitted to it, explored it, even vented it, so how dare you preempt me. I thought by staying quiet about my doubts and confusions, I'd done what a good husband should, quashing my dissatisfactions and greater jihading for appearances. I'd long since begun to feel like we were not working like we used to, that we weren't close like we had been, we didn't connect like we once did, but I responded to these sentiments like I responded to anything else: by assuming they were evidence of some kind of moral failure, and therefore best dealt with by being denied. All my disquiet was just selfishness, for once you got married, you stayed married, and I had a great wife—smart, fun, beautiful, cool, funny—while many people couldn't even find a spouse, so shut the fuck up Haroon and be thankful to God like the masjid taught. Moreover, what would discussing it do? Make matters worse. Therefore her honesty got processed as a kind of treachery. For Hafsa began to say what I'd been suspecting, and once you say something out loud, it means you can moot what might happen next. One night I woke up to see her on the floor, an image that resurfaces not infrequently even now, at any time of day, even as I've tried to keep it down, because it hurts so damn much.

She was crying. She must've been up and crying for some time. She was going through all the cards I'd given her, poems I'd written her. They were real, or had been real, or still were. But I did not tell her I was awake, let alone reach for her, console her, speak to her. I shut my eyes and tried to sleep, which I failed at like I failed at husbanding. My job was to keep her happy—and she wasn't. That spring, we saw a series of therapists. I will never forget that one day a therapist asked us each how committed we were to the marriage, on a scale of 1 to 10. In retrospect this seems like a really dumb thing to ask anyone to do in front of anyone else. Her number was much higher than mine.

There were brief changes, of course, moments when the old Hafsa and Haroon were resurrected. On her birthday, ten years to the date we went to see *Monsters, Inc.*, I insisted we go out, us and only us, and we had Japanese on Bell Boulevard. It was a really nice forty-five minutes, and we ran out of things to say. That in and of itself wasn't dispositive. But it was not up to the moment either. I should have just opened up and said it all. I should have crossed the distance between us. And I'll tell you what: a good husband would skip the travel, the distractions, the distances, the obsessions, stop pursuing gigs that pay next to nothing, and put wife and the chance of a family first.

My Hail Mary presented itself the following spring. I took advantage of scheduled presentations in Spokane to create a trip for the two of us, which would include Seattle, Vancouver, and then Anchorage. We'd bust out of routine. Spend time together. She later told me she'd been miserable the whole trip. She said, much later, it was because we never addressed the elephant in the room. Our relationship. We were focusing on what was around us instead of what was between us. Whereas I'd thought that the time away would somehow make the past come back, that we were better off not unpacking our grievances, that we'd be happier if we just made some new memories to crowd out the bad ones.

After that trip, though, it seemed we were done. Which is when, of course, I got the job of a lifetime; all those years of working in communities for such a pittance, endless efforts and strivings, had paid off. New America Foundation, a prestigious DC think tank, was looking for someone to help do outreach to Muslim communities, and I earned the job. I tried to frame the move to Washington, DC, as a chance for Hafsa and me to start afresh. In the meanwhile she suggested a trial separation, which I figured was her first step out the door. Because I was the kind of person worth leaving. The old anxieties I'd had had metastasized—I was now incapable as a man in yet another way, unable to keep my wife with me. Though I'd spent weeks resisting her proposal, I reconsidered when I realized that, if this was really going to be over, then I should prepare myself for what was to come. Even as we unpacked in our Arlington apartment, I told her I was with her. In going without her. We should be apart for a while, I concurred. She was deeply grateful for this concurrence.

I now believe that, for her, the time apart would let us clear our heads, and come back to each other in love all over again. I was not only bad at communicating my feelings, but terrible at understanding hers. To encourage us in the punishment that is unpacking, I'd put the radio on. It was Mike Posner's "Cooler Than Me." Unprompted, she walked over to me, pulled me up, and began to dance with me. As if none of this had happened. As if we were two students in love in Greenwich Village. Adia, we are still—we are. Still. Hafsa pulled me closer and I could smell her perfume, count the freckles on her face, wrap my arms around her, and then it hit me, all of it, and maybe she was doing this to reassure me, to show me what was inside her, that we'd get through this. I couldn't though. I ran to the bedroom and sobbed into a pillow for how long I don't know. I've never cried so hard, so long, so painfully, so wretchedly, in my life. Until the very next day.

The next morning I dropped her off at Union Station for her return trip to New York, not to see her again until the day—we'd picked no particular day—we'd reunite. She hoped it would be only a few weeks. I, of course, suspected it was already over. That misunderstanding was fatal. Better to make the move than have it made for you. Then you remember that in a few weeks you've got to take a bus full of Muslims, many of whom know you and your—is she still your?—wife, in tandem with her brother-in-law, to Spain for a historical tour. You brought this shit on yourself.

· 18 ·

HOW TO BE AN IDIOT

MAHMUD GAMELY BALANCED HIS commitment to our paying customers, and his loyalty to his wife—Hafsa's younger sister—by sending another employee in his stead. While I was tour-guiding the splendors of Spain, Hafsa went to Central America for her own vacation.

Our tour started in Seville, in a very contemporary hotel, whose stylishness would have wowed me had I not been so tormented inside. Whereas most of the group stayed up late, overcharged by the excitement of arriving for what I'd promised would be an exceptional experience, I went to bed early, hoping I'd be rested for the next day's activities. By and large this meant escorting the participants on state-sanctioned tours where available, and then amending, objecting to, or overruling everything Iberia's often partisan propagandists, witting or not, wanted tourists to know about the Muslim era. That was the very reason people paid handsomely for me to come along—because I could and would.

That first night, though, augured poorly.

Usually I do not dream or do not remember dreaming; I suspect that, to balance my tendency to overthink all my waking hours, my body takes my brain wholly offline for the night. Except this time. My hotel room was at the far end of the first floor; it wasn't overly large, and was dominated, as hotel rooms tend to be, by the bed—whose chocolate leather headboard stretched all the way to the ceiling, nearly matching the very slim wooden puzzle pieces that made up the floor. The glut of brown made the room seem more cramped than it was; the bathroom was in contrast blindingly white. But none of that explains what I was shown.

The highlight of Muslim Spain is, in this former expert guide's opinion, the Great Mosque of Córdoba, which I had excitedly planned to guide my way through solo—a difference from the first tour, when I let the locals take charge. I'd mapped out precisely how our tour group would arrive, what streets we would take, what ancestries and architectural flourishes I would highlight, and even where I'd pray illegally when the opportunity presented itself. This Great Mosque is modeled on the Umayyad Grand Mosque in Damascus, which was modeled on the Prophet's original and very humble mosque in Medina. Centuries later, the rebuilt Prophet's mosque, costing hundreds of millions of dollars, is an unmistakable homage to Córdoba's. The end is the beginning is the end.

An ethereal structure, Córdoba's mosque had been forcibly converted, after the city's conquest by Christian armies, to a church and in fact still served as one; a cathedral was even built incongruously in the center, creating a schizophrenic affect, delicate Semitic monotheism all around, encircling a gaudy Trinitarian heart, like a hand from the Sistine Chapel had reached down and excavated a portion of Muslim history for the purpose of inserting Catholic revisionism. Muslim prayer is, as a result, forbidden. You lost and we won, which is true, and unfair, and fair. Back to my dream now.

And then there I was, alone, inside the mosque part of the Great Mosque of Córdoba. I had a three-quarters view from the ceiling. Far below me was me, a person-shaped smudge lost in a forest of spindly columns in candy-stripe marble. I was observing me like a security camera might. The air tasted so old I thought I might be inhaling the exhalations of the mosque's doomed congregation, from whatever day in 1236 Muslim prayers were last held there. No one else was present. I spent a fair amount of time trying to make sense of my apparent imprisonment in an overrun mosque. And while it was unclear how I'd gotten in, with deep assuredness I knew I would not be able to get out.

Because I was dead.

I knew it with the surety our most upsetting dreams leave us with. It wasn't the Great Mosque of Córdoba, but a funerary imitation, some postmortem way station toward a more devastating destination. Maybe I was meant to fester in regret until God made me move on. Maybe the building was my punishment, my straitjacket, my endpoint. I woke up startled, the sheets drenched with sweaty terror. My phone said it was 5 a.m. My dark-roast-coffee hotel room was pitch black, but turning on the fluorescent-office-lamp lighting only made things worse. Too small and Spartan, monastic and maybe even Catholic, a slap in the face I did not need. I sat up against the crinkling headboard and tucked my knees against my pounding chest. What would it mean to be stuck in a mosque that wasn't a mosque, centuries after the last congregations had been evicted?

Come morning I joined our forty-plus customers. I beamed and joked, pretended I was okay and it was okay, showing them Muslim Spain as I'd vowed. And what I could not show, what had been erased or destroyed or denied, I conjured for them as best as I could, spinning them a picture of the great things that had been and never would be again.

Hafsa and I had spent our last evening together in Virginia looking at photo albums. The last time we would be side by side, her body scrunched up against mine. There we were, marching against George W. Bush's naked aggression in Iraq. There we were on the beach in Mexico: on the first day, shocked by usurious in-hotel prices for everyday beverages, we located a Walmart just beyond touristland, took a suitcase there, and came back pretending we'd just landed. Gatorades for the win, and the week. It was before I'd gotten so sick; looking at the photographs, I remarked on how much heavier I had been. Other pictures. There we were baking in the Mostar summer. Photographs. Two-dimensional. They were going through my head as

I drove her to the train station the next day. I'm sure they were going through her head as well.

We held hands the length of the drive, from the apartment we would never live in to the train station she'd leave from. She was weeping behind her sunglasses, but I didn't know what to say. After she disappeared into Union Station, I called Ali, because I didn't know what else to do. He'd no idea why I was calling and couldn't hear me anyway because the minute he said, "Hey, salam," I realized what I had to say, and I could not. I hadn't accepted it myself. I began bawling. I believe the only thing I said was: "I'll call you back." I've never cried so hard in my life. If you told me I would have reason again in my life to cry so hard, I might rather take my life. When my mother died I wept, but she was in so much pain that I felt we had only given her what she needed, as hurtful as that was for us. But this? I had done this.

We made last-ditch efforts to revive what we once had. She and I outside a café on Seventh Avenue in Brooklyn, talking about whether we had a future. After I came back from Dubai (the first time), we drove all the way out to Coney Island, to an Uighur restaurant, and had a fantastic meal. It was what I loved best about us, an easy evening, calm and cool, natural, reasonable, inevitable. The food was ridiculously tasty. But when I went into the bathroom to wash my hands, I must've taken my ring off. I thought at the time I'd left it in my trusty Camry. I dropped her off at her apartment, and with a forwardness I had not had with her in a very long time, I held her head in my hands, kissed her, told her I'd be back, I'd fix this. Later I searched the trays and bins of the car for my ring, but I never found it again.

Maybe I left it at that Central Asian hole in the wall, and part of me now hopes I had. If our marriage was to end, at least it concluded there, gone before we were sure it was, a memory I still cherish, a last glimmer of good. Some people say religion is for people who cannot confront their mortality; it is faintheartedness. Perhaps the idea of a life hereafter is a cheat. But I could come to terms with my mother's passing because I could not imagine anyone would want to live plugged into machines, and I was greatly consoled because I knew, given what I'd seen of her, the dreams after she was gone, the things people said they saw in her, that I might have a chance to see her again. There was an again. But to divorce someone is to not only abandon and expunge her, but to crush the part of yourself you gave to her, and to heal, to move on, to function again requires the unconditional removal of certain feelings from your heart and soul. Not only to murder these sentiments, however deep they go, but to assassinate the person to whom they belonged, the person who fell in love, which in turn makes you feel that whatever else you feel, and however strongly, in any future, is less genuine than it seems. A whole stretch of my life consequently seems like a memory that belonged to someone else, and was deposited, for reasons unclear, in me. Hafsa had been my life. I think I was hers. I'd met her when I was twenty-one. She was nineteen. All I'd known, nearly all of my adult life, was her. With her, through her. And now she was not only gone, but I'd pushed her away, and wasted the time I had with her on a whole range of stupid shit, none of which took my life anywhere, brought about anything, changed anyone. To confront these feelings I had to first admit to them.

I began to write—and I started, to my initial surprise, with high school, well before I could even imagine Hafsa. Home is where you go when there's nowhere else left. NYU, the Islamic Center, all that we'd achieved, heading to Columbia, even my year at New America—these included her. My only reliable memories, then, were of struggling to fit in, of having to decide whether I was Muslim or American, a binary that is moronic, and yet it resurfaced, and it was then as if I had not ever decided, or rather as if I must decide all over again. Had I chosen differently, would I have been spared this heartache? Had I talked through my feelings, would I have known better what it takes to be in a marriage? Knowing something, as Imam al-Ghazali might have put it, is still not being something. Had I dated widely, would I have been happier?

I cannot listen to Mike Posner. I cannot read certain poems. I cannot go to specific places. I don't cry. I just can't do it. I feel a twinge of pain, above my stomach and beside my heart, and I re-coil, instinctively, in the way something in you yanks your hand from the flame before you know you've been burned. Those words, those songs: doors I dare not open. They lead me not only to what I lost, but my complicity in the entire ordeal. In the time when Hafsa and I should have been trying again, or coming to terms with what happened, I was dematerializing. I hardly went to work. My mind began to perform loop-de-loops. I couldn't shower, wouldn't eat.

Her absence was the greatest hole my life had ever known.

Near the end of that summer, days after Hafsa and I agreed to divorce, hashing out the terms in an e-mail conversation—so we'd have a written record we could both refer to if necessary—I received an e-mail from someone who said we'd met before. In Missouri, years back, at one of my public presentations on Islam-something-something. She was commissioning essays for a magazine she was undertaking, and I wanted to write, so I said sure, but with all my seesawing from one extreme to another, the piece I sent her was remarkably intimate and open, less an op-ed and more a desperate cry for help. Moved, I think, she opened up, too, and we began a back-and-forth. When she cited Derrida, I expressed surprise. She wasted no time calling me out. "Why should I not read Derrida?" she said. "Because I wear hijab?"

Zhaleh had left a marriage to a man whom she loved, but who'd been angry, even abusive. I lost a marriage because I wasn't looking. I poured out my heart to her, which brought us ever closer together, but that unsolicited candor was the last thing I needed. She needed. She needed it anyway. Me too. When she let me know she had to attend an industry conference in Richmond, Virginia, for the weekend, I drove down from DC, picked her up from her hotel on Sunday afternoon, intending only dinner—her flight was the next day. She was on my couch, just inches from me, wearing a long kurta, something with bright reds and blues, and for the life of me, I could not imagine that a woman as beautiful as she would be beside me with desire. That beneath her modest clothes she could hide such a figure, that someone who looked like that would want to take my clothes off. There must have been some mistake. We were just sounding boards for each other.

I took her confession, she took mine.

She had soft eyes, flawless skin, long hands, piano fingers. We watched *Downfall*, about Hitler's last days in the bunker. She had a thing for things Deutsche. Then she turned to me, smiling, biting her lip—it was like a postcard from paradise, the coy smile, the red of her cheeks, a strand of scandalous brown hair slipping free from under her scarf—and said, "I want to bite your cheek."

Who am I to stand in the way of another person's hopes and dreams?

She reached over, her hijab very much still wrapped around her wavy dark hair—I must have a thing for brunettes—and grabbed my cheek with her teeth. She didn't break skin, but she could have. Should have. She didn't leave Virginia for another seven days. She read me poetry. She recited it to me on the balcony. She wrote it with me on the couch. She had a way of finding the most wonderful and heartfelt music, songs that could get me through anything. (She left me, but she left me Florence and the Machine.) She played these songs at times and in situations that surprised me. She was remarkably open. Liberated. Stunning. Deeply pious. All at once. All of her worked on all of me. I spoke openly to her, without hesitation or impediment, the things I had wanted to say, do, try, indulge but had been too ashamed to admit, too humiliated to attempt, that I thought I would have been marked perverse and unseemly even for thinking. She took me shopping and made us spend too much money on clothes. She said she had been asked to become a model, but her very North Indian parents made it clear she would not. She was not allowed to leave the Show Me State because that was not what good girls did. She knew which books might be fair candidates to be the great American novel. She urged me to write my own. She shared her own. She shared too much. Something so intense cannot last.

By the time Hafsa said that we should try again, that we'd parted too hastily, that we were not in the right frame of mind to make a judicious call, that there was still a deep and fantastic and special love between us, a regard that endured over so many years and in the face of so much hurt, I'd fallen for Zhaleh. This might seem the primary genus of cheating, though Hafsa and I had separated months before, and agreed to divorce beforehand, so it wasn't de jure. But it was de facto. If you do decide to walk away from a relationship, you can only do so knowing you gave it your all. You should revisit the relationship out of respect and love for this person who dedicated so much of her life to you, so you can both honestly conclude that it was not meant to be. Or, rather, not meant to be any longer than it had been. Then your conscience is clear.

But then you're supposed to have time off to recover, not jump into the next thing to prevent yourself from facing the consequences of the first thing. Though that's what I did. Worse, I believe I was genuinely in love with both of them and didn't want to have to choose. Romantically agglutinative. A Muslim stereotype. Several of my friends were waving red flags. But I was too needy, too thirsty, too color-blind. Zhaleh and I might've loved and moved each other. But we hardly helped each other. My own guilty conscience was expressed unchecked to her, and she had to internalize the feeling that perhaps she'd precipitated the conclusion of my marriage, or at least canceled any chance of resumption. And Zhaleh was already severely depressed herself. We might be in the kitchen and she'd point to a knife and say, "Don't you sometimes just want to end it?" She'd caress the knife slowly; this was not itself unusual: her every movement often seemed a little too lackadaisical. She'd remark on how beautiful it looked, how wonderful it would be to see it work, how good it would be to go, to see her blood work its way out of her, the last life in her life dry up on the blade.

· 19 ·

THE BIGAMIST

TORN BETWEEN OLD AND DEEP feelings for Hafsa and new and fiery feelings for Zhaleh, I reached out to an elder from upstate. He told me I
wasn't praying enough. "Believe in Allah," he demanded. Telling a
person who's crumbling from the inside that he's not Muslim enough
is telling someone already down on himself that there's yet another
reason to feel worthless. Not only are you a failure romantically, pro-
fessionally, and biologically, but also spiritually. Which translated to
eternally. But somehow I found an ounce of courage and pushed back.
For if being a terrible Muslim was the cause of bipolarity, depression,
or other such ailments, then how come I met so many terrible Muslims who weren't depressed, manic, or suicidal?

I searched for a psychologist and picked a Pakistani Muslim
woman, in part because I thought her background would be a help in
counseling me. We could hit the ground running, so to speak. And
we did, because she instantly understood many of the things I was
telling her, the meaning of my references, the things I was too shy to
admit except obliquely. She was damned good too; I was astonished
by the quickness and correctness of her insight. "Do you want to kill
yourself?" she asked, the day of our first session.

"Like, right now?"

She sent me for medication, far more than I'd ever been told to
take. I was "undertreated," as she put it. Through my meetings with

her, plus the honesty desperation elicits, I began to see the motivations behind my actions, the anxieties behind my behaviors, the failures powering the successes. I read intensely on my predicament. I became a little kinder to myself. I made it a habit to buy two books a week. One to treat myself. One to improve myself. A small gesture to reward myself instead of seeking women in whose arms I could console myself. In *On Depression*, Nassir Ghaemi argues that bipolarity produces five behaviors. The first three are

1. Shopping binges. (Shifts in revenue streams had taken that option off the table.)
2. Impulsive travel. (I'd agree to go anywhere, no matter the time I didn't have.)
3. Hypersexuality. (Requires more than parenthetical comment. To wit, below.)

My psychiatrist thought I needed years to just date, normally, casually, to feel like I had the chance to know who else might be out there, to get to know myself, to have fun, to live in a world where every thing did not have to mean Everything. But I should also add that I could discover nothing else that could plug me back into the world, no other jolt or current powerful enough to revive my desire to live, than the companionship of women.

For a lot of people, the obvious answer is sex—physical intimacy has a way of making you feel good, and good about yourself. But there were three problems. First, Islam—no casual hookups allowed. Two, I was recently divorced but still loved my ex-wife. I still loved her, I still felt married to her, and I wasn't so sure I wanted to be unmarried to her. (Awkwardly, I was also in love with someone else.) Three, me. The idea of just having a physical relationship with someone, even a one-night stand, felt wrong; it felt like using her, or debasing myself. I couldn't separate physical intimacy and emotional commitment. To date someone was to consider marrying them. If I couldn't see myself marrying you, then anything else felt dishonest, grimy, exploitative.

I wasn't just angry at myself for wanting women—why the hell doesn't my wife suffice?—but I was angry at God for making me this way, and then imposing on me a religion whose attitude to sexuality seemed to run counter not only to what I wanted but how the world was working. If I hadn't believed I needed to be married to be with someone, then maybe I wouldn't have put myself, and Hafsa— and now Zhaleh, too—in this position. My therapist and I talked about this a lot. As far back as I could remember, I'd been thinking about sex. Maybe because it was taboo, I mused. She urged me to dig further.

I literally could not remember a time when I didn't find women attractive. But I revealed to her what I'd never revealed to anyone. A person had forced me to do something that embarrassed me, humiliated me, disgusted me. When the request was first made, I was speechless. I thought I'd misheard. I did what was asked, with closed eyes and a fervent wish I was elsewhere. Was this incident the origin, my therapist wondered? I countered: Might it just have added to and complicated who I was? I was young, but I was not *that* young; the obsession seemed to well predate the incident. But I could not tell and, even now, cannot tell if there were other such incidents. When we're not taught about boundaries, about the value and dignity of our bodies, we're rendered vulnerable to anyone who preys on our ignorance.

But I was undergoing a very different struggle at the moment. I'd come to believe, based on my relationship with Hafsa, that she'd seemed to lose interest in me, that any and all women would reject me, that I was fundamentally unattractive, some kind of repulsive, and this merely corroborated what I had always believed about myself, and why I had sought things from outside myself to give me a sense of self. The sensation predated the breakdown. I'd doubted Hafsa's feelings for me even in the times when our relationship was strong. The tables were turning.

What I once lacked in abundance I now possessed in spades.

In the coming months, I'd have to give up my dream job at New America Foundation, surrender most of my savings, and then yield to indebtedness, from where I have yet to return, lose my wife and much of my social circle, but suddenly, abruptly, I was entirely at ease with women. I don't know if it was heartache that loosened my tongue, or the sight of a person in obvious distress that opened others up to me. I also found women much easier to talk to than most of the men in my circle, especially the Asian or Muslim ones—they seemed to be more interested in what car they would buy next, or what house, or what gadget. How long can you talk about a house? This provoked a greater jihad that, like most jihads, ended badly. First, I was no virgin, inexperienced, clumsy, or insecure.

Dates could go from zero to violation of Shari'ah in hours. Theoretically, of course. I don't think "dating" is even the right word. It should not have been hard to sense what my therapist was telling me, that these very relationships—if that's not too generous a term— were preventing me from confronting what was wrong with me, from coming to terms with and rebuilding myself. My therapist pushed me to resist these behaviors by understanding what preceded them. I didn't know if all this was just bipolarity, or me, or whether the one inflamed the other, but eff it, I had nothing else. Going from work back to a Virginia apartment filled with furniture from a life that had come to an ignominious end? Which brings us to Ghaemi's fourth and fifth symptoms.

4. Divorce is one of the more common outcomes the manic-depressive faces. If before, again. And again?

5. Last and definitely least (harmful), the waterfall of words. I challenged myself to focus this flow on projects that would be of long-term benefit, instead of scattering my attention on a thousand creative projects, speeches, and essays, exhausting my energy, which would reignite the depression, which would provoke the behaviors that instigated the mania, ad infinitum. I could afford not to be a creative ambulant. There was a quieter, more fulfilling pride in working at something day after day, creating something slowly and thoughtfully,

and the amount of energy and time this required, the commitment to mapping out a book (this one), or a novel (working on it), or a lengthier essay (Google search), took away some of the whiplash.

I also wrote for myself—to understand myself. Problem is, revealing the purpose of the coping mechanism takes away its effectiveness. Comprehending the (doomed) dam that holds the great pressure behind it is not enough; you must carefully dismantle it before it blows open and blows you away. Without blowing it open and blowing yourself away. When I'd first met Zhaleh, she wore hijab. Within a few weeks, she sent me pictures of herself, showing her hair or wearing a short-sleeved shirt. This may not seem much to you, but this was what only her family was supposed to see. Or her future husband. Was that how she conceived of me? Not let's get married so we won't sin, but let's get married because I want to get married. When she first came over, it took her a few hours to remove her hijab but she did. Within a few weeks, the toxicity of our relationship had poisoned her. She mooted abandoning hijab.

She thought she'd start drinking.

I never thought my husband would be someone like you, she said, but I love you. Once, she told me I'd ruined her. Because I'd destroyed her faith. Or, maybe, as she began to suspect, it hadn't been so deep as she presumed. I loved her too.

Islam's theology is Oneness as uniqueness—"There is nothing like even the like of Him."[1] Neither does space capture Him—God is not only not everywhere but not in *any* where—nor time; He precedes and succeeds, though my reliance on such words betrays the insufficiency of human language. What relationship we should have with God follows from these negations and exists because of them. Islam

---

1. Qur'an 42:11.

rejects the common dismissal of divine interest in human affairs; not only does He care, but He doesn't have more important things to do. God is not a person: "Neither slumber seizes Him nor sleep."[2] He does not have to prioritize; insofar as there are no limits to His power, the idea that something could be too unimportant for Him to listen to, because it would take His attention away from some other thing, is preposterous. He knows our actions and hears all our pleas. He hears all of everyone's. He doesn't have to consider which to answer first, except as He wishes. He wasn't just hearing me out, though, just responding or delaying responding to my prayers. He'd designed me, the person who was praying to Him for help. He was responsible for me. And then He'd judge me?

There was a verse in the Qur'an I could not get past, which blocked my every attempt to speak to Him. God recalls how He addressed all of us, the entire human race, everyone who lived and has yet to live. Before we were placed into bodies and chronologies, with the racial, ethnic, and gendering implications that follow, we were sentient souls who had at least this one conversation with our Maker:

> Your Lord drew forth from the Children of Adam their descen-
> dants and made them testify concerning themselves. "Am I not
> your Lord?" They said, "Yes! We do witness."—Lest you should say
> on the Day of Judgment, "We did not know."[3]

We know. We've always known. We're responsible because it was audible. And the echo is within us, waiting to be noticed, if only we could clear out the competing noise. That's why He sends us prophets. Who after all would heed a prophet's weird words unless those words compelled him inwardly? By Muhammad's birth, Mecca's Abrahamic monotheism had long since become entangled with poly-theism. Though not everyone had gone along. Some Arabs aspired

---

2. Qur'an 2:155.
3. Qur'an 7:172.

to God alone. These were *hanifs*, primordial monotheists, who longed for the One though they'd not heard His voice.

Abraham was a hanif. He went into a fire for his faith, and in response to his yearning, God reached out to him—making of him and his family a mighty legacy. Muhammad, too, was a hanif. That was why he returned time and again to that cave outside Mecca, why God eventually answered his search with the Qur'an. He deserved it. Revelation comes to those most fitting. Who are legion. The numbers 124,000 or 224,000 are sometimes offered. No people, or maybe no place with people, was left without a prophet to preach to them. And what Muhammad taught was no different than what David taught which was no different than what Noah taught. When I led classes on Islam, I'd pick up my pen and release it a few seconds later. After it struck the ground—with an underwhelming, piddling sound—I'd tell the room: "The pen is Muslim!"

The difference between Muslim pens and Muslim humans? We humans know, deep down, that God created us, but we can deny it and forget it or at least divert ourselves from it. We are good at lying to ourselves. Hiding ourselves. Pens can't. They know God exists, and they have no choice but to obey His laws. In Islam, everything inanimate is animate, insofar as the most basic building blocks of existence—quarks? strings?—spin and hum in praise of Him. Humans can disobey God, at least for a while. Pens can't. Gravity conquers the pen. We on the other hand can build an engine strong enough to fight gravity. But only because that, too, is a law through which God built the universe: our free will is divinely gifted and operates within the parameters He leaves for us to discover.

I knew I had to submit, but there was one thing stopping me. Why is there a pen, and why should there be any gravity to bring it down?

In Yann Martel's *Life of Pi*, a young Piscine, a juvenile hanif, asks a Catholic priest why we exist, and the priest appeals to God's love of us in roundabout answer. For many of us, the mechanisms of life's emergence—chemistry and biology, astronomy and cosmology—are insufficient to answer why we are here. How we got here, in other words, is not the same as why we are here. In *Why Does the World Exist?* Jim Holt mused: If there is a God, does He wonder why *He* had to exist? A Muslim might answer: Since God calls Himself, among other names, Aleem, Omniscient, and since He has always been Aleem, because of course He has always been, then His omniscience includes eternal knowledge of why He has to exist. The tormented mind cannot but espy this tidy conclusion with envy. Why does He get to know why He is, and *has* to be, but not me?

In late autumn, Hafsa came by the apartment that was supposed to be our chance to start over. We'd all but parted ways, e-mailed our terms of divorce; her purpose was to take some critical personal effects, few of which she'd taken with her in our trial separation, back to New York. I spent the time at a nearby Barnes & Noble. About two hours later, Hafsa texted that she'd finished. I hoped she meant that she was done collecting her things. I wrote back, "When are you leaving?" I anticipated we'd get coffee. I was having second, third, fourth thoughts. "We left half an hour ago," she replied—her brother was driving. When I got back, the sun was already in decline, I found a slightly emptier, sadder one-bedroom. Hafsa had left my wedding ring, a little silver thing in need of polish, on the dark mahogany of our—and now just my—bedside table. Twelve years of my life collapsed into a band of metal, all the feelings, hopes, dreams, the expectations of a life forever, now ended, an outline of a void. Everything turns into nothing. One day I'd lose it somewhere in Coney Island. But not yet.

I did what any idiot can be expected to.

At least she wanted me. And vice versa. Since my marriage had dried up and died, the sudden torrent of intimacy was overwhelming, impossible to abstain from, even as my therapist insisted it'd turn catastrophic. When Zhaleh left my place a few days later, it was pretty clear I should not have asked her to come at all. I already knew she was not in the right place to pursue a relationship—she could not stop speaking of suicide, of regrets, of whether she wanted to be the Muslim she'd been or some other kind—and she knew that I was in a bad place. Agreeing to a divorce is not the same as having recovered from the divorce. Zhaleh and I fought, bitterly, angrily. We made up. We fought again.

A few evenings later, my brother called. I haven't had time to tell you that he was in the middle of his own journey. He was moving to Dubai. His wife and my two young nephews would join him several weeks later, once he'd settled in. It was a big shift for him, and for me—I'd just lost my wife and best friend, her family (who'd always treated me as one of their own), and now most of my family too. During our call, I heard the ping of an incoming call. It was Zhaleh. I transferred over. She could see what I should have seen. Even if the time had been right, we might not have worked. But this was a bad time, making this a terrible idea. She told me she could not do this, should not do this, that I needed to know whether I was with Hafsa or with her. I transferred back to my brother, only for him to say he had to shut his phone off. Time to take off. "Wait," I wanted to cry. How could I begin to tell him? The line went dead.

A few days later, and I could be found on the Orange Line, but not going to work, or even my therapist's office. There was a copy of my suicide short story on my nightstand and another with me, as you may remember. Wistfully I wished I was with some beautiful woman, dressed in an autumn jacket, her long legs in olive or midnight blue or charcoal gray pants, her scarf bunched up around her neck. We would order a pumpkin spice something, live the dream that is gentrification, and walk gloved hand in gloved hand toward some other, better place. That was the only thing I felt I ever wanted, and when I thought about who'd be there with me, it was Zhaleh, but she was gone, and I'd chased her away, and everything else was gone—or going. There would be no other person, no romance ever like this one, no warm embraces in the declining days, no magical evenings. Nobody would love me like Hafsa did. Nobody would love me like Zhaleh did. Nobody was even around to care.

To anyone who knew me from afar, my life was going splendidly. More and more people attended my speeches. My writings made it to ever more prominent platforms. I was working with some of the smartest analysts and policymakers in America, and I had only recently turned thirty. In fact, just days before, a prominent American Muslim leader had said I might be the Muslim Obama. I said, "Isn't Obama the Muslim Obama?" and he laughed milk out of his nose. My separation from my wife was a closely guarded secret, and the relationship with Zhaleh even more so. Depression, bipolarity, illness, all of it behind Twitter humor and tailored suits. Maybe only my dramatic weight loss indicated something was off, but even that I'd blamed on a new exercise regimen and a strict diet. Most people were impressed by my discipline. That's how little anyone sees. They think because you are well without you are flourishing within. I wasn't even well without.

I don't know that I can tell you what it feels like to decide to jump off a bridge. There's deep sadness. A certain anesthetic disinterest. And blessed relief. I might be hurting, worse than I've ever been hurting, but I'll only be hurt one more time, and instead of blindsiding me, this time I know what'll come. The ground, eventually, conclusively, finally. I'd had other ideas, of course. Carbon-monoxide poisoning, but I had no garage. A prescription-drug overdose, but what if I survived, damaged? This felt right. I'd considered smacking concrete with my father's BMW; I'd had very concrete thoughts of jumping off the top of Wanamaker House in Philadelphia. This was destiny, overdue, if anything, no different than shooting down a mountain, one foot locked onto the board and the other waiting for the right moment. I'd fall free, fast, and faithful. The pen is Muslim.

In his legendarium, J. R. R. Tolkien had the first Elves awaken under starlight, before any sun and any moon—every word they spoke, from then on, the birth of their language, sparkles with this history. When the Vala Oromë, a mighty angel, came to offer these newborn, firstborn children of Eru shelter in heavenly Valinor, some Elves balked. I adored these Elves who refused the chance to go to paradise, who wished to stay behind in darkness, Easterners who did not want to go west, who did not buy into the arc of history, who refused the metanarrative. Tolkien wrote them out of history. I hoped I'd meet Tolkien in the next life, so I could ask him why. They didn't disbelieve in Ilúvatar, after all. They just didn't want to be forced into making choices they had had no choice in. God had made them in darkness and starlight, so why was it wrong for them to want the glints of heavens above and not the floodlit overkill of Valinor?

Perhaps they were better Muslims. Perhaps they were in love with their waterfalls. Perhaps they wished to be forgotten. Perhaps they were tired of every single moment of every single day having to mean not just something, but Everything.

There was a Così's on the right and a pharmacy on the left, but the commercial outlets soon gave way to homes, trees, an incongruous hotel. Topography turned treacherous, and I made a wearying uphill climb, onto a level road one side of which was taken up by scaffolding. In New England, the trees would've been fire-engine red and construction-cone orange by now. Connecticut might as well have been Cuiviénen. I'd tried to go along. I'd listened to the summons. I tried to leave my starlight and waterfalls. Muhammad, though, was just following orders. The sudden flatness, the exposure to the great sky above, the emptiness and quietness of this span, this was the right place, unusual, unexpected, perfect. One foot over the other. But I don't ask myself why I took my phone.

God made me bring it. I was standing at the edge, halfway across, not a car in sight. For a big city, DC is awfully empty. My left pants pocket vibrated; I was surprised not only that I had my phone, but that anyone would be contacting me. Probably it was something stupid. A reminder of a bill I had to pay. Curiosity got the best of me—what would it hurt to look before leaving? I almost wanted it to be bad news. More anger. Rage. Something else I'd done wrong. Written in the slightly cartoonish, gently rounded font that makes the iPhone almost precious, were three simple words, meant to be a preview of the full message, an invitation to unlock the phone, but that was enough room to show me everything Zhaleh had written. Her. Her? Her.

Zhaleh: *Are you okay?*
Me: *Why do you ask?*
Zhaleh: *Are you with us, Haroon, or are you among us?*

I paused a moment until I understood her meaning.

Me: *Among us.*
Zhaleh: *Oh God.*
Me: *?*
Zhaleh: *I had a dream last night that I was in an apartment. You were standing on the ledge outside. I was banging on the window to stop you from jumping but you couldn't hear me.*

I didn't respond. I couldn't. I was dumb. So she asked again.

Zhaleh: *Are you okay?*

·20·

EMIRATE STATE OF MIND

THE TEA WAS, as I should have expected from a store specializing in small cakes with multicolored dollops of high-fructose-corn-syrup frosting, terrible. This struck me as a grave injustice, never mind what had just transpired. My legs still felt like jelly. My hand shook so much I couldn't make myself drink the disappointingly tepid alleged hot beverage I'd hoped to calm myself with. I read her texts over and over again, then and before, my back against the wall of that bridge for ten or fifteen minutes, trying to understand why she had reached out to me, what kind of connection she had to Him, and why, if I couldn't go back to her, she would come back to me.

I called Ali. I did not say, over the phone, what had gone down, but he could not have forgotten our conversation from the night before, when he asked me to promise not to kill myself without speaking to him again. And so, when I asked him to come meet me immediately, he left work—immediately. Probably because he could guess what might have gone down, he called another friend, Abdullah, who was in the process of boarding a flight back to North Carolina. One can imagine the consequences of a hirsute imam exiting an aircraft at the very last minute, insisting he must stop someone from killing himself. But he did. Ali showed up first—Abdullah sometime later.

"I got here as fast as I could," Ali said. "What happened?"

I told him I was going to kill myself, not exactly how or when, but that it was going to happen, that it was on the verge of happening, not that it had almost just happened. "Don't, Haroon," Ali urged. Which sounded sager in the moment. "Can you call your doctor?"

"Yeah."

"Right now."

"Like, in front of you?"

"Jesus, Haroon."

Ali dropped me at my therapist's office—not without making sure she'd come to the door and I'd gone inside with her—and then he and Abdullah met. Colluded. Conspired. She spoke to them separately, and they all agreed, without giving me much (viz, any) say in the process; I should be hospitalized, which decision filled me with unimaginable dread, fear I'd be locked up forever and never let out. I even protested that I could not be parted from my laptop. It sounds so silly now, but the inability to respond to e-mails presented itself as the worst thing in the world, possibly because the alternative was to admit what was happening to me. But I was admitted, and Ali visited each night, and that softened the blow. Not that visitors were allowed, mind you; he told them he was a chaplain. They might have presumed he was a *hospital* chaplain, as in *the* hospital chaplain, but never volunteer too much.

The Muslim chaplain had become a commonplace. Legacies.

While I sat in the hospital, pondering how I'd fallen this low— several of my fellow patients, including a young Saudi princeling, did not believe I could be there for any medical reason, and decided I was a doctor surreptitiously researching them—Abdullah, Ali, and my brother laid the groundwork for a trip to Dubai. They planned on me spending six weeks convalescing, and my boss at New America gave me permission too—I told him I was facing a severe illness. That was technically true. I'd be back, refreshed and renewed, by early February. We'd stop terrorism and reset America's relationship to the Muslim world. I thought it would be so easy. Take a break. Come back shiny and clean. It was three days in the hospital, and I pushed to get out, and wished a week later I'd stayed for months. The proof, as it were: the first thing I did when I returned home (apartment) from the hospital was to try to talk to Zhaleh, even as she knew the broad outlines of what had happened and, as you can imagine, assigned herself a prominent role in the entire sordid business.

To be with another woman while losing my wife might have filled me with more guilt and disgust than anything I'd ever done, but I still couldn't cut it off. This second time around went as terribly as you could suspect and ended not just with her breaking it off, as before; instead, she broke it off, as before, and e-mailed Hafsa and overshared what had happened between us. It was the least I deserved for what I'd put the two of them through. But I didn't crack. I didn't go run to find another woman to fall in love with. I didn't seek out a bridge to jump off of. If I knew at least the connection between one behavior and another outcome, then I could begin breaking the pattern. I apologized to each of them; Hafsa issued a cold acknowledgment and cut me off. Rightly.

Sometimes we see ourselves making the same decisions, and despair of any transformation. But that's because we can't see the destination for the road we're on. I left Washington, DC, a city I had begun to associate only with misery, and drove to New York, to be with family, friends, in anonymity. I wandered the streets and listened to music. I changed my phone number so I wouldn't talk to people I shouldn't. I agreed to go to Dubai, to get even farther away. Turkish Airlines carried me there on New Year's Eve. I landed before dawn and was, an hour later, at a hotel on Shaykh Zayed Road, where my brother had a furnished apartment. I woke up at 3 p.m. to nuclear-detonation sunshine. My first trip was to a Union grocery store, where I was tasked with buying two and only two items, hummus and poppy seeds. It was an inauspicious beginning.

Nobody seemed to have any idea what hummus was, and when I moved on to the poppy seeds, the Pakistani clerk appeared puzzled by the English-language request. So I offered a more elaborate Urdu formulation, *khashkhash ke dane*, which is not an inaccurate translation, though it might literally mean heroin seeds, which is the meaning I am assuming he assumed, since he raised his eyebrows, ran around a corner, and entirely vanished. In that regard, but only that regard, my trip to Dubai was a failure. Late in January, I flew to Oman to visit a friend, a very Christian banker who'd done very capitalistically for himself, and we spent a few days together, relaxing near and occasionally in the Arabian Sea. In both countries I stood in the sun as long as I could. Before it was gone. In mid-February, I reboarded a Turkish Airlines flight, wearing a T-shirt, thinking I'd retrieve my coat at Dulles. Our Istanbul stopover involved an open-air transfer, when it was, of course, winter on the Bosphorus.

After radioactive brightness, eschatological cloud cover, acerbic rain, not dropping but cluster bombing, fat, hard, wet, and cruel. I froze, in more ways than one. Ali met me at the airport but I knew, even before seeing him: it was too soon. If I returned to New America, or otherwise tried to resume my normal life, I would fall back into the same holes. I longed for the endless speediness of the place I had just left, the cocaine-white cars and shiny underground garages, escape from the burdens of public Muslimness and private turmoil, the chance to be alone with myself, embedded in the Muslim Las Vegas. But selling my car, paying off the balance due on my lease, explaining to my bosses that I was going for good, burning bridges while depleting checking accounts, all that took a month or two; I would not be back in Dubai until early April. In the meanwhile, Ali frequently had me over. His parents, who took a liking to me (the feeling was mutual), knew something was up, and played along. My therapist kept close tabs on me. She even sent me to see another therapist.

She said it'd be good for me.

This second specialist, who worked in the very same hospital where I'd been detained, had been blinded giving birth. Her labor went so badly, she'd lost her eyesight. I wished I'd asked her why she didn't loathe her daughter for ruining her life—or if she did. Or if her daughter hated herself for what she'd done. Or if they stood in solidarity and blamed God and the doctors. We only talked about me, though. When she asked me about my being suicidal, I confessed that I still was. Not so intensely, not actively, less of a I will kill myself and more of a I'm okay if I die.

"This doesn't just go away," she explained. "You can't snap your fingers."

"Aren't you supposed to make me feel better?"

"This, what you're feeling, it's not all of you. But it is part of you. It is in you." It is one of your names. Haroon. Writer. Bipolar.

"So what am I supposed to do with that?"

She told me I'd never gain the upper hand until I did one thing. "You have to love yourself."

I must've grimaced; the suggestion offended me. We are supposed to obey God, not love ourselves, and even if we did not worship God, at least we were not compounding infidelity with egomania. "I don't." I can't. I won't.

"Surely you love something about yourself," she implored.

She suggested I begin writing down what that might be. I wanted to ask how I could write nothing. She believed that I could tell my own story, and that in the process I might find something about myself that would make me want to keep me around. This sounded even worse than the first request. You want me to record what I love about me? A Muslim is not supposed to love himself, let alone dwell on himself. That's self-indulgent post-Christian nonsense, the shameless solipsism of a civilization that has gone overboard in its regard for itself—navels gazing at their own navels. But if she was right, if I could not love myself, then I would spend the rest of my life on that bridge.

· 21 ·

JET ENGINE OVEN

I HAD NO DESIRE to be in America ever again, but that meant I had no idea what I was going to do with myself in Dubai. I was broke, unemployed, and though I'd started writing again, there couldn't be enough writing to fill the day, let alone make a living off of. The first few days I'd gone swimming, but I wondered how much swimming a man should pursue. Then my brother suggested I rent a car. A few weeks later, when he moved from the hotel where he and his wife had so generously offered me a room, to a large house, keeping a car became a possibility.

I received my (monthly) rented Toyota Camry from Hertz's office in Motor City, an unrealized neighborhood across from Arabian Ranches. I got a different color every thirty days, and a different license plate too. Of the things I loved most about Dubai, not least was the chance to accelerate, albeit in an economical vehicle. DC had been the first place I'd moved to after the introduction of satellite navigation, which I became so reliant on whenever I did drive that I never got a sense of the place. I went wherever the purple lines told me. So in the Emirates, I refused GPS. I spent days getting hopelessly lost, until I knew Dubai and Abu Dhabi and even their next-door neighbor, Oman, like the back of my hand. It might've been convenient for my brother, but those sundry Toyota Camrys saved my life.

Two caveats, which I hope the good rulers of the UAE do not in future use to deny me entry into their fine country. First, I'm not sure it was legal for me to drive there. When I went to the local office of the Department of Motor Vehicles, I inquired as to whether my American license would qualify me to motor in the UAE. "Yes, it is okay," the kind, faceless bureaucrat who exists in various genetic iterations, all of whom are descended from Adam's fifth son, the world's first uniformed agent of an annoying but unarmed branch of government, told me. "So I don't need to apply for a UAE license?" He turned sour. "Yes, you do." "But you said my American license is valid?" "Yes it is." We went back and forth several times until my brother muttered, in Urdu, that ignorance could be bliss.

Second, as an American, I was permitted a thirty-day stay on a tourist visa. Then I would have to leave. But if I exited the UAE I could reenter for another thirty days and repeat as necessary. The nearest country was Oman. It was two hours of driving really fast and my brother hardly had the time; this then I'd do for myself, and could, thanks, Camry. You'd begin by driving out of Arabian Ranches but turn left, down a wide deserted highway, not toward but away from the great big buildings and into the wild. One of my friends, a law student in Kosova, said she'd never seen the desert. Could I make her a video? On that first drive to the entirely unfairly underrated Omani Sultanate, I stopped in the breakdown lane to give her just that. Okay, and this proves Islamophobia is racism, because I did what any genetically Muslim individual would do: I did make the video but didn't stop. I shot the video with my right hand on the wheel, my left hand across my chest, less dangerous in description than, inshallah, in execution, the window down, hot air blasting into my face like someone had turned a jet engine on inside an oven. Here the sand was alone with itself, massive piles of grains, sculpted by the wind, more Day-Glo tangerine than mustard or yellow, so illuminated it was impossible to perceive without sunglasses.

One could not imagine life here. Yet Moses and Muhammad, did they not hear God in the vastness and the emptiness? At night I whizzed by bioluminescent towers of impetuous height and structural derring-do. I found all kinds of restaurants, journeyed to remote bedouin villages, went to more places than most Emiratis might. I began to uncover old friends—like New York, Dubai is a crossroads of the world. Closest was Junayd, my friend from NYU days, who'd done business school and then done damned well. Or I made new friends. One day, a new friend, Kayvan, and I snuck into a hotel to access the beach facing the Arabian Sea—we swam the morning away—and then found a battlefield where, just one year after the Prophet Muhammad had died, his best friend, Abu Bakr, sent a caliphal army after a rebellious tribe, fighting with its backs to the sea, but in futility. Thousands of small stones grew out of the sand, obeying no pattern, each marking a martyr, each a story that had ended here, so far from home, at what might have seemed to them the end of the world, but still they went and fought and died, because they believed in Muhammad when he told them their eyes would see lands of which their ears hadn't the chance to hear. There we were, my Pakistani American self and Anglo-Persian Kayvan, with his long brown rock-star hair and thick beard, both of us in floral board shorts, and an elderly Emirati, outfitted in the old-school style and discomfited by our presence. He wondered if we had come to mock sacred ground. Kayvan lifted his iPhone and played a famous reciter's rendition of the heart of the Qur'an, Y. S., to honor those who gave their lives; the old man's dry lips turned up into a rich smile, and he produced an unhesitating thumbs-up. On the way back, we stopped in a village for snacks and noticed a crush of cars on an empty street—an Emirati wedding was in full swing, and we were graciously invited in.

I drove the entire time. I didn't mind; I preferred driving over being driven. I'd always liked speed. But the highways in Dubai are big enough to land A380s on. They go four, five, six lanes across, and they are space-telescope smooth. Gas is cheap. Everyone else is permanently accelerating too. I began to drive in ways I'd never imagine daring to back in sedate, settled, declinist America. With, for example, a paper road map on my lap, unfolded, to aid in navigation. Turn signals as suggestions. Lane changing the width of the highway in one sexy move. Reversing on an on-ramp. Parking on the side of sand dunes. What, really, does "One Way" mean? Was it because I didn't care if I died? Or was it because I wanted desperately to feel, to come back to life, to be alive? There is succor in haste. Peace of mind that comes from being unable to think of anything else except the road ahead. When any stray thought might literally kill you. I learned where the speed cameras were, so I could gun it as soon as I was out of sight, or ensconce myself in the blind spot of a faster driver, trusting he would get, and could afford, the ticket for both of us. Allah smiled on my Pan-Islamism; in my months of Emirati renaissance, I earned only one ticket, and that not even in one of my beloved Toyotas. I did this all with social media disconnected, freed, in every sense, of the expectation of constant intervention, of the need for total aware-ness, complete knowledge wedded to a total inability to make any difference in the injustices one was so vividly exposed to. I did not have to defend Islam. I did not have to give speeches. I did not have to explain why going to war with a country that did not attack us and then blaming me for the outcome was unreasonable. I did not have to pretend to be anyone.

I was largely unknown and unheard from. And unheard of. I did me, as you might say.

Do not get me wrong. There was, as a certain therapist had inti-mated, no snapping of the fingers. Suicide and I were still on speaking terms. I ached inside. But I didn't have to pretend for the outside. I was too far away to be pulled back in. One day Zhaleh e-mailed me, saying she was thinking of something I'd said about my mother. I thanked her in reply, but left no door open. Two months later, she e-mailed me to apologize for revealing our relationship to Hafsa and told me she would always remember our "friendship." All of us should have more such friendships, I thought. But do not think I had sud-denly become strong either. Rather, I was aware of my weakness, its own kind of bravery. Had she been in proximity, I would've maybe started up with her again. But you cannot begin to heal unless you stop picking at the scab. Any continuation of the discussion would go badly. I left no door open. I didn't respond. She made it in all the same.

Zhaleh had been deeply involved in "traditional Islam," the Sufi side of Sunnism. More than that, though: God loved her, of that I'm sure, and something of her plentiful *barakah*, the Barack in the Hussein Obama, her grace and blessedness, ended up on me. A few weeks in and I saw her. So to speak. I dreamt I, wearing shorts (rather inappropriately), arrived at the Islamic Center at NYU, except the ICNYU was an Ottoman mosque. I wandered past the prayer area and into a boardroom, with stale furniture and muted sunlight peeking through pulled shades. Zhaleh was there; she introduced me to the man beside her, Nuh Ha Mim Keller. I had never met or even seen him before, but I'd read his book, years ago, about how he'd converted to Islam. All she said was, "This is Haroon; he studies Iqbal." Then a mute Keller offered me a gift, wrapped in rough brown paper: dark metal bracelets, wound round and round.

They looked a little like three-dimensional pinwheels, but the material was hard, strong, dark. I don't remember if I thanked him, or wore them, but I took the dream to mean that I should go see Keller, who was based in Jordan. Not too far. But a stretch. As a younger man, I'd once winced at the sight of the worshipful Muslim, obsessed with fetishized ritual. If only one read the right prayers at the right moments! Pronounce this before you enter the bathroom, and God won't burn you alive for eternity! Remember to ask God to protect you, but remember, if you die, it's what He wanted. I disdained superstitious and incantatory mysticism, reserved, it seemed to me, for people who did not want to fight, to argue, to build, to succeed, to struggle. I'd outsmarted all of them and in and through my genius, my predilection for action and construction, a new world would be born, history rerouted. Whereas a mere text message, uninitiated and unasked for, had saved my life. This did not stay unnoticed in my mind. But when I shared my dream with Junayd, who lived in Abu Dhabi, he asked, "Why not visit a scholar here?"

As in, We all know you can't afford to fly to Jordan stop embarrassing yourself. The Rolodex I'd built up over years of career Islamsplaining gave me connections I expertly exploited and, via faraway Calgary, I secured a conversation with a prominent scholar in Abu

Dhabi, ninety minutes to the west. The appointment was scheduled. I drove there, averaging sixty-five miles per hour plus thirty-five, to attend a class this *shaykh* taught on philosopher-turned-atheist-turned Sufi imam al-Ghazali. It took him thirty minutes to leave the mosque just because so many people wanted to greet him. An hour on and I found myself in his home, a newer version of a traditional Muslim residence. There was a public half for guests and a private half for his family. A large group, most of us strangers to each other, sat around the edges of a massive salon, carpeted with fine Persian rugs, and ate from communal plates. Dinner began at midnight and guests did not leave until 3 a.m.—to be a Muslim is to be an insomniac. Finally, with guests departed, my energy flagging, he invited me to his library; there must have been a thousand hardcover books. A millennium's worth of knowledge resting on cherry shelves. His desk was in the center.

I sat across from the shaykh, who invited me to speak with the help of a translator who sat directly across from me but made himself as unobtrusive as possible. I introduced myself with my dream, the one set in Córdoba, me finding myself abandoned in the Great Mosque, knowing, sure, convinced I was dead. In the Islamic tradition dreams have power. Maybe if he could make sense of my vision I'd know he was the kind of person I should talk to, and maybe if he heard what was in my head he'd know something of what was wrong with my mind. He listened to the whole dream, and then asked several questions, filling in details. But these questions had nothing to do with me, and only the minutiae.

"And that is all you saw?"

I confirmed that it was.

The shaykh looked at me, smiled—he thereafter never stopped smiling, actually—and said, very matter-of-factly, "You thought you were a Christian." He nodded at his own conclusion. "This is what the dream means."

Either I said, "How did you know?" or my expression did.

"You thought you were Christian, but you have always been Muslim," he elaborated. "You never left Islam." He looked at me to make sure I followed. There was no sound other than his voice. The translator kept to himself, politely looking down at the cut of his *thobe*. Maybe he was used to this, epiphanies offered every night, life-changing directions dealt out by the dozen. "The mosque in Córdoba, the one you saw in your dream, that is your heart," the shaykh explained. The *qalb* is the only thing that can contain God. But the heart is equally a reflection of what else we might be possessed by. "Even though you tried to turn your heart into a church, you could not, and even though that mosque isn't a mosque now"—historically and immediately accurate—"you and I both know it's still a mosque."

I sat speechless, unsure where to go with any of this, part of me thinking I might head out and come back in a week, when I'd processed these last few minutes, the rest of me believing we might be in some kind of gunpowder-empire, late medieval or Muslim steampunk, his chamber a doorway through which this apparent human being was slipped messages from one dimension to the next. With his glowing smile filling his face, his turban resting unperturbed on his head, his eyes still full of energy, he handled everything I threw at him with a gentleness and fraternity I'd never experienced in another Muslim, let alone a shaykh. I told him how Islam defeated me, time and again, sharing complaints most previous interlocutors had dismissed as petty, or would judge blasphemous. I talked about my love for Hafsa, calm, cool, natural, irrevocable, and my deep desire for Zhaleh, passion, intensity, about the practical simultaneity of these relationships, about how I was stupid enough to think I could chase two different things at once, about my pasts: how I drank, how I found refuge in women, how I tried to be an atheist, about my medical diagnoses, my psychological turmoil. About my ongoing desire to be dead. About my plan to jump. Then I stopped, concerned. He was still smiling. But not speaking. I dared not interrupt the silence, but he took so long I was afraid he had left this plane of existence and might be back much later. After a few minutes had passed, the shaykh's turn had come.

"Talk to God, Haroon."

Not, however, what I expected. In fact it was precisely what I feared. I'd heard this patronizing bullshit before; he was the same as anyone else. Go to the mosque—then you won't be depressed! Allah loves you, that's why He punishes you! "I can't." In fact I already told you. "I don't get why. Not five times a day, not once a day. Here and there but—"

His turn to cut me off. It was his library, after all. If he was angry, though, it didn't show. "*Talk* to God, Haroon." There was that beaming visage. In fact it was hard to look at him, because there was too much love in his aspect. "If even for five minutes a day."

But he had not said what talking meant. "Praying?"

"I am asking you to give yourself five minutes," he repeated.

"Of prayer?"

"Of anything."

I was now officially lost. I felt like he was blaspheming with me and I was about to be let in on a wicked secret, which I didn't think I could bear receiving.

"Sit and reflect, listen to poetry, read Qur'an. Just make it five minutes a day." He shifted from advice to experience, and looked away, not beyond but within, to some place he knew and I could not imagine. Yet. "One day," he promised, "five minutes will become five hours, but you will not know how."

And then he stood up; he hugged me and, as we parted, handed me his cloak. He walked into the darkened private chambers of his home, and then the last thing he ever said to me, his voice echoing in the darkness, his body almost impossible to make out: "You have to love yourself."

· 22 ·

MATTHEW AND SON

I HEARD THE CALL to prayer through the windows, the back side of our building facing the direction of the mosque. It was so hot outside, the sky looked ill; I'd all but fainted by the time I reached the mosque, a five-minute walk away. The sun here did not shine, it slapped, punched, drained, aggressed. Though I rushed through my ablutions, startled by the icy cold water, and kicked off my orange and black Adidas slippers as fast as possible, I did not make it into the mosque in time for most of the midday *salat*. The only upside was that the mosque invariably cleared out afterwards, there being no subsequent services till sundown. I had a front row all to myself.

I dropped into prostration, talking to God, just like the shaykh had told me to. Figured it was worth a try, right? But I just did what I'd done countless times before. Rote prayers, mechanical formulae. This was not how people talked, though; it was how they lectured. I'd been recommended the former. Somewhere in the course of my mumbled prayers something snapped. Desperate to just let it all out, maybe, or unable to content myself with the same old, same old. It still felt wrong, but not enough for me to countermand myself. It's not like He didn't know every single thought that crossed my mind anyway, the things I thought when I did not lower my gaze, when I was burned out and broken.

I started asking for what I wanted. A way out. An end to the up and down. The endless fucking up and down. I began apologizing for what I'd done, and soon the regrets turned to pleas, knowing that I could not continue to live in such a miserable way, haunted by my faults, wounded by my decisions, hoping every few hours that I might die, that nonexistence was the only adequate solution to existence. I asked Him to remedy me, to right the wrongs I'd done to others, and I began to count them up, and that was when, or rather how, it happened. My mind fell to Hafsa and to Zhaleh. "I wronged them," I whispered, over and over, my mouth almost kissing the green carpet, the cold air going through my khakis and into my bones. "I hurt them," I cried into fresh, clean fibers. Hafsa and I were done, the pain from which was the chiefest cause of my desire to die, but not the only one, of course. Zhaleh, who was entirely too soon, who I still cared for too. "I wronged them," I whispered, almost violent in my remorse, my head down, my breath bouncing back. In desperate ramble, speaking without thinking, I blurted out, "I hurt them and I hurt me too."

You might remember Jonah—the Messiah, Jesus, said his sign was like Jonah's. Jonah, the son of Matthew, is one of twenty-five prophets named by the Qur'an; these and the many, many more prophets who go unknown and unnamed, prayed with Muhammad in Jerusalem during the Night Journey. He's called Dhun-Nun, "the companion of the whale," but that's not an affectionate aside. For Jonah preached and preached, but Jonah's people didn't listen to a Word he said. When he'd had it with their indifference, he took passage on a ship. But prophets don't get days off: they're the original professional Muslims. Great big storms struck, the ship tossing and turning, up one wave and down another, the timbers creaking and the sails fraying, and so the passengers began to draw lots, trying to determine who'd brought this ill fortune upon them.

Jonah was not just blamed for the storm, but thrown overboard in hopes that his sacrifice would save the others. God didn't let him die, though. A giant fish or whale—the Qur'an doesn't specify—swallowed him whole. For three days Jonah lingered undigested, an Abraham in an acid bath. There, in the belly of that aquatic beast, Jonah heard the creatures of the sea praising God. These ichthyologic *adhans* reminded him of who he was. Jonah, peace be upon him, cried out in anguished repentance, a prayer known to Muslims the world over. "There's no god but You!" The testimonial of faith shared by all prophets, the thread of Islam tying Adam to Muhammad. "Glory be to You," Jonah added—the same glorification all nature engages in—"for I have oppressed myself."[1] *Inni kuntu min adh-dhalimin.* The singular, *dhalim*, is from an Arabic root meaning "darkness." Because oppression is darkness. To put something in a category in which it does not belong. Square peg, round hole.

To oppress another is to deny him his rights. To oppress yourself is to deny yourself your own rights. I had heard the story a thousand times. I probably offered it in sermons. But it was as if I had never heard Jonah's prayer until that afternoon in Dubai.

I paused in prostration, alone in the mosque. Stunned. For you can only wrong something, it occurred to me, if it has rights. I'd wronged others. That I knew. Obviously. The guilt over my actions was destroying me, or driving me to destroy myself. Regret may be the worst pain in the universe. But the mistakes that caused the regret were the bigger problem. I'd never quite made this connection before. That I had rights, that I'd been *unfair* to myself, not only in how I was treating myself—which, as I understood, included how I treated others—but in how I related to God. There were physical laws operating in and enabling the universe, which I would often point to, rhetorically and publicly, as proof of God. There were moral laws, too, I would come to see, and they have their consequences, which are a proof for God as well. "Make not your own hands," the Qur'an warns, "the source of your own destruction."[2] What else explained how I'd been doing?

---

1. Qur'an 21:87–88.
2. Qur'an 2:195.

You have to find something to love about yourself, she'd said. It sounded so meretricious. But he'd said it too, the shaykh: love yourself. Love your neighbor as you love yourself—Jesus. None of you is a believer until he wants for his brother what he wants for himself—Muhammad. "I am one of those who oppresses himself" is a fair alternative translation of the second half of Jonah's prayer. Islamic tradition describes sin as a kind of *self*-oppression, as acting in ways unbefitting the actor, as insufficient selfishness. And who oppresses himself except the one who doesn't care for himself, who doesn't love himself, who doesn't believe he matters? Oppression, as the Qur'an suggests, is worse than slaughter.[3] Could it be that wronging myself was worse than trying to kill myself? The one causes the other. In wronging ourselves, we debase ourselves. We kill ourselves slowly. But how do you stop, except that you fall on the floor and cry it out, and why would you do that, unless you think what you had to say had some importance, that your fate was of relevance?

If our religion is our return to our fitra, our original condition— the prelapsarian Adam inside each of us—then of course it's wrong to sin. But not based on abstracted investigations into sterile texts. I wasn't depressed because I sinned, but much sin came down to my depression. During my worst depressive episodes, my indifference to prayer grew into palpable distaste. When I reached for Zhaleh, sure, it was because I was drowning. But it was also because I was afraid to be with myself, to listen to myself, to accept myself. Had I realized mental illness was real, I would've been pressed to address it. No one leaves a broken bone untouched.

Now I must be clear in my causation. Am I arguing that bipolarity is caused by sin? No, I am not. Except I also am. What we think of our place in the world—recall Jonah, who forgot who he was destined to be—has everything to do with how we inhabit it. Your idea of your self is indispensable for the rescue of that self.[4] No woman or man is an island. Your leg is broken, you need a doctor. The problem

---

3. Qur'an 2:191.
4. Qur'an 37:139–148.

with depression, though, is you think you don't deserve the doctor. You think you deserve the broken bone.

While we were still together, Zhaleh had enthusiastically recommended Nuh Ha Mim Keller's *Sea Without Shore* to me. I took the book to Dubai and, as with pretty much every book in my life, started reading it months after I vowed I would. Good timing, though. I turned to Keller when Zhaleh reached into my sleep and introduced us.

In one of my favorite passages, Keller asks why the world is the way it is. His response requires us to reflect on God's nature, known to us in great measure through God's names. He is God, Allah, as much as He is Rahman and Rahim. But He is also but not limited to "Jabbar," the Overwhelming; "Kareem," the most Generous; "Wudud," the most Loving; "Musawwar," the Evolver. One of my favorites is "Samad," which some have translated as "Eternal Refuge."

Keller argued these names described qualities that are Him, but also that these qualities originate in Him. God was the most Loving and Merciful before He created creation, and will be after He has ended this creation. He, *causa sui*, must always be. Too, vengeance, wrath, justice, and so on—all these qualities exist in the world because the world He created was made to reflect Him. And why? For God to be worshipped, Keller argues, for us to have a real relationship with Him, we must first be able to understand Him, to know Him, to grasp the idea of Him. But how can the finite grasp even the idea of the infinite, except through analogy—or intimacy? Therefore God evolved a universe through which we know of mightiness, fairness, evolution, and so on, not just conceptually but experientially, so that we may know Him more completely and more fully, and even pursue a genuine connection with Him. One might see this as a circuitous argument, of course—namely, that the world is the way it is because God was (and is) that way—and I would not begrudge such a judgment. But at some point you must exit the roundabout and reenter traffic.

Something may be true for more than one reason. And all such reasons, too, may be true. Martin Heidegger called human beings *Da-sein*. We're never abstractly impartial, never purely objective creatures. We only are (*sein*, German for "being") when we are in a place or condition (*Da*) and cannot know anything apart from such conditionality. When we hurt, the world *is* hurtful. What therefore we experience of the divine—the Kellerian read through the Heideggerian—depends on who we (think we) are, what we think we are, how we think we are, where we think we are. There are other divine qualities, I might add. Like *qabd* and *bast*, or expansion and contraction. Bipolarity is one particularly intense way to *know* something of these sides of God, of His qualities of increasing and decreasing. Though these are faces of God, these are not all His faces. And they are never His only faces.

My favorite mosque happened to be on the beach, near the Burj al-Arab hotel, the giant sailboat that was Brand Dubai's tallest building for some time. I found this mosque during Ramadan, my first ever in a Muslim-majority society. I spent as many nights as I could there, almost always heading out after sundown, trying to outrun the stoplights on Umm Suqeim—which has, too late for me, been turned into another highway. If you headed farther down Jumeirah Beach Road there were small strip malls and sexy restaurants, tucked between or carved out of homes. But between those and the Burj there was a gap, a little outpost of an older Dubai, where the houses might be grand, but you could not tell, because they were surrounded by high walls. A holdover. The part that missed the makeover.

Through dark, nearly deserted streets, belying the skyscrapers just a half mile away in both directions, I could walk to the beach and hear the ocean heaving even in the middle of the night. I'd listen to waves unseen; Elves in the dark promised that, on the other side of this ocean, was Valinor. *Mujhe jane do*. Like Círdan, I am ready now. My feet itched but I knew the ablution fountain would spray them clean. I spent several evenings there, just thinking. Occasionally praying. I had a mandate to prescribe myself a pace I could sustain. I carried Keller's fat maroon book from this mosque to others, finding myself rereading key passages over and over. After *isha* prayers were Ramadan's special prayers, *taraweeh*, in which every night a thirtieth of the Qur'an would be recited.

Maybe Kayvan and I would go get coffee and *shisha* after. I'd eat something more. Junayd might join in. Then back to a mosque, another mosque. *Qiyam al-layl.* Standing in the night. This was only enlightenment as it ever really happens—you walk through a door after years of effort, and find there are new doors still closed to you. The Kellerian exposition answered the why—as in, why the world is the way it is. But I began to feel a new doubt, which threatened everything I'd achieved in Dubai. Had it not been for religion, even just religion as I'd been taught it, would I have been so depressed? To struggle against this darkness inside me, a fight I sensed (rightly, unfortunately) would never end, I needed to translate the abstract to the personal. Not just why, but more importantly, why *me*—the question which, all along, I had been unable to answer, and driven mad by my inability to. Why me the way I was, *Da-sein*, being but being as suffering? Why me raised in a language and a culture that did not just inhibit self-awareness, but discouraged thoughts of self-repair and self-recovery?

Why hadn't God brought me into being elsewhere, elsewhen, elsehow? I've been through a lot of pain in my life, too many surgeries, procedures, and diagnoses to count. (Two dozen at least.) But for one's mind to be plunged into depression only to climb spookily high and to cycle rapidly between these, soaring then plunging every few days—that is probably the worst of them. I felt existentially nauseated. I was dizzied by the back-and-forth in my head, the sense one morning that I could have both Zhaleh and Hafsa, that I could pull it off, the sureness that I would have neither of them, that I was the Muslim or the infidel, plainspoken or duplicitous, the belief that even if I was in the hospital yesterday I could be on the plane tomorrow, followed by the certainty that I deserve to be in the ER the next day. "My Lord is as my servant thinks I am," God once informed

Muhammad.[5] I should like to add: Your servant might be as he thinks
You are. "If you did not sin," Muhammad once told his followers,
"God would destroy you and replace you with a people who sinned
and asked forgiveness—so that He could forgive them."[6]

Now, "destroy" is a hard word to contemplate. But that's what I'd
done. I'd hated who I was. What I was. What I could not be. What
limitations were placed on me. For a long time, Islam was a religion
of love, because love was the only language through which we could
explain and experience the demands of a jealous Divine: Thou shalt
have no other gods. He is worthy of worship, but you are worthy of
worshipping. There's no more loaded term in the Islamic grammar
than "kafir." But the kafir isn't someone who lacks faith. The kafir is
the opposite of a believer—one who is thankful. *Shakir*. In awe at the
privilege of existence. This sentiment is not exclusive to the monotheist; many a secularist describes wonderment at the world as the
driving force behind her desire to explore and understand. There's
a reason I was attracted to *Star Trek*—the unlikely but undeniable
confluence, though perhaps those of us who are spiritually inclined
go one step further.

Because we exist. But we did not ask to. Atheist, agnostic, theist:
doesn't matter. You can and will still ask the same question all the
same. We can all ask, too, until we're lowered in the grave, "Why
me?" I likewise was made, the making having been long ago concluded. In ways that left me suffering for many of my years. But perhaps there was, in that, an insight and a wisdom I could not otherwise
have, even if many times I'd wish I didn't have to have it. I'm not
suggesting the depressed or otherwise afflicted can simply think their
way out of illness. Except that I am. How we think about ourselves
has a lot to do with what becomes of us. How we think about ourselves determines what we believe about the universe and its Creator.
I could ask, Why me? until the day I died. Why I was made, why I was

5. Found in Bukhari, via hadithaday.org: http://hadithaday.org/hadith-qudsi
/i-am-as-my-servant-thinks-expects-i-am, accessed January 15, 2014.
6. This particular hadith is found in Muslim ibn Hajjaj's collection, no. 2687.

broken, why I was hurting? And then I'd die, and then what? What if, instead, I asked, Why *not* me? Why can I not simply *be*, however imperfectly? The kafir denies God's signs, actively and with malice. With charity toward none, he hates not only God but himself. Who cries, Why me? and flees, when he should scream, Why the hell not me? and, if he finds the world indifferent or inimical to his cares, his concerns, his people, force the world to stop and listen.

A Muslim is not a coward, Muhammad said. Maybe he has to pretend he's in a movie to get there. A few weeks later, on my way to Jerusalem for two weeks, I stopped in Istanbul and, by this same logic of doing what the audience would like to see done, got myself teargassed—which I do not recommend but would do again. Stand and fight. The kafir faces Camus's great question—Should we kill ourselves?—and cannot answer except affirmatively, because his constitution is thankless. For he refuses the gift, even though he already is it. That threatening deadness inside us can tear us apart. But it is inescapable. If the world was created from nothing, and it was, then it is created in distance from God. We are not Him. We cannot be Him. We must be ourselves. Our lonely, terrified, mortal selves. Individuality demands alienation. God, many Muslims will say, created the world so that He may be known. As above, so below. Perhaps the self is only sated by a Self, but there's only so close you can get. Because the self is meant to be itself. I would have to come to terms with a mind that sometimes told me to die. The gap, as it were, between me and me.

·23·

WHO SHOT THE SHATRI

ABU BAKR AL-SHATRI WAS FAMOUS, for which reason there was almost no chance of him leading prayers in American mosques, which were too small and too strapped for cash to afford such a mellifluous Qur'an reciter. But in Dubai? On Ramadan's fifteenth night, my brother and I navigated our way to Rashidiyya, a neighborhood not far from DXB, and parked his SUV in a sandlot under the elevated Green Line. There with time to spare, I was so enthusiastic I was jittery; to be led in prayer by someone who'd for me thus far existed solely digitally? I wore a powder-blue *kandoura* with a kaffiyeh in silver and cream.

There was an openness in Dubai you could not find in the West, and even less so now. (Try walking around in New York City in shalwar qamis.) In Dubai, though, nobody cared. I had accumulated Punjabi kurtas, whimsical Turkish T-shirts, and the ubiquitous flowing garments that might've been what people here wore centuries ago, when they could not pore star-struck over prayer schedules, eager to find out when their favorite reciter would be at which mosque. I had spent much of my dwindling income on kaffiyehs. I'd learned to tie them in the local style, and had every conceivable color scheme. I spent extraordinary sums of money, relatively speaking, on the local colognes. I dabbed my finest on me that night, so overjoyed was I that I might be able to experience

Islam in a way I never had before. But once prayers began, we had a problem: our imam was not Shatri.

This was the right night, I told myself, based on the fliers we'd consulted. And certainly we could not have gotten the mosque wrong. There were too many thousands of people packing the space. Never before had I experienced a religiously induced traffic jam; I liked that here, God caused gridlock. Maybe, my brother guessed, "Shatri will lead *taraweeh*," what we'd really come for. How desperately I clung to this hope. I'd been enjoying a Dubaiian spin on Ramadan. Every mosque is in immaculate condition. Every reciter would command celebrity in America. They even perfume the mosques here: you walk out smelling better than you ever have. Given all this, and that this was my only Ramadan in a Muslim country thus far, Shatri's absence was heartbreaking. Because once *taraweeh* started, it was the same imam. The wrong imam. The not-Shatri. While I appreciated this other imam's mastery of Qur'anic craft, I hadn't left an hour in advance, braved unfamiliar roads and nigh-comatose post-*iftar* drivers promiscuously drifting between lanes at unhealthy speeds while pondering the afterlife to listen to someone I'd never heard of.

His name, I found out much later, was Idrees Abkar. Maybe you like him and now don't like me very much. But consider my point of view. I was frustrated I'd apparently missed my shot at Shatri and then I was more frustrated because I couldn't stop feeling frustrated; focus on the prayer, I urged myself, and I focused so much on focusing that I lost it entirely. This was the fifteenth night, where the hell was Abu Bakr al-Shatri, why does my Islam suck, and why do things never work out and where did Zhaleh go and why did I ruin things for Hafsa and me and I totally just went to a bridge and almost jumped. After taraweeh comes *witr*, which is just Arabic for "odd." Three cycles of prayer. (God, as One, is odd.) In the final cycle, before the penultimate prostration, the imam leads the congregation in audible supplication. Typically this involves the regurgitation of a series of prophetic pleas sung in a style nearly indistinguishable from Qur'an, though they are largely not of such provenance. Most such *duas* I'd been through were perfunctory affairs, me racing to translate the Arabic of each supplication in time to know whether I should say "Ya Allah!" or "Ameen" before the imam started on the next entreaty. Not this time.

In a postmatch interview, a top-ranked tennis player once described what it was like to lose to Rafael Nadal. "I am one of the top players in the world," this athlete said, not to brag but to underscore what came next. For, he admitted, he had no idea what had happened on the court, except that all his considerable talent had come to naught, he was crushed by some kind of magic he had never before encountered, and to which he had no response. I do not, to this day, know what Idrees Abkar did. Except I was there for it. In his spoken supplication, the dua right before witr's end, Abkar started talking to God, in a manner that suggested he not only forgot but didn't care we were in the room, or maybe it was him yearning for the thousands behind him to ascend briefly to where he permanently resided.

If we could be inside his heart, if we could be offered transportation to the Rock, to fly from our Jerusalem to his heaven, this is what we might have absorbed. Abkar was not leading us in prayer. He was talking to God and we happened to be behind him, squeezed in so tightly we could hardly find places for our foreheads on flawless plush carpet. We were realizing that he was realizing, in the course of his supplicating, that he was talking to Him, and this nearly did him in. "I am speaking to my Creator." "I am speaking to Him because He created Me." What kind of person, given a gift, complains about it? Abkar started crying. Bawling, truly. What, after all, does it really mean to say "Allahu Akbar" and begin a prayer—talking to the One who made you? It would be bewildering. And amazing. "You. . . ." He whispered. Then he mumbled it. Then he screamed it. Then he tried it again because he could get no further. "You," he managed, in between roiling sobs, "brought us from nonexistence into existence."

This thought entering him stabbed us too, but he kept on, no rest for the bewildered, him tearing us open and firing a water cannon of tears into our hearts. Grown men began to weep. We were broken. But we knew it. We felt it.

We couldn't resist it.

Abkar made what was foundational into what was conclusive, thundering it, panhandling for it, returning to it, swearing by it, running a giant circle around us and spinning us around with him. "You created us," he said, and then what he said next I will never forget. "*La ilaha illa anta.*" "There is no God but You." He said it, over and over again, until not one of us was not shaking, breaking, struggling to stay on our legs, held up perhaps just because there were so many of us, but that was only where he began, for with that out of the way, he asked, and how he asked, how painfully and unashamedly he described the miserableness of our souls and the griminess of our deeds and the insufficiencies of our actions that we felt there was no veil. Why should there be? We were supposed to be absolute monotheists, the people who keep our one finger raised come what may. In the months to come I would look on the music of drunken Sufis and the poetry of intoxicated saints in an entirely new way. Their sins reflected a piety far greater than our modern puritanical fidelity could summon. They lived a life immersed in God. I experienced the seminal principle of Islam in a way I could have never imagined. The direct and unhampered access to God of His creation, given by the Lord of All the right to speak to Him, and the means to it.

When I was growing up, I had a fantastic and formative Sunday-school teacher, a part-time doctor who was a full-time community leader. "Imagine if you were to describe to an unborn child the world that was coming," he said to me. "She would not *be able* to believe you." That, he said, was the challenge facing Muhammad in trying to describe what happens after death. When Abkar's supplication concluded and the prayer ended, nobody moved. For fear of breaking the spell that, we knew, would have to be broken. For every ascension to God, there is a return to the world. If this did not end, if this connection were not snapped, then we would be in paradise. We sat nervously still. Some of us sniffled. Wiped away tears. Were surprised to realize they were ours. Stared at the floor, like it might tell us, Yes, that just happened.

Shatri came the next night. I went out for shisha.

·24·

GAZI HUSREV BEGGING THE QUESTION

JUNAYD LIVED NEAR DUBAI MARINA, the drive to which, at twilight, with the lamps of Dubai kindling, was almost tangibly otherworldly; you could be forgiven for a moment if you thought you might enter Rivendell, not a modern, planned, worldly metropolis. I very happily joined Junayd there as often as I could, sometimes for dinner, or this time for coffee. I parked on the street, because I found a spot for free. I wore a Bosnian soccer jersey, because I liked it. When we finally sat down on the waterfront with our drinks, the jersey prompted him to ask about the tour of Bosnia I'd led about a year ago. It felt like it had happened to someone else.

Mahmud accompanied me on the trip, even though he knew Hafsa and I were already separated, and probably divorcing, and it would be the last time any of these tours would happen. After we landed in Sarajevo's tiny airport, and proceeded down the stairs to the modest customs section, Mahmud asked, "Do we need visas?" I looked at him incredulously; was it possible this question had not previously been asked and, more importantly, answered? Fortunately for him, me, and the twenty some customers who'd paid thousands of dollars, we did not need visas. We stayed at the Europa Hotel. I'd be up at fajr to pray at Gazi Husrev Beg's mosque, and I'd be back there when the group went to bed early, or I'd just go out when they stayed in.

I excitedly recalled my own favorite place in Baščaršija, where I'd smoke under a Palestinian flag in the courtyard of a former madrasa. Sami Yusuf played on the loudspeakers. I met a man wearing what my mother would've call a shocking-pink polo—with jet black, it's one of the two colors exclusive to desi Crayola—his robust biceps bulging through the sleeves. He looked like he'd been born in and intended to die in a club; he was also my age. His family had been killed early in the war and so he took up a gun to defend his home when I was still mourning Kurt Cobain. But his first question to me—through a translator, but what I want you to keep in mind is what he'd been through and the vastness of circumstance that separated us and the religion that bound us—was why Pakistanis were late for everything.

In my wistfulness I must have made Junayd wish he'd gone. A woman at the table just behind ours, who I suspected was listening in for some time now, interrupted the reverie to ask me, "Are you Bosnian?"

Now, reader, in my life I have been confused for nearly everything: Iranian, Turkish, Moroccan, Puerto Rican, Mexican, Emirati, Israeli, Afghan. Those are not terribly surprising. One time an Indian thought my name was "Arun" and decided to offload his very anti-Muslim views onto me until, an hour later, I swore I too wanted to stay in touch with him, entered my contact into his phone as Haroon, and he thereafter crossed the street whenever he saw me coming. One of my high school friends, a kid I'd known for seven or eight years, once asked me to drive him to his brother's soccer practice and take them both home. But when his brother came out of the school, looking for us, my friend called him preemptively, and guided him to our vehicle. "See the SUV with the black guy driving? That's us." And I looked around and saw no SUVs and felt lost until I remembered I was driving an SUV and—oh. Another time I was confused for Ghanaian, by a Ghanaian. But I did not ever think a man who looked like me would ever be confused for a Slav by someone who turned out to be a Slav herself.

We had a friendly conversation about Bosnia, about how much I wished to return there, and then we returned to our respective friends. Half an hour later, she left and I confessed to Junayd, "I should have asked for her number."

Duh, his eyes said. So. "Why didn't you?"

But I'd hesitated. Would being so forward, in a Muslim country, be interpreted badly? But since I saw people out on dates all the time, I asked, "How does everyone else do it, anyhow?"

"Sometimes," he said, "if a woman is with someone, like her friend, then her friend will make herself scarce for some time, giving you an opening. It's a sure sign she's interested, because you don't have to ask in front of her friend."

I nodded. I understood. I imagined the conversation I could have pursued. I'd ask her out and then make her pay. I would explain that I was a very moderate, modern Muslim man who so detested the legacy of patriarchy that he refused any manner of chivalry, and that was the only reason, not because I was in overdraft. But then I frowned because I realized . . . "Just like her friend had gotten up like right after she and I stopped talking?"

"Yeah." Junayd cackled. He was enjoying this. "She probably wanted you to ask her out." Or, a little more than probably.

"Why the *fuck* didn't you tell me?"

"I didn't know how to."

"What does that mean?"

"Well, I couldn't just point out to you that she was waiting for you to ask her out with her sitting right next to us."

"To mujhe Urdu mein kyun nahin bataya?" *Haramzada.*

"Oh yeah." He chuckled, realizing, as I'd reminded him, that as he was from Karachi and my family was from Islamabad (ish), and that although the motherland's official language is English, we shared a national language in which he could have spoken to me. "I'm sorry. I forgot we speak Urdu. She seemed into you." Thank you, *madarchhod.* Junayd finished with a flourish. "She was really hot."

I will not ever let him live this down, mind you, for the Junayd who would otherwise never cease to proclaim his pride in his

Pakistani heritage suddenly saw his *qawmi zaban* abandon him—but that was, even though it didn't feel like it at the time, of secondary significance. On our walk to my latest Camry, he said, "You were really willing to ask, though? Like you wanted to take her out?"

"Are you serious?"

"Okay, fine, I mean, I get why you'd want to, but would you be ready?"

Junayd had work in the morning, so he said salam soon after. I lingered. Ever since Hafsa and I had separated, I'd had trouble sleeping. I might be up till four in the morning; the later the night got, the worse I got. Come every evening, I came to feel my day had lacked purpose, that my life had no meaning, that really there was no point to living, and this feeling of futility presented in daylight hours as a desire to die and in the late night as a kind of painful alertness, an almost raw feeling of disappointed vigilance. I strolled lazily around the marina, hoping I might bump into the Bosnian, though it never happened. But something else happened.

Instead of waiting for her to come to me, why not go to her? I loved traveling; wanderlust (and lust). My preparation for Spain had been so much fun I still smiled just remembering; I greatly enjoyed finding random bits of trivia, and corroborating these, or merely indulging them. Did you know, for example, that at one time the Portuguese city of Faro was known as Santa Maria bint Haroon, or Saint Mary the Daughter of Aaron, a wonderful fusion of Catholic and Muslim, Indo-European Iberian and Hebraic-Arabic Semitic, because for a very long time Portugal had been largely Muslim, and because, in the Qur'an, Mary is often referred to by her descent from Aaron's line.

If I found the right job, I could have enough money to bounce between new and old destinations, undertaking the adventure I'd had to convince myself I already starred in. I would rent a car and drive from one end of Europe to another, from Lisbon to Kazan. Perhaps return to Sarajevo regularly. I'd travel with a pen and a notebook as open as the world was supposed to be. I could be alone with the world. I could be far enough in the shadows that maybe God would

not see me, or get bored and move on. So I turned to NYU Abu
Dhabi, a satellite campus of my alma mater where, as fate would have
it, Junayd's wife was now working. She asked me to visit.

The day I parked my car beside the main building, I might've
teared up—NEW YORK UNIVERSITY was spelled out in Latin and Arabic script; on the other end of the parking lot was a large mosque.
We'd fought, Junayd and I and many others, just fifteen years earlier,
for a single room to pray in. Just a room. And here I was at an NYU
campus, listening to the call to prayer pervading even classrooms. I
met as many people as I could, professors, students, administrators. I
spent part of an afternoon chatting with a woman who was helping
to bring the new campus to life. She was American, too, kind and
helpful, and suggested I meet her colleague, Teuta, who worked in
some-department-or-other but wasn't on campus that day. I assumed
Teuta was Teutonic, because, of course, I am a moron.

I also assumed Teuta was the key to a job that would make my
dreams come true.

Teuta and I arranged to meet in Marina Mall, in a coffee shop
located on a platform in the middle of one of the atriums. I got there
early, leaving my car in the world's most nausea-inducing garage,
a seashell spiral that turned around and around on itself until you
puked or parked. Teuta arrived on time. She shook my hand and sat
down directly across from me, both of us in high-backed chairs and
visible to all the mall traffic flowing past us, a small marble island in
a human river. As she began to describe her role at NYU, however,
it occurred to me that she had nothing whatsoever to do with my
areas of interest. She was remarkably accomplished—but still, there
was little crossover. Why then had we been introduced? She'd never
help me get hired.

I wondered if the meeting was an attempt at matchmaking. If
so, though, why pair Haroon with some random white lady? (Very
attractive white lady though.) When I mentioned I'd just returned
from a short trip to Jerusalem, to study at the Shalom Hartman Institute as part of the pilot cohort of something called the Muslim
Leadership Initiative, Teuta began recounting her own recent trip to

the holy city, which was supposed to have culminated in a visit to the
Noble Sanctuary, but she'd been denied entry, despite having worn a
respectful hijab. She even started crying. There in Jerusalem, I mean,
not in front of me. This white woman, I thought, must really be on
some Orientalist trip—why else would she be that upset? (How could
I be this dense? you may also be asking. Again.) It was only when she
began to recount her visit to nearby Sharjah to watch *pahlwani* wres-
tling, wherein large, nearly naked West Asian men grease themselves
up and have at each other, that I became suspicious.

"Wait. Where are you from?" I interjected.

"New York."

"No, I mean your family."

"We're Albanian."

White Muslims being like white chocolate—somehow they're
still brown. I'd made the fully reasonable and simultaneously totally offensive presumption that her phenotypic fairness indicated
Judeo-Christianity. Thereupon I concluded that this was a date, or,
okay, maybe I just hoped it was. But I realized I had acted entirely
inappropriately and dressed absurdly, given that this might have been
a potential romantic encounter. I had been looking for a job, but that
didn't mean the only thing I wanted was a job. The next day Teuta
and I began texting, and found remarkable convergences. "Not much
I'm doing groceries looking for cashews," I'd write. A minute later:
"OMG I am eating cashews right now."

These were no mere coincidences. No, world-historical forces
had propelled us to this point, moved and killed large numbers of
humans so that we might have cause to be amazed by each other.
Like Napoleon had lost the Battle of Waterloo in order that England
might retain its hold on the Perso-Arabian Gulf, so that Dubai's primary language would be English and Anglophones from America
could end up there two hundred years later and figure out they had
the same interest in nuts. And other marginalia that, when you are
even somewhat besotted, can only mean that the universe intends for
you to have babies together and live out your old age watching Net-
flix until one or both of you expires. Her uncle lived in Brooklyn just

blocks from mine, where in just a few months, entirely unbeknownst to me and at the time unimaginable and unfathomable, I'd be living. Because this wasn't the happy ending.

Or even the ending. Every time I would be in Abu Dhabi, something would (in)conveniently come up to prevent us from getting together. Or she'd mention she was coming to Dubai tomorrow, then message me at the end of tomorrow to say she got busy and so she couldn't make it and sorry she didn't text earlier to let me know. I got the message. And dealt with it. Because I'd tried. Like Babar tried for Central Asia. Seven or eight times. At the time, of course, I couldn't see the real lesson. Rather than understand that marriage was not the end-all, be-all of life, that I needed to learn how to be okay with myself, instead of finding a woman to complete me—as if it was partnership with a single human being that made us fully human—I was convinced that the solution was marriage on different terms. A wife more suitable for me, and I, a better husband, and then I would not want to die.

I did meet Teuta one more time, briefly, at another part of the marina, facing the beach. She'd reached out because she'd heard I was leaving Dubai. The convalescence had come to an end. I'd hoped Dubai would be a second chapter, a chance at reinvention. Instead it sits parenthetically, an aside I am deeply fond of but which never stood quite on its own. My stay in the Gulf turned out to be very much like leaving the marina, which exists on a kind of stage, looming over Shaykh Zahed Road beside it. (SZR, as it is known for short, is no mere traffic conduit; it is a highway big enough to parallel-park aircraft carriers on.) To return to Arabian Ranches, you must drive straight down an ordinary two-lane street punctuated by traffic lights (and now a streetcar too), which road eventually splits, the left lane winding down and toward sapphire water and the right leading onto a high, twisting on-ramp that takes an impossibly long distance to turn you 180 degrees around and onto the Shaykh Zayed Superhighway.

You must drive very cautiously on this ramp, for if you go too fast, you won't just hit a concrete barrier but potentially push through it, which means falling a great distance down to the ground, whereafter

I imagine your car would explode as in an action movie. But you also know that there is at the end of this descending on-ramp only the briefest of straightaways, over which you must really floor it, pick up some velocity, or otherwise you will be unable to merge into the unforgiving traffic that rockets mercilessly toward Burj Khalifa. Of course, just as I got going, in fact only a minute after I had slid into the harrowingly fast traffic, I had to leave, because mine was the first exit, onto Umm Suqeim Road. No sooner had I gained entry then I had to bow out.

Years after my family had decamped from Somers, Connecticut, I had a chance to go back. My mother was buried in Enfield's Muslim cemetery, and after I'd finished reading Y. S. for her, the chapter she died to, I drove fifteen minutes in the wrong direction to see what had become of the place where we'd lived together so long. It had been nearly four years since she'd passed. Hafsa and I had just begun to hit turbulence, and I was rattled enough that I needed something before her, and before us, to hold on to.

In a gunmetal Camry—are you surprised?—I drove down Turnpike Road, accelerated up Mountain Road, and then took the second left up the long hill, all the way to the end. I reached the cul-de-sac, and crept my car up what was once *our* thirteen-hundred-foot driveway, well aware of the dire NO TRESPASSING warnings I myself had nailed up so long before, signs I'd never conceived could be used against me. The new occupants had painted our white windowsills black, though that left me more emulous than envious. My former home was darker and, as a surprising result, kinder. I got out of the car and walked a circle around the house, from the swimming pool to the outcropping of rock on the other end that I'd transformed, when I was much younger, into a fortress.

I wanted more, though. To peer through the windows. To be in my room. I'd remember when I worked up the courage to ask Carla out, and thought thereafter life would only get better—a man is only not alone when he is with a woman. I'd look at all the rooms I imagined decorating or redesigning. Like when we live somewhere, we do so permanently. I hoped to walk in, light a fire in the chimneys we never tested, pass hot beverages to whoever happened to be home and tell these replacements how much each oversized room meant to me. I'd do such a good job of describing what the place meant to me that the new homeowners would ejaculate—in the way they did back before everything was innuendo—"Why'd you leave?" I'd finally belonged somewhere, and then right when it seemed I had it all figured out, Carla closed the door in my face.

I believe it was Nicholas E. Meyer, of *Star Trek* fame, who said that had high school lasted one more year, he would've ruled. Was he somehow me? I'd thought I made it at New York University, forgetting that it was just four years; I should have had plans for after. I got my dream job in Washington, but too bad it was when I was falling to bits. I made hegira to Dubai, where I could exhale years that had gone nowhere. I wondered if whatever great-great-grandfather left Mesopotamia for the Punjab felt the same way. But I had to leave Dubai before I was ready to, forced by circumstances made of finances. "But that is not for them to decide," Gandalf said. Did they know he was just like Sauron, not a man, not even an elf—"All we have to decide is what to do with the time that is given us."

There were many wonderful things about Dubai, but none of these fit my skill set, or had room for me. Not even NYU Abu Dhabi. I guess it wasn't meant to be. There was nothing there for me, nothing I could do full time that would permit me to build a life there, or as I preferred, a life rooted there but reaching everywhere. I grew extremely concerned by the fact of having to leave, and desperately searched for other places to live besides America—I tried hard for Istanbul, for example. No such luck. I remember landing at JFK, standing outside Terminal 1, and being surprised that it felt familiar. But the greatest blows were yet to come.

My career wasn't just interrupted. Once back, I applied for countless academic positions, hoping I'd get something that'd allow me

to finish my dissertation before the clock ran out, but I received almost no responses, never mind the courtesy of explicit rejections.
From Mississippi to Oregon. Zilch. So while I wanted to complete
my project on Iqbal, the prospectus for which I'd already submitted
and defended, I could not. There was no way I could dedicate the
time and energy needed to write five full chapters, to complete the
research necessary, to sit in the library for hours on end, when I had
to cobble together enough freelance assignments, speaking gigs, and
other projects, just to address my debt, never mind build a life anew.
Maybe then Dubai had just delayed the inevitable. Or made it worse.
Maybe I'd be stuck in the same ten jobs, none of them adding up to
even one proper job. Maybe I would be back on another bridge in
another few years, and this time, who would stop me?

So when I received the invitation from the Muslim Public Affairs Council to speak at their Los Angeles conference, I told myself
I wanted to go, and maybe I did. But more importantly, I had to; the
hamster was back on his wheel. The last MPAC panel I'd spoken at
had danced around almost the same topic: the Arab Spring. It was
now 2013, however: the empire was striking back. The day I flew
out, an historic snowstorm whitewashed the Middle East. "Look," I
tweeted, attaching a shot of the Dome of the Rock dressed up like
a Christmas ornament, "the Arab Winter." Global warming, someone responded, or the end of days? (Yes.) If you're expecting an easy
epiphany, you might want to stop reading. It took almost twenty years
for thesis to meet antithesis and begin a synthesis. I would not come
from the clothes I put on, the women I was with, the drinks I drank.
For a man who had to star in movies to get himself out the door, I can
think of no better place to finish than Los Angeles.

·25·

MUSLIM PREFERS VIRGIN

THERE'S AN UPSIDE TO EVERY DOWN. In the course of my freaking out, I'd begun to hope the choice of a Friday the 13th flight to Los Angeles might correspond to an emptier aircraft. But capitalism beat out paraskevidekatriaphobia. Passing the ticketing counter revealed a serpentine line. Then the national-security indignity. Most people wouldn't stop eyeballing me until the TSA had radioactively strip-searched me. Thereafter my nervous fellow travelers went back to ignoring me, and I spent the hour before takeoff trying to remain calm. I dared not listen to music on my phone, which usually helped in these situations, because I couldn't risk draining my phone of even a percentage point of battery life, because without it I'd be alone with myself on the flight, and there's nothing tougher than travel, nothing scarier than the hollowness that gathers as you take off, builds as you fly, and all but swallows you by the time you've landed.

This being America's principal northeastern port of entry and largest city since 1790, there were however no surplus outlets anywhere. I was in fact so desperate to get my phone the 7 percent of battery life it had lost in the time between leaving home and getting on the plane that I lustily eyed the power outlet oddly placed halfway down the jet bridge, only stopping when I realized how that'd look and whether it'd end in Guantánamo. The trauma of modern Islam.

You haven't done anything wrong, but you must assume, in public, that you have. I busied myself with the kinds of exercises people pursued before the invention of apps. I ogled aircraft. There was an overwhelming Singapore Airlines A380 (flown the plane, never the airline) and an El Al 747 (yes & yes) skittishly parked some distance from the terminal, while, from far away, I espied Pakistan International, which, awkwardly for both parties, aesthetically converged with Israel's flag carrier. And then I saw my red-and-white plane.

A few years ago, I'd gone to Australia. I went there to speak about—what else—Islam. I got stupid excited because I thought we'd be flown on Qantas, and I'm the type of weirdo who really gets excited about airlines, but we took Virgin to Melbourne. Not a bad thing at all. On this trip to Los Angeles, I'd be flying Virgin (America) again. I cannot tell you how relieved I was to board at last, having run out of diversions. But as I sat down in the aircraft, an unexpected calm possessed me. I didn't require music to take my mind off myself and other things I was afraid of, or just continued to think I was, because an object in motion presumes it still is. Virgin America was partly to credit. I liked their lounge-like mood lighting. I liked their leather-jacketed stewardesses. I dared to dream I'd one day reach such altitudes of desirability that I might graduate from polite requests for aisle seats to sternly specifying airlines. "I prefer Virgin," though, might not have gone over so well. But who wanted to go, say, Delta?

Even the corporate overlords at Delta probably thought it a punishment to fly their own airline. Virgin America's safety demonstration video made me think, for a moment, that we'd outsourced the FAA to Bollywood. Though one of the characters in the Virgin video was a nun trying to get her phone into airplane mode, otherwise we were subjected to this airliner's catchy spin on the same flight-safety catechism—what to do in the event of cataclysm—that is the closest thing our world has to a nonlocal universality. When you fly many Muslim airlines, takeoff is preceded by a recitation of a traveler's invocation, a plea to God for a safe going and coming. Virgin succeeded its alert with advertisements, like a sponsor's pitch after a sermon, which was really the sermon. After telling us what to do in the unlikely event of us, I don't know, slamming into the earth at several hundred miles per hour, I was being marketed to.

I'd recently published an academic essay about air travel, and wished I could've included this moment. In my essay, I'd shared how airlines originating from Muslim-majority societies feature faith in ways most fellow Western-but-not-Muslim travelers might find unfamiliar. My argument was that Islam does not negate the boundaries of sacred and secular, but the way Muslims do their religion challenges what many think religion could or should be. The imposition of a particular Protestant sensibility on all theology and every praxis. For if religion should be private, what do we do with headscarves, which create the public, so much as they are created by it? On nominally secular Turkish Airlines, there are options to listen to religious music or Qur'an recitation. I'd never seen anything similar on Western airlines, however, save this one nun. I'd never sustained any interest in political Islam, which in the years since my first exposure to its principal theoreticians had led the Muslim world further down a lizard hole. The private rigidity of the personal Islams I inherited had also failed me. But neither could I embrace a progressivism or liberalism that merely stamped whatever the left found morally appropriate at that moment as having been Islam's ultimate intention all along. The airline that opens with Islam and offers the Qur'an but travels all over the world, and includes all kinds of people, some of whom are sometimes not on good terms with each other, that might have revealed me to me.

The kid who was perhaps never more himself than outside Medina, debating whether he should pick Jesus or Muhammad, because it was not the "either/or" but the "and." In Dubai, Hafsa and I had a conversation over Skype, and agreed, but this time we meant it, that divorce was the right thing to do. I came back from Dubai and a funny thing happened. We met up several times, to catch up on our lives then and going ahead, separate, but not severed. I found consolation and more, in this conclusion; a wonderful person had chosen to be part of my life. We could not, of course, be friends. But despite how bitterly the last months had gone, that did not describe who we were, together or apart. The last time we met up for coffee, some-where in East Harlem, we discussed books we were reading, poems we found moving, movies we believed funny. We cracked up at each other's jokes. What that ex post facto coda was, I do not know. I don't need to. The ring is gone. My regard for the feelings it bound is not.

All around me, the smarter/cheaper/hungrier folks had brought something to snack on. I'd believed my airport last supper would suf-fice: a McDonald's Quarter Pounder no cheese, large fries, a ginor-mous Diet Coke that cleared its neighboring region of planetesimals, a Starbucks grande Awake tea, a chocolate chip cookie, a power bar, two bottles of water. It'd been $6.52 at McDonald's, by the way, but they took my receipt to make sure I paid for the meal I claimed, so I wouldn't be able to deduct that bill from my taxes. There was $11.00 for the *Atlantic* I'd purchased days before, which had an article about John Kerry's Israel-Palestine peace process (which had predictably failed but was important to my planned remarks), gum I bought and lost before we landed, and a 20 oz. Coke Zero. Not to mention $25.00 to check my bag. When my appetite overwhelmed me, I yielded to a peanut butter and jelly sandwich so perfect I wanted to swing my legs under the chair like a little kid. I wrote more, visited the bathroom several times and wrote some more, none of it my talk for the next day, the future or not of political Islam.

Before I knew it, having typed my way into the carpal tunnel, we were told to power down our electronics. I wasn't ten feet post jetbridge and one flaxen-haired someone special caught me checking her out though that was an accidental side-effect of my planning to use the bathroom behind her while determining how to walk around her. There'd be another one, I reassured my bladder, because this was after all an alpha world city. Bathrooms are, however, California's electrical outlets. We don't always find what we're looking for. Even when we need it most. The whole point of my telling you about this trip is simple. It is to illustrate what had changed, and what had not. You might hear it in the rhythm of my words. It is looming, right there. First, let me tell you how this journey would've ordinarily, or previously, gone.

Hey, I'm actually not that down, I would've reasoned, at some point in my flight over America. I'm legitimately having a good time. Life is good, I'd begin to think. I am good. Not just good, great. This is exciting. Excited^excited. I'm awesome, incredible, indomitable. I'm not on drugs. Drugs should be on me. I can do anything. So I'll do everything. By the time I'll have reached the hotel, from which I have no escape because they're too cheap to rent you a car, and you're too insecure to ask for one, you're filled with deep self-loathing. This isn't a punishment God imposed on you, but that you imposed on you. So you do something to rescue yourself, but you only hurt yourself. For what in mania is seen as merely the next step to the conquest of the entire world—let's flirt with someone, buy something I can't afford, drink something I'm not meant to—becomes in depression the penultimate step before defenestration.

Sometimes (most recently in Jerusalem) you find yourself measuring the hotel window to see if you fit through. But if God did impose this on you, if He made you to contract and to expand, well then on no bearer of burdens does He place a burden greater than he can bear. What would it mean to be unipolar? At some point, when you've gone through enough, through headaches and heartaches and stomachaches, you realize that you want to keep going. You try to temper the highs and nurse yourself through the lows. You develop strategies, big and small. Ideas for how not to go up too high, or come down too low.

FIRST

Assign yourself a monetary value. It cuts off your mania before it goes too far. "Yes, I would love to, but this is my fee, and I but rarely budge." You hold fast to it. You refuse to go otherwise. You will miss out on gigs. But you prioritize what you have to do. And you don't allow yourself to be cajoled or guilt-tripped into programs you can't afford to pursue. You are therefore happier, not in the exuberant and nearly uncontrollable sense. But sometimes the fee is reasonable, the program worthwhile; you're sure you're going to go. But I'm still me; to get over the anxiety of the speaking gig ahead of me and the traveling required to get there, I amp myself up, psych myself out. And what goes up, in my case, keeps going up, until it crashes on another planet and then wakes up terrified, alone, with difficulty breathing.

SECOND

You arrive in your hotel room, put your head on the floor, and cry. I'm not just describing, I'm prescribing. I begin with a formal prayer, but the main event, what I'm really looking forward to, is when my lips are speaking to Him with my words. All the crazy, stupid, embarrassing shit. I want these. I fear that. I am humiliated by this. I hope for that. I am afraid to _____. God the psychotherapist and the prayer rug the couch. The courage of late-afternoon sunshine and the despair of nightfall. People make imbecilic decisions late at night. Or text exes. Why God urges Muslims to pray during part of the night. (Why, too, I have come to suspect, God urges Muslims to pray more when traveling.)

At first I did not enjoy the prayers, but at some point in the course of every such exercise, I'd tear through the layers that made it so hard for me to admit myself to myself. I would let loose a torrent of words and feel Him carrying them, their burdens, replacing them with a softness and ease in my heart. Some people told me I could not, or should not, do this. But (1) He already knows what I'm thinking—He's God; (2) He can handle it, or otherwise He wouldn't be God; (3) if it's wrong, and I don't think it is, He's still God. Five or ten or fifteen minutes, and I was not at peace but inside it. I'd said it all and could breathe again. I could write, or read, or sleep, or watch TV, and I didn't feel guilty for spending sundry kinds of time on me, for defining me differently, for doing things otherwise. When you have been through enough, you're enough. I never saw Abu Dhabi Shaykh again, not ever. I never met Nuh Ha Mim Keller, not once.

Some months after returning from Dubai, I completed my participation in the Shalom Hartman Institute's Muslim Leadership Initiative, or MLI, a program bringing North American Muslims to learn about Israel, Judaism, and Zionism—in Jerusalem. When the news of my participation first broke, I was subjected to a wave of criticism I'd not conceived possible. Far worse than the pushback we got at NYU, for example, and anyway, wasn't I the same guy who'd been marching *for* Palestine at NYU? A lot of people couldn't understand that my political commitments hadn't changed, but my belief in isolation, in exclusion, in repudiating those we disagree with, had withered. But I could not survived it had I not nearly died by my own decision. The old Haroon would never have had the guts to go. He wouldn't have had the confidence to believe that just because everyone else did things one way, it didn't mean that was the right way—for him, or the world. You can choose to keep your head down there, where it's just you and God, or you can choose to get up off the floor again.

THIRD

Not only did I imagine myself in stories to make living nonfiction easier, but I found that I was always storytelling. Creating them, consuming them, crafting them. Crafted by them. The Creator created us to create. The plot thickens. Where once I was caught in tensions between Muslimness and Westernness, Americanness and Pakistani-ness, now I embraced these as complementarities, or if not, then as various aspects of a self that did not have to be reduced, in the manner of a crude calculation, to one result, one label, one type. Or sometimes I let myself have the stories told to me.

I've no greater fear than thoughts of offing myself when I'm alone and away—plus, who'll talk me out of it? Me? Another way to not face oneself is to face something else. Anything else. I've, as such, tried to include one movie on every subsequent excursion, especially abroad: Abu Dhabi, *Pacific Rim*; Istanbul, *Man of Steel*; Cairo, *The Mummy Returns*; West Virginia, *The Hobbit: An Unexpected Subtitle*; Dubai, *The Wolverine*. I'd planned to see *The Hobbit: The Desolation of Smaug* in Los Angeles. Following Bilbo Baggins would be like letting pop culture give me a hug. Coping mechanisms, you could say. They make us stronger when we're weak. They make us happier before we become too sad. They make for good stories too—I watched this movie in that place, and so, if I have to go back to that place, as I often did for work before and again after Dubai, the memory is not of isolation but of a movie seen at an excellent price. Adventures are good. Which you can incorporate into your speeches in front of confused Muslim audiences who'll be like, Did he just share that anecdote about a woman on the plane shit now our children know sex is real?

Revenge is a dish best published. Once I was in a Stop & Shop parking lot and a gaggle of blond girls swarmed toward me in a wave of spring-break exuberance, beautiful, bright-eyed, and possibly intentionally uniformed, yellow shirts and yoga pants. They carried glitter-marker signs, which read in curly girlie twenty-two-point letters DO YOU NEED A HUG? and why does this shit only ever happen to me plus yes but I can't touch you but thanks for letting me know what paradise kind of looks like. I dove into my Camry at the time— Nazgûl-black—and pretended like I wasn't the lamest person ever for declining. I should go to heaven just for that.

He already knows I think that.

FOURTH

I had an old friend pick me up from the hotel just after check-in. Let's call him Muhammad (since there are several thousand in SoCal). "LA," Muhammad swooned, "has been good to me." Good to me, too. Not only because I found a store selling the exact same kind of sneakers I'd designed and fancied but because I had at least one grand realization. Frequently the locations of these are themselves epiphanic. Take a place described by most as immature and superficial, and it is likely to carry me to the depths of my self. When he'd at last dropped me back to my hotel after a long night out on the town, I plugged my iPhone into the hotel room's speaker system, stared up at the ceiling and almost had a panic attack because I had not had a panic attack.

This trip something happened to me that had not before. I left a residence in New York and felt at home. "Move here," someone said.

"Get me a job," I countered, "and I will."

We call it *fana*, the moment when the moth, disoriented by the candle, enters an orbital death spiral. When you are so overcome by God's infiniteness that you are extinguished. Nothing remains of you but a ring of smoke. Some Muslims, the rugged individualists, the Iqbals and Ghazalis, the Xs and Alis, believe that the point was not to go through the fire but to come out intact on the other side. A Hartman rabbi once said to me, "I can't pray with the people I talk to, and I can't talk to the people I pray with." He meant that the kind of worship services that appealed to him were Orthodox. But that was between him and Hashem. The people, the mentality, the mood that he was connected to were more progressive. Neither helped him in the other part of his life. This was the effect of my *fana*, my nearly burning up in a fire that I and the world kindled; I came out, though, to the other side. By heat and test I had been fused.

I spoke at the conference. I went out the night of, and the next night too. Some friends in my moments of greatest vulnerability had told me their great crises were springboards to grand things. When I was in Dubai I imagined reinventing myself, because it was easier—it was somewhere else, after all. It wasn't America. It seemed simple, neat, convenient. Fail here, reinvent there. But to be returned to America so abruptly—had I had just one more year in Dubai, I am sure I would have ruled—well, I thought that was the end of any ambition in me. Just the thought of rebuilding my life *again* paralyzed me. What if I just trampolined into the same disasters over and over again? What if the next time around, or for every next time around, I would fail and be failed, go bankrupt and keep going bankrupt?

Once more in a September, a year after Dubai, I passed out on a train. At least I was sitting down. The doctor ordered a brain MRI and a stress test. The former showed indications of microstrokes, accumulated over the years—but nothing definitive. The twenty-four-hour take-home stress test was worse: my heart stopped beating for six seconds. A more invasive exam showed a massive heart defect, which necessitated an emergency angiogram, which produced still more confusion. One cardiologist guessed I had Brugada syndrome, which

could be confirmed with an infusion test. They'd shock my heart to
the point of failure, and then they'd know if it was liable to failure.

This was safe? But that test told us, as you can by now guess, nada,
and then nobody knew what was wrong except that something was,
and also, of course, some of the tests were also wrong, so there I was at
thirty-five having a heart monitor put in, the cardio ward's version of
a shrug of the shoulders. "If you have a heart attack," they reassured
me, "at least we'll know what happened." My friend Wajahat told me
that hackers could disable a heart monitor from afar. He thought this
funny. My lymph nodes were soon judged enlarged, and it was lym-
phoma that had killed my mom. The insurance company denied me a
full-body PET, and a biopsy was declined after the next investigation.
"I can't feel the lymph nodes," the doctor said. Reassuring. But what
are you going to do, wait for death?

My reputation as a navigator meant I was tasked to pick up my
cousins from the airport one frigid October day. I was asked to drop
them off at an uncle's house, where they'd be staying. That's where I
met her. Her intention was only to surprise my cousins, because she
knew them from Pakistan. She surprised me (too). Two years later I
got down on one knee and asked. It was different this time, not only
because she was different, but because I was. (Also, she said yes.)
That's what I didn't see when I'd first landed in New York, and what
I hope you always do. I was not trapped because I knew it could end.
The opposite. I was freed or, in my own dialect, decolonized. All of it
would end. There will be more shocks and blows, of course, and one
of them will kill me—at the end of the day, all our flights land just
short of the runway.

Islam was no longer a straitjacket into which I forced myself, nor
a nonnative language I learned from others around me, but a grammar through which I vowed to write my own stories. In Los Angeles,
Muhammad drove me through neighborhoods touristically, but I was
appraising them domestically. Guesstimating distances, memorizing
routes, noting cafés that could be workspaces. He asked me, concerned, why I was so quiet—was I unhappy? But I was thanking Him
for the chance. For selfishness enough to want things for myself here

in this world, even as I needed to transcend here, for it is in the end to triumph or to have made the effort. In desire is our every and only dignity. Once Muslims shaped the world. Now we have become afraid of our selves. We either only apologize, or never apologize. We are spineless and gutless, or harshness and darkness.

Here in Los Angeles, I explained to Muhammad, I'd found for the first time that I could imagine what it'd mean to move across the country, to build a life, with the full awareness that every such beginning has an end, that I might be expelled, as Dubai had spat me out, that relationships end, friendships disappear, love changes us, but love changes too. And I wanted this nevertheless. To try, even to fail. I hungered for it. To experience as much of it as I could. We dream because when we die, we wake up. After Muhammad dropped me off but before the flight back, I splurged on a Whopper and daydreamed until we landed. I'll live near the water, the sea that's ever calming to me, temporarily domiciled beside eternity profiled, God in between the peaks and troughs, but you don't need to see Him to know Him. Or yourself. The waves that crash, that fail, that fizzle, that dip down and lift their heads up again, that's how it is—you evaporate like water and rain down far, far away, the clay from which you're made becomes the forehead on the ground becomes the body in the dirt becomes something else somewhere else entirely, and then, when God Himself asks what it is you want, where would you look except to this, to here, which you remember as a dream, but a thing so fleeting, so fantastic, so foreign, is still the only thing you have to turn to. In it are signs. None of us belongs here, yes. But all of us are meant to be here.

ACKNOWLEDGMENTS

ADNAN ZULFIQAR FIRST pushed me to write. I start with him because the buck stops with him.

At *Religion Dispatches*, Evan Derkacz and Lisa Webster took a chance on me. Caitlin Hu and Meredith Bennett-Smith at *Quartz* respected me enough to let me write what I believed needed to be said. Amina Chaudary at the *Islamic Monthly*, a friend and an honest critic, graciously permitted me to reproduce part of an article for that magazine—on Abu Bakr al-Shatri—here. Amy Caldwell received a manuscript and made it a memoir. She didn't just make this book far better than it could be. In pushing me to be more truthful, she helped me see parts of me I never would have otherwise.

Eboo Patel had my back and Ayad Akhtar picked me up when I was down.

Wajahat Ali's confidence in my story led to another, right when the amazing Ayesha Mattu and awesome Nura Maznavi issued a call for submissions. (Waj, let's get tear-gassed when Sarah's airborne.) Karen Greenberg wanted me to soldier on even as I pushed in a direction that, she noted, no one else was following in. I thank Peter Bergen for his mentorship and for his dedication to writing, research, storytelling. I wish I'd had more time to learn from you. Nosheen and Nabila—your feedback was invaluable. Your ears and your patience more so. Ali has always been there. His is the friendship few of us can be so honored to have. I love you, but I still don't forgive you. Murtaza Hussain, because now I know I'm not crazy.

This story had to end at a certain point in my life, which meant I could not cover all the things that have changed me and changed for me. But they have changed. Yehuda Kurtzer is the kind of teacher I hope I might become. Yossi Klein-Halevi challenged me, intimidated me, and pushed me to find a relationship to Islam, to Muslims, and to the world, that I could not have found otherwise. Abdullah Antepli, I wouldn't know where to start. You saved my lives. Ali Eteraz, I pray you are well, wherever you are. Muddassar Ahmad has built things most of us believe would take generations to accomplish, consumed by the very same fire Iqbal was. Speaking of whom. Iqbal, yes, and Rumi, Bedil, Ghalib, Mahfouz, Dard, Shariati, Izetbegovič, Roddenberry, Foucault, Tolkien, Qadi Mansurpuri, Imam Ghazali. My Eärendils in the sky.

Ami, I miss your kindness, patience, dignity, piety, warmth. You taught me to love learning, to take pleasure in reading, to honor this faith and my ancestry. Abu, you taught me that I could do anything, compete with anyone, stand beside everyone. You taught me to fight. May God reward you both with the eternal company of the prophets and scholars, the saints and martyrs. To my future children, just because I did it doesn't mean you can.

My brother, Umar, and my sister, Saema—I would not be without your prayers, sacrifices, compassion, and concern. You've been there for me in more ways than I could count. To Uncle Bajwa, Aunti Kaneez, Uncle Ali, Aunti Azra, Hafiz Zubair, and Brother Ahmed—God reward you for the sacrifices you made, day in and day out, to teach us this wonderful religion. So much of what I learned of Islam, I learned from you. Most importantly you made me want to keep it. No matter how hard I tried to give it up.

John: 9:48. 2–3 = Negative fun. It was, totally. Christina: It meant more. Ben: Fire at Will. (I'd say "all good things"—because they really were, all of them, good things.) Jeff: Play on, player. Miss Robbins and Mister Malone: Truly teachers. Mr. Stoddard: We never got to say good-bye. Rest in peace. Peer: Come back. Brendan: For beating me. Camrey for the company. Shaheen for being right, even though it's a bit late for all that. Faraz, because you made me want to try again.

In the UAE, Samir: The next road trip you're driving though. The very friendly folks at the Starbucks and Tim Horton's off Shaykh Zayed, where much of this book came together: Muna, Arif, Abdul-Hadi, John. Your constant good cheer were welcome companions when the writing grew painful and the points seemed spurious, if not indulgent. Maybe they are, but it's not your fault. It's Adnan's. Julia for the coffee and company. Pascal for shisha. Tatjana for making the marina.

Ayman—thank Allah for Twitter. Masood for every night I couldn't sleep and all the food I'd never be able to afford. Angela's hegira inspired me. "What else can I read"—your disappointment at my disappointing answer is a significant reason this book even is. Willow Wilson is my *shaykha*. Jana for anonymizing.

"You lit a fire under me," she said. It was the other way around all this time. I'm sorry I did not see. Juwairia, you brought joy back into my life. For however long we have in this world, I pray we have it together. Preferably on this couch, which is not only the greatest thing in the world, but where we belong. Ami and Abu: For being an Ami and an Abu.

Messenger of God, in my darkest hours, when I did not know what to believe, when I did not believe even in myself, your love for me, for all of us, kept me. When I was sick in a hospital bed, when I was illest and broken, when I did not want to live, I sent salam and you responded by bringing me salam.

My Lord and Maker, might I be able to thank your beloved, in person, at heaven's gates?

I know that's a cheat, but it's a good one.